D1496448

FLORIDA STATE
UNIVERSITY LIBRARIES

MAY 16 1996

TALLAHASSEE, FLORIDA

THE
CHIGA
OF
UGANDA

MAY M. EDEL

WITH A NEW INTRODUCTION BY
ABRAHAM EDEL

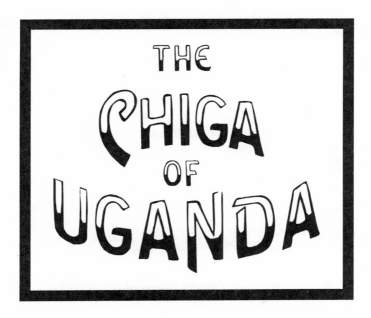

THE CHIGA OF UGANDA

SECOND EDITION

Transaction Publishers
New Brunswick (U.S.A.) and London (U.K.)

DT
434
.U242
E3
1996

New material this edition copyright © 1996 by Transaction Publishers, New Brunswick, New Jersey 08903. Foreword and Chapters 1–8 were originally published in 1957 by Oxford University Press. Chapter 12 originally appeared in *Political Science Quarterly* 80, no. 3 (September 1965).

All rights reserved under International and Pan-American Copyright Conventions. No part of this book may be reproduced or transmitted in any form or by any means, electronic or mechanical, including photocopy, recording, or any information storage and retrieval system, without prior permission in writing from the publisher. All inquiries should be addressed to Transaction Publishers, Rutgers—The State University, New Brunswick, New Jersey 08903.

This book is printed on acid-free paper that meets the American National Standard for Permanence of Paper for Printed Library Materials.

Library of Congress Catalog Number: 95-33213
ISBN: 1-56000-248-4
Printed in the United States of America

Library of Congress Cataloging-in-Publication Data

Edel, May M. (May Mandelbaum), 1909–1964.
   The Chiga of Uganda / May M. Edel ; with an introduction by Abraham Edel. — 2nd ed.
      p. cm.
   Rev. ed. of: The Chiga of western Uganda. 1957.
   Includes bibliographical references (p.   ) and index.
   ISBN 1-56000-248-4 (cloth : acid-free paper)
   1. Chiga (African people)—Social life and customs. 2. Chiga (African people)—Material culture. 3. Kabale District (Uganda)—Social life and customs. I. Edel, May M. (May Mandelbaum), 1909–1964. Chiga of western Uganda. II. Title.
DT434.U242E3 1995
306'.089963956—dc20   95-33213
                                                                       CIP

CONTENTS

ACKNOWLEDGMENTS

CHAPTERS 1–8 come from *The Chiga of Western Uganda* by May Mandelbaum Edel, published in 1957 for the International African Institute by Oxford University Press. This material is here reproduced with the kind permission of the International African Institute.

Chapters 9–11 come from a hitherto unpublished manuscript of May Edel's by permission of Abraham Edel.

Chapter 12 is reprinted, by permission, from *Political Science Quarterly* 80, no. 3 (September 1965): 357–72.

PREFACE

THE present volume contains the entire text of *The Chiga of Western Uganda* by May Mandelbaum Edel (1909-1964), published in 1957 for the International African Institute by the Oxford University Press. This is amplified by *The Material Culture of the Chiga*, a hitherto unpublished manuscript from the papers of May Edel, and by an article of hers that was originally published in the *Political Science Quarterly* (1964). All of these writings are based on fieldwork she did in Uganda from October 1932 to January 1934.

Another source for securing a fuller account is the weekly letters that she wrote me from Africa. They provide many fresh insights and cultural items that are not dealt with in the book. They have been utilized by me in writing the Introduction.

She also wrote papers on Africa dealing with special topics— for example, "Property among the Chiga" (*Africa* 2: 325-341) and "The Bachiga of East Africa" in *Cooperation and Competition among Primitive Peoples*, edited by Margaret Mead (McGraw Hill, 1937), as well as in other cooperative volumes. She also wrote on the moral ideas of the Chiga in *Anthropology and Ethics*, a book on which we collaborated (Charles C. Thomas, 1959; Transaction Publishers, 1970).

A full bibliography of her writings on Africa and on other areas in which she worked, as well as her theoretical reflections, can be found in Ruth Bunzel's memorial note in *American Anthropologist* 68, no. 4 (August 1966).

ABRAHAM EDEL

Philadelphia, 1995.

INTRODUCTION TO THE
TRANSACTION EDITION

IN THE 1930s, when May did her doctoral work at Columbia University, the central figure in anthropology there was Franz Boas, commonly called by his students "Papa Franz." Boas had come from Germany in the late nineteenth century on an expedition to study geography in the northwest part of North America. He then believed that geography played a determining part in the life of a people. But he found that this did not hold for the Eskimo, who worked out their own life pattern sometimes contrary to what geographers would expect. One had thus to study the full life ways of a people, their full culture in its specific historical setting. He worked especially at that time on the Indians in the northwest of North America. He realized, of course, that "civilization" was spreading in all directions, that the Eskimo mode of life would be altered by their contact with the peoples of western Europe, now moving into western Canada and through the United States. This imparted a sense of urgency to descriptive anthropology: it had to capture the view of the past before the past disappeared. And it should be captured not only by reports of the people themselves—the older among them would still remember the ways that had gone by—but by students going into the field to observe, question, and report. Indeed Boas had his doctoral students do their dissertations on the basis of the fieldwork they themselves did. And the Anthropology Department got visiting professors from Europe who had done fieldwork in various parts of the world. He had encouraged Ruth Benedict and Margaret Mead to work "in the field," and in the 1930s their works were published, for example Benedict's *Patterns of Culture* and Mead's *Coming of Age in Samoa*. Boas was also aware of the importance of educating the public generally about cultures and cultural differences. He did a number of popular books, chief among which were *The Mind of Primitive Man* (1911), *Anthropology and Modern Life* (1928), and *Race, Language and Culture* (1928), a collection of papers written between 1887 and 1936 (published in 1940).

May did her undergraduate work at Barnard College in the late 1920s, and it was a course given by Mead that first alerted her to the field. She decided to major in it. She was in a group of students, guided by Leslie Spier, that went out to Indian territory in the state of Washington, and she wrote up her work in that expedition. During 1930–31, for her doctoral thesis, she went to study the Tillamook Indians in Oregon. In the town of Garibaldi she found only an old woman who remembered the stories that used to be told among their people, but she had difficulty in enunciating clearly because of the state of her teeth. Boas simply advised May to get a dentist to deal with her teeth. May was thus able to get from her the stories of the old days and the myths of the past. In the Indian cultures the telling of stories generally played the role that the reading of books plays in our culture. Under such conditions, special "story tellers" had developed long and precise memories; stories were told to the young in successive generations in almost word-perfect form.

May's study of the Tillamook was oriented to language, but of course the stories she received gave information about the beliefs and mode of life, just as the ancient Greek stories of the gods and heroes (as in Homer or the tragedies) gave some picture of early Greek life. After this American Indian study, chance led her to develop a strong interest in Uganda. Ernest B. Kalibala, from Uganda, was visiting at Teachers College, Columbia. He had translated a book by Sir Apolo Kagwa, who had been prime minister and regent of the Baganda in Uganda in the latter part of the nineteenth and early part of the twentieth centuries. Boas asked May to help out Kalibala in preparing the work for the press. She found that there was quite a complex situation involved.

In the first place, a great part of the material had already appeared in a large volume by the Reverend John Roscoe. This book had been written under unusual and comfortable circumstances. Roscoe was a friend of Sir Apolo Kagwa and stayed with him for some months in the royal palace while he was preparing the book. The work was rich in the actual presentation of the native customs and beliefs. As his interest was directed on one or another topic of Baganda life, Sir Apolo got an informant for that area to come and live in the palace until Roscoe was finished with him. As a result the book was not the product of observation but of material delivered. It was original material, but the authenticity of the informant's version or his personal perspective was not checked by life in the village. Moreover, when Roscoe's book was done, Sir Apolo translated it into Luganda (the language of the Baganda). But he found himself dissatisfied with it and so wrote his own *Customs of the Baganda*. Yet, as May points out in her introduction to Kalibala's translation of Sir Apolo's book, Sir Apolo did not deviate much from Roscoe's account and his work as a whole "reflects in no way the fact that the author was a participant in, and had intimate knowledge of, the culture he is describing." She explains this in part by the fact that he was writing for his own people, who knew their own culture. The result was, however, that Kalibala's translation and Roscoe's book gave very much the same account. May thus saw Sir Apolo's book as essentially an annotation and expansion of Roscoe's. Hence, Kalibala's translation was cut down to give only the parts that Roscoe had not covered, to which was added a summary (in square brackets) of any of Roscoe's material that was necessary background for Kalibala's points. This work was completed in 1930–31 though not published till 1934 after May had returned from Africa.

In any case, the material piqued May's interest in Uganda. She did not intend to work among the Baganda, because they were already by that time somewhat "Europeanized," but to go to the Chiga who dwelt at the borders of Uganda and were reported to be unaffected by British ways, although in the relation of European powers it was acknowledged to be British territory. She applied for and got a grant for the Chiga project, and by the fall of 1932 she left for Africa.

May had selected a British protectorate for her work rather than a French or Belgian one. The French and Belgians saw a protectorate as an opportunity for the spread of their own culture and for exploiting native labor; this meant direct rule over the native population. The British let the natives go their own way provided that the British got what they wanted in the way of products and taxes. The exception was religion: British missionaries were a prime factor in the penetration of the culture in British territories. And along with them, or after them, came the doctors, nurses, administrators, and eventually the scholars. But the fact that the British tended to rule through native chiefs rather than by direct intervention meant that in Uganda natives continued largely their previous agricultural mode of life.

In Britain, immediately after her Atlantic crossing, May gathered materials and supplies for her work. Differences in climate required different preparation. She got in touch not only with anthropologists—for example, Malinowski—but also missionaries who had worked in East Africa. In doing this—in effect a touch of fieldwork in Britain itself—she learned about attitudes toward women there. From London, she wrote on October 18, 1932:

> This crazy town has the kind of shops which take an hour to fit a bush-jumper, which ought to come in standard sizes like Macy's and take ten minutes. I've bought the funniest clothes— shorts, and slacks, and mosquito boots, and a teral [?]. (It's what one wants instead of a pith helmet) which is two complete funny-looking felt hats one inside the other. All of which junk I shall need and fifteen porters to carry it, no doubt!...I got tips on diplomacy from the nicer of the returned females. She says one has to be a nice dumb woman—interested in something like the women and children—and one should be able to do tennis and bridge and such to be a social success. They're still in the sticks, the English public school idea of womankind and it's hard to combine with what one's doing. She actually took notes on *white* ethnology—found them quite amusing.

From London May went to France and Germany, where she also had discussions with fellow anthropologists. In Germany the eminent Africanist, to whom she was (nominally) responsible under the foundation grant she had received for African fieldwork, was Professor Diedrich Westermann in Berlin. She met him in his home. He told her in the course of conversation that the Nazis were causing trouble in the universities by attacking Jewish professors, but seemed to feel no imminent threat in entertaining a Jewish woman scholar.

At Genoa she embarked for Africa. The ship sailed through the Mediterranean, the Suez Canal—she went ashore at Cairo, her first view of an African city—then down the Red Sea and around the "corner" to the east coast of the continent. She landed at Mombassa, then went inland to Nairobi and finally to Kampala. This would remain thereafter the base from which she would get her supplies. Here she consulted missionaries and government officials to get a knowledge of the various areas in which she might work. She considered the districts of Kigezi and Toro. The latter was a possibility, although it would have involved the use of French, it being in part Belgian territory. She could speak French but decided against Toro because it was already somewhat "Europeanized."

In Kabale (in Kigezi) May consulted missionaries and government officials who had lived for a long time in the area and knew it well. She wanted a location as "un-Europeanized" as possible, one where in the course of their lives the people had little to do with Europeans. As she discovered later, this was not wholly possible because the British levied a head tax on the natives even where the latter were ruled by their own people and lived in an isolated area. This meant that the young men had to work about a month a year to earn enough to pay the tax, and so had European contact where they went to work. But the older men and women and children did not have this contact, and so met her expectations.

Having decided on the district, she had next to concern herself with the question of language. The language of the Chiga was *Lutchiga*. Fortunately she found a native school teacher in Kampala who knew that language, and who happened to have a month's vacation. She hired him to come for the month to Chiga territory to teach her the language; he did so seven hours a day, after which he had to go beck to Kampala. She was now on her own, the only white westerner in the village. She discovered much later that the people were a bit afraid of her at first, and some even thought she might be a British spy.

A good technique to get closer to the people, she found, was through the children. They were curious and came to look at her, whatever she was doing. She gave them candy, and once they discovered it was sweet, even older children came along with their younger siblings. Bikonko was a three-year old who stayed around a great deal, and asked for candy. She learned the word he used in asking, and from the varied use by others decided it meant sweet. She tried it out calling a person "sweet," and the little boy laughed. This narrowed down the use. Pretty soon, by a variety of experimental techniques, her vocabulary began to grow. An older girl, Eseri, began to stay around most of the day when she was not needed in her family; she began to pick up English expressions from May and try them out. May accordingly hired her, as a companion, and began to ask her questions about her life, her family, the people. Eseri eventually moved in with May as an assistant in a variety of tasks—in some respects as a housekeeper, in some as an informant, in some as liaison to the village. Eseri eventually wrote to May when May returned to the United States, and could be asked questions about uncertain linguistic points.

Eria was May's houseboy. He was in charge of the porters who brought up the day's water from the lake that lay down a fairly steep hill, and made a fire so it could be boiled to ensure purity. There were about a dozen porters constantly employed. Some worked during the day; others during the night, tending a fire which kept away animals. Fortunately there were no lions in the area, and only once during the year was there a prowling tiger to be scared away by banging pots to make a loud noise. The common wild animal was the hyena, but it was cowardly; it ran away from people, but tried to get cats for food and sometimes it succeeded.

May had chosen the site for her "house"—a rough small structure made of mud for "cement" and boughs of trees, lined inside with sheets from packing boxes—on top of a hill with a view of the nearby lake. The reason for not being near the shore was the presence of malaria-carrying mosquitoes. The natives to a great extent had grown immune to this over generations, but Europeans, in addition to taking preventive pills, had to exercise caution. Up the hill mosquitoes were less frequent during the day, and the fires kept them away at night.

Like Eseri, Eria remained in May's employment during her whole period among the Chiga. At the end of May's stay Eria and Eseri were married. Later on Eria was to become a leader in the community. Leadership was a matter of respect, for the Chiga did not have any kind of internal political organization, just kin authority relations. (These are presented in chapter 3.) Leadership, however, was needed in dealing with the British. Many years later, when the British withdrew from Africa after World War II, May happened to see a television scene of tumult in Uganda, and there, in a crowd obviously concerned with organized action, was Eria clearly telling the crowd what to do.

May wrote of her introduction to the territory and the people:

There is no kingdom, no classes, etc., but there are cattle and such. They're quite wild in many ways. There is no European cultivation here—settlers are not allowed. The hills are covered with native farms, with beautifully laid out patches of large millet, sweet potatoes, and assorted legumes. No bananas—it's not

really warm enough, being very high. A sweater was very grateful all morning! The people wear cowskins—just one skin or
two—and not sewn, merely knotted on the shoulders, completely
open down one side, and often swinging indiscretely out of place.
The women wear only skirts, and anklets—millions of them.
They are said to be very nice, are relatively unknown—I knew
not even their name (Chiga) and sound like an interesting cultural type. They would be most convenient to do, as they can be
worked from my headquarters here, at least for a good part of
the time. There are plenty of them about.

May found the countryside impressive with its "rolling hills
and plains, forests that look like the African jungle, and tree-dot-
ted elephant grass country, papyrus swamps galore." The district
commissioner welcomed her, made all necessary arrangements,
and warned her about health care. He also lent her a gun—"a little
revolver in a lovely wooden box, but he says I won't need it, and
he's willing to wager I'll give it back in a few weeks. He thought
it might be nice to have at first in case I should be frightened at
strange noises." Then she adds, "In any case, I'm still happy, though
a little scared by the proximity of my great task, which suddenly
seems very difficult. It merely means buckling down."

The work involved facing a mass of disparate tasks. Her belongings had to be put in order; she had to work on Lunyoro grammar; and she had to read some of the books on the area that she
had picked up. Photos, which she took from the start, had to be
developed: it would take too long to send them for development,
so she had to cultivate the art herself. She also went down the hill
to the beach where men were idling, and made arrangements with
an Indian for canoe transport. She found that good will was easily
achieved by freely giving cigarettes ("a brand specially purchased
for the purpose, and costing one bob a hundred"). Bathing in her
tub raised the problem of getting the water. This was done in old
petrol tins and carried up to her tent by boys who were eager for a
job. Drinking water was a more serious problem. People there had
developed immunity to germs the water might contain, and they
were not likely to be careful about getting it to the right boiling
point. So she had to reboil it. There was also the question of light
in the tent after dark. She had brought lamp equipment, but the
petrol raised problems, and for a few days she was reduced to an
ordinary kerosene lamp.

Interestingly, medical matters started her relationship with the people: "I've already been called upon for 'dawa'—I gave a child a brown mixture lozenge for a cold. I should have given it more, but I couldn't explain about the hours for taking it." By the beginning of January 1933, an ordered mode of life was established. May writes, "Shall I give you the really detailed program?" Getting up is at seven o'clock. There is morning tea in English fashion, then breakfast, then to work till 12:30 on the language. There are, of course, different tasks on different days. One is occupied by writing notes, such as to a mission lady to arrange for fresh vegetables, another to interview a gentleman who knows the language well, and a note "to my new neighbors to thank them for some mutton they had sent down yesterday." These messages are carried by one of her porters whose pay is only 30 cents of the local currency (about a nickel in American money). "Tomorrow I must get up early; and have so instructed my boy (remember he speaks no English), as I am walking the twenty minutes up the hill to the camp, there to get a lift to town at 8 o'clock. And then to the Mission for a long talk with Dr. Smith; and so to lunch with one of the ladies here—the government doctor's wife. Originally they were Mission people—But when you're offered twice so much, *and* a pension, what can one do? But at a dinner party the other night Dr. Cook brushed the brandy sauce off his plum pudding."

In a letter early in the new year (January 7, 1933) May reflects on problems of method. She decides on the use of questions to the people rather than first making observations of behavior. Of course what one gathered from what people said would be checked against their behavior. In her present position there are numerous informants. The only difficulty, she anticipates, will be in religion, because this is tied up with magic and the Nyabingi cult—a black magic order which some years before had tried to stir up trouble against Europeans. As a result it was banned. She suspects even innocent forms of magic may be kept from her, such as magic to make gardening successful. Her mode of proceeding (which eventually proved successful) was to get as much information from old-time British residents, and then ask questions of the older men among the natives.

Of the language May writes:

The grammar is very neat but very complicated, the vocabulary very rich and full of long words, the phonetic shifts regular but far too numerous for an outsider, and the ways of handling ideas rather foreign to us. Locative adverbs have a way of being nouns, to be followed by the genitive, for example—the inside of the house, not in the house. And there is a declension of demonstratives. All of which I can grasp, being so trained, but find it much more difficult to memorize the words and use them than I had hoped. I shall proceed by all the methods I know of, writing out sentences painfully constructed in order to give orders to my boy, who has now grasped the fact that I am anxious to speak his language rather than Swahili. And so it will go on. Pray for me.

On January 12 she went for a walk along a circular route and observed the fields at which the people work. "It's easy to see how these people get by without villages. The fields are small and close to each other; there were many people about in them, despite the hour, all shouting to each other. They responded very cordially to my greeting. I expect to make friends with some of them very soon now. They are, as a lot, most attractive—not in appearance but in expression and humour."

For my benefit, May describes the curriculum of the school. It consists of arithmetic, hygiene, English grammar, Scriptures, geography, Lutchiga grammar, agriculture, Swahili, reading and writing, and English reading. Students with good manners are picked for high school, which adds chemistry, some physics, English, and Church history. For her own reading in the language, May will use the gospel according to St. Mark, which is the only thing she can find printed.

Eight days later (January 20) the weather is warmer and dryer, and already May is ready to try out her use of the language in speech. She starts with the carpenter, and asks how he makes boats, to whom he sells them and for how much, how he happened to become a carpenter, who makes his tools, and so on at considerable length and variety of inquiry. She expects out of this also to get initial ideas of exchange. She is struck by the fact that the boats are used chiefly by men, and reflects that that may be because the men now have greater leisure, since they have cleared the fields and it is the turn of the women to do the planting, which is largely of millet.

On Sunday she went to see a carpenter who makes all the dugouts on the lake. "He presented me with a chicken, showed me all his tools and how he uses them, and followed this up with the invariable request for clothes. I'm writing to Nairobi for cheap khaki—there's certainly nothing better to endear me to them all." A couple of days later she interviews an old man who was-one of the most important of the Chiga. Mutambuka, leader of one of the clans, was now old and blind:

> He has about 17 living wives, having had 21 in all, and was long one of the most important men in these parts. He has a tremendous household, with more small children than I've ever seen before, all tumbling about fairly naked. The place was not so filthy as a smaller one would be. There were squads at work making beer in many large pots. He spoke to me for 4 hours, Blasio interpreting. If what he told me is true, there was no unit here higher than the clan, whose leader had what judicial and war-leadership authority there was. But of elaborate religious or even land-tenure-arranging functions there could be found no trace.

On January 29, Blasio, May's teacher, went home. From that time on, for the whole year until May was back in the United States, she was on her own, except of course when she visited administrative officials or missionaries. On January 29 she was out at the leper colony, visiting Miss Langley, who was the head nurse there. The colony is on an island some distance away:

> It's one of the most beautiful places I've ever seen. The house is on top of a high hill—away from the hospital and the villages—and all about are the rolling mountains of the mainland, running into the lake in dozens of fantastic little peninsulas. The lake itself is studded with tiny islands. The only thing keeping the view from perfection is that there are no trees. The hills are merely grass covered, with only an occasional clump of bushes for relief. Just now Miss Langley is down holding services—I can hear the singing from here. She's left the dog—who is never allowed among the lepers—as a guard—not that one is necessary. It's the most tremendous animal you ever saw. An Irish wolfhound, I believe—it's only a puppy—but really about five feet long, and correspondingly heavy. And it has all a pup's playfulness—which is rather a worry to me.

I went along to the services this morning, though I could follow but little of it. The people's good spirits are astonishing. But...the disease is horrible.

Interestingly, closer relations with the Chiga began once May was on her own. On February 3 two girls came to visit her. They spent the morning sitting in the sun and making baskets, carrying on a desultory conversation. "I'm going to the native church on Sunday, and they're coming back here again afterwards." May writes, "You should have seen their amazement at my typewriter— particularly as they know how to read. All the Christians do— they have to be baptised—C. of E., not R.C."

The limit of authority here was the clan: "interclan wars oc- curred over such important trifles as the theft of a cow—And its leader, who held his position by inheritance from a long lineage, was at once general in warfare, and arbitrator, with sway dictated and supported only by general consent and prestige, but none the less effective, on quarrels within. The women came from without, to take their place as members."

Cows were the visible symbols of wealth, but agriculture occu- pied their time and supplied the food. Women ate the meat of the cow, but not of sheep and goat. A man would not marry a woman who violated that tabu.

On Sunday, February 5, May went to the native church. "They celebrate afterwards by dancing—which would shock some of the mission here dreadfully if they knew it. I enjoyed it thoroughly... it's a simple pumping, with arms in the air, but very syncopated in rhythm, and with a 'break.' For my special benefit they also did a sort of shield and spear dance—two men at a time—a sort of chal- lenge and combat thing—very dramatic.... The music is a simple phrase repeated over and over again, with clapping, and without any harmony."

May began to make friends with the girls rapidly. They came over to her place on a Sunday morning to work on making bas- kets. And she gave them bead necklaces for a gift (bought from the Indian traders at ten for a shilling). To learn their way of mak- ing baskets May tried her hand at it under Eseri's observation. (Eseri was astonished at the smoothness of May's hands—but working on baskets diminished that!) May planned after that to go on and learn how potting was done, then tanning skins and sewing the elaborate skirts that women wear.

On February 13 May had lunch at Eseri's. Eseri cooked corn. She went on to tea at Miss Langley's, where there was a gather- ing: "An English Lady So-and-so and her daughter, tourists, and a doctor from Entebbe with his family. He found I knew not lice, and, being a great humorist, ordered the attendant to show me one, which he did!" May's relations with Eseri were beginning to be closer—in fact Eseri now allowed herself to gossip about the people in her village. To encourage this, and at the same time to learn about kinship relations, May began to take genealogies from Eseri. Eseri also told her of her suitors; there had been two so far, but her father rejected them because they were not wealthy enough.

Within the next two months May's use of the language improved considerably, as she began to visit the people's homes more frequently and converse with the men as well as the women; she was looked upon almost as "one of them." In a letter on March 17, she wrote: Maybe my Lutchiga is improving, because I actually tried to start sentences in it when talking to English people!" And shortly after she wrote that she could speak Lutchiga "fluently and incorrectly."

On March 20, May went on *safari,* a walking trip to examine neighboring places; Eseri came along. This of course required equipment as one had to stay over wherever one was at nightfall, which might be out in the open away from any settled parts. Hence, she had twenty porters, who carried her tent and equipment as well as their own. May found that even the old men could understand her speech. The trip lasted about three weeks; it was not until April 13 that she was back and resting up at Miss Langley's. Since Eseri had been with her on the trip and listened to her conversations with people, Eseri now had a good idea of what sort of things May was interested in and could help get the required information in her area.

In the latter part of April, May decided to move into Eseri's village and build a house there. She would thus be an insider rather than an occasional visitor. She arranged to build a Chiga-style hut for sitting in and cooking in, and a small one for the staff to live in. "I shall thus be nearer the scene of action...which will have the advantage of evening visiting and rainy-day visiting, as well as more chance for intimacy.... Also I shan't miss the fuss if someone dies, as happened last night—and it wasn't proper for one to call." She would keep her tent for sleeping in.

Her safari had convinced May that her village was sufficiently typical of the Chiga as a whole, and she decided to stay there for the time she had rather than move among several villages. In fact her belief in greater intimacy in one place proved correct. She became almost accepted as a member of the clan, people talked to her more freely, the men as well as the women.

While her house was being built, she stayed with May Langley. She wrote of the mission people: "They're a very funny mixed lot.... They're all being nice to me, I must confess.... It's such fun to meet people who, being awakened at night by the rumblings of a distant earthquake, think the end of the world has come!"

The kind of problems encountered when trying to get the building done give an excellent picture of the complications faced:

Right now I'm sitting at a little table at Chabahinga, looking over the lake. This morning I selected ten men, who've gone off to cut wood for building, and five others who are making rope—twist in papyrus—it's astonishingly strong. Tomorrow I shall get boats to carry the posts to the village I've chosen—it's called Bafuga—where I already have most of the genealogies and such—Then the D.C.'s [district commissioners] come out to make sure I don't pick someone else's field and cause a shauri [a fuss, quarrel]—and my establishment will be up in very short time, if we're lucky—or rather, good managers. Meanwhile this is being fun, because I'm doing it—or shall try to without the assistance of any chiefs or such. This morning we also prepared a mass of small millet I'd bought at the market. It had to be sifted to remove tiny pebbles and such. Some is being set in water to sort of sprout—that's for brewing. The rest is merely being spread in the sun, for grinding and such, to be made into some sort of native bread, which I've never yet met. I've discovered that the gruel drink I wrote you about can be very good when it's properly made. I'm preparing to stock a lot of it, so guests can be properly entertained. Anyway, there will be the big feast I shall give.

Actually, May found the bread not so good because she did not like the flavor of millet, but she found the rest of their food quite satisfactory, and the green vegetables much better than spinach.

On May 21 May moved into her own camp at Bufuga:

It's really surprisingly nice. The boys fixed up the inside of the big house with 'tables'—matting on sticks set in forked posts—to hold all the 'bintu' (Bantu for things, but uniformly used in

East Africa to mean belongings, luggage, and such) and it looks much cosier, much lighter, than I'd hoped.... the village is quite pleased we are finally 'entering'—and I expect, today being a general knocking off day, that we shall have loads of company. Eseri is going to cook a large mess of peas so that we will be able to serve something out, as etiquette demands. Unfortunately, although she's ground lots of flour, we haven't had time to stir the gruel, which is at once food and drink here—like a malted milk, no—Perhaps we'll make some hot. And I shall give away loads of salt and tobacco.

Many advantages followed from being in the village. For example, sixty people danced on her "front lawn" after church, and she gave out lots of salt and necklaces; May wrote down part of a story they told, and listened to a concert. One evening she was invited to the evening meal at Eseri's, and another evening elsewhere. The people liked her and asked when she was coming to visit. They gradually learned to come to her place single, merely to visit.

In general, she found it was an each-for-himself culture, anarchistic except for fear of priests (and government). Laughter was an important social weapon, enough to keep women from eating sheep and goat meat.

In her new home, closer to the people, May was able to find out more readily about their history and customs. There had been actual war between the clans:

> people are still afraid to go very far off lest they be killed, as once they would have been. And each has its land rigidly defined—confined to distinct hills. Also the leader, whose position is hereditary, was a sort of high priest as well as war leader. But in very little was he 'ruler.' The clans have subdivisions, and each is a clan in miniature, with only a little less inclination to war.

At this close range some of the more intimate ways were more easily observable. The natives wear cowskins which are cleansed by rubbing with butter. There is a proper way of scolding, not just giving vent to feeling. It is said to involve the "giving of shame." Again, a sister's son can marry a brother's daughter, but a sister's daughter cannot marry a brother's son. Involved here are motiva-

tions about the dowry; a man gives away his daughter in marriage, not the mother who comes from an outside clan. There would
be no profit for a man to have his son marry a sister's daughter; in
effect he would be giving the dowry to himself. Furthermore, the
decision whom his daughter will marry, while the father's, does
require the approval of his fellows. But the dowry goes to him,
not to any other of the kin. Economic motives can enter in various
ways: for example, a father may refuse his daughter to suitors
because he does not have the wherewithal to brew the necessary
beer for the ceremony; and this may happen just because there
was a bad millet season.

There are all sorts of prohibitions, not only with respect to food
but also with respect to building. For example, when May's hut
was being built she wanted to see what the roof was to be like.
There was a bar over the entrance, to keep women out. (No woman
would sneak in, for no man would marry her if it was known what
she had done.) Because May went in and had a look, she was
correspondingly regarded as an outsider, not of the village group.
And that was something to overcome.

Beer plays an important part in Chiga life. It is required in specified gifts on ceremonial occasions; its brewing occupies the whole
village at a particular time. But at the same time it is a source of
trouble, because the people tend to overindulge; this makes some
of them quarrelsome, and fights may break out. The British authorities had tried to ban the making of beer, but with little suc-
cess. They were wary at the season in which beer was made.

Marriage ceremonies are important festive occasions, at least
for the men. The procedure is elaborate, and much of it prescribed—for example, what is worn, who sits on whose lap and
how, and when it becomes permissible for a brother to have intercourse with his brother's wife (after she has become pregnant).

By mid-June the weather changed. "The dry season is here with
a vengeance which means a really glaring sun all the middle part
of the day. It's really hot out in it, but fortunately it's not the kind
of oppressive heat that pursues one into the shade. So except when
actively engaged I can manage to be very comfortable indeed."

One day her cook came home drunk—he had gone to town to
pay his taxes. May wanted to scold him, but Eseri refused to tell
her how to do it in proper Lutchiga style, which involves a "giving of shame." Eseri, with increasing independence, decided also

that it wouldn't do to distribute the beer indiscriminately. So they made only a moderate amount, for family only. May thus learned the techniques, without coming up against the authorities.

In June, May also wrote one day that her house had been burned down. Fortunately, the people got her goods out in time—all the neighbors came on the scene at once, though it was night and many were already in bed. Fortunately, her important possessions (money, papers, clothes) were in her tent, which was untouched. For future safety, she decided to have watchmen at night.

One day there was an elopement: a girl ran away and no one knew about it in advance. There was merry-making heard from three peninsulas away, so people presumed that was where her husband lived. This provided an occasion for inquiry into the ways of dealing with sex and marriage. The linguistic form of talking of a marriage was not that a person "got married," but "we are marrying (someone off)." Girls practice elongation of the clitoris up to the time of marriage. The bride has to sit on the husband's hand, naked, and probably virginity is tested as well; this is the limit of intimacy on the first night of marriage. One of the women asked whether white women had breasts with nipples, and May assured her that all bodies, whether white or black, were the same. This woman, after that, was quite ready to talk about sexual practices. Eseri, on the other hand, was modest in this respect. What May wanted, in these inquiries, was to distinguish what were simply current practices from what had institutional significance.

For a while May used an informant, named Kezitcia, to gather information about matters that were not directly available to her. She learned about religion, omens, and prohibitions, about the different grades of practitioners—diviners, magicians, and priests, and what they did ceremonially and how they acquired their powers. The government had gotten rid of the highest order, but the other practices were found, surreptitiously among some individuals. The yearly dancing and beer parties in honor of the spirits no longer took place, out of fear of the government. A "middling order" of spirits were still surreptitiously honored in ceremonies stealthily; these ceremonies took place at annual festivals at which a selected group of old people took part. But even familiar practices, like sacrifice to one's own ancestors, an act of piety readily permitted, is done with apprehension.

Because of the fire, and the fear that it might have been set as a hostile act, government officials decided to send a local chief to stay with May's entourage. He turned out to be just a youth, and he stayed with May's group until his house was built. He had in fact nothing to do, so May tried to use him as another informant. She did get considerable information on language use from him and from others, particularly on social and religious requirements—for example, "You must wear a white skin and turn it inside out" or "the mother wears the leaves of such-and-such in her hair." But on the whole, the young people spoke of such matters from hearsay, not from their own social experience, since many of the older ways and rituals had been abandoned. Again, May tried to distinguish the customary from the imperative.

Much of the work proved quite detailed—for example, how you flick your wrist up to split papyrus properly; the difference between the various ways of preparing fields for different crops; the names given to people and times and animals and places; tools used and objects made; detailed techniques; details of planting, herding, and cooking; what and how objects are owned, borrowed, inherited, sold; the greater importance of agriculture over herding; and so forth. Ownership was individual for some things, communal for others; but for some things there were slight family and communal claims. As for conduct, there was a distinction between bad manners, illegal acts, and religiously tabu practices.

One day in the middle of August May visited Mutambuka, "He didn't deny he had been one of the most powerful magicians in these parts; and we were for the most part able to understand each other without too much cross-questioning and repetition." They were interrupted by other people coming around so on this occasion they did not get far. He was an intelligent old man, not influenced much by the new situation. He had served as a subchief until his blindness became too pronounced. May also saw different halves of two weddings:

one at the girl's father's, the first half—where I was pleasantly excited at the spectacle—she hidden in the house and rhythmically wailing, the girls dancing just outside the gate, with the neighborhood looking on, and then, toward sunset, a real battle— the boys have to remove her friends from the house by force, and then the girl herself, while the waiting relatives of the husband screech and jump about. Sometimes a bone gets broken and the thatching half removed. Everyone's crowded into the courtyard to watch, and dashes madly back when the scrimmage seems to threaten the onlookers. Finally, with much hiding behind mats, and covering of heads with skirts, she's hoisted on a 'brother's' shoulders, and the crowd marches off.

At their destination there is much dancing before they come, and gifts are given to the groom. When they arrive, the girl is left on a mat outside, while all make merry in the courtyard. The boys leap and twist, while the girls clap and sing. When the girl is carried into the house, there is more dancing outside, but most people go home. Later the bride is taken into the front for the real ceremony; at daybreak the bride's people go off, leaving her struggling to go, too. Consummation takes place later in the morning, and the girl is supposed to fight against it.

Property rules are definitely patterned. Property is personal, but the group has limited veto powers. Land is acquired by clearing it, and it may be lent or even alienated. Its owner is the head of the household, but when a wife or borrower cultivates the field, it is known as hers or his. The person who did the work owns the crops. Sheep, cows, and the like are the recognized "wealth" and belong to the master of the house. Clothes belong to the individual. Household items—hoe, crops, baskets—can be used by the women; but a wife if she goes away, can take none of these. But the wife's son will inherit such part of the cattle as she brought to the marriage: a brother acts as regent for the sons.

Knowledge is open if it can be learned by watching, but trade secrets, for example of magicians, have to be bought. Hunting and watering belong to all members of the clan who live there, except where a person has built a well, which is then his. As noted earlier, a father may refuse to marry off a daughter to a suitor, but requires the approval of his fellows to accept the suitor. But the cattle dowry is all his, and in the case of divorce it and its offspring have to be returned. Since the cattle may have been used for another child's dowry, divorce has the potential of upsetting others' marriages as well. Cattle thus help provide greater stability for marriage.

A few of the comments on Lutchiga are of grammatical interest. For example, there seems to be a greater centrality of the verb, as contrasted with our starting with the subject. For example, where we say, "It is difficult" or "I find it difficult," they will say, "It difficults me."

May found Eseri very helpful on linguistic questions. They explored such matters as their calendar (which May found highly inaccurate) and their names (and possibly perceptions) with regard to color. They had no difficulty distinguishing colors or grouping them, though with some variation among individuals. But the only color names they had were those applied to sheep, cows, and men. Nicknames were common. (We may wonder whether nicknames might operate as a kind of sanction, since they might sometimes arise from actions commented on.) May discovered that she was sometimes referred to as "a woman who falls" which was probably directed at her way of creeping down hills.

May collected botanical specimens, which she dried out (or waited till they dried out) and then mounted on heavy paper. This tin box was found many years later in the attic, under a mass of papers so that it had escaped notice. The Anthropological Department in the American Museum of Natural History in New York was overloaded at the time, so eventually the box was given to the Botanical Gardens in Philadelphia. The seeds no doubt sprouted in due course, and were technically described; or perhaps more likely, were preserved on the sheet with a fluid covering to keep them from crumbling.

In mid-October May turned to a quite different job—to take bodily measurements of the people. This had been part of her original assignment, to satisfy the physical anthropologists who sometimes cared little about the culture and wanted the physical comparison of different peoples. Boas himself was very interested in the question whether size was inherent or depended on the food supply. It tied up with his concern over the claims of racial differences, often by those who had ideas of superior or inferior peoples.

Another job in October was to see how far the Chiga extended and how different other groups of Chiga might be. There was another group in Belgian territory that adjoined her people. Accordingly, in early November she went into this Bahororo country, which included a visit down to Lake Edward. She found the people sufficiently like the Chiga, so she decided not to do any comparative study, but to devote all the time to the Chiga. Her decision was strengthened by Boas' view that it was better to add a month to her stay and get a fuller picture than to do that month elsewhere and get only a brief view there.

By Saturday, November 4, she was so steeped in the ways of the Chiga that, as she wrote, "Such is the force of habit—I was just about to set the date in Lutchiga." She packed up and said her farewells. On the day she was leaving the Chiga, Eria approached Eseri's father for permission to marry Eseri.

May retraced her steps—from Kabale to Kampala, down to Nairobi and Mombassa, then the Red Sea and the Canal, and on through the Mediterranean. From Paris she went to Germany; she was under obligation to report to Professor Westermann, whom she had visited in Berlin on her path to Uganda. The situation in Berlin was far different from her earlier visit, for the Nazis were now in power. Westermann no longer invited her to his home; he feared that neighbors might report that a Jewish woman was visiting him. He met her in a public situation. And he also talked in a loud voice about how good things were in Germany, because (as he explained later) there were two storm troopers nearby. Her duty done, May went to London, where fellow anthropologists who had worked in other parts of Africa were interested to have a report of her experiences. Finally, she sailed for America, landing there on January 25, 1934.

ABRAHAM EDEL

Philadelphia, 1995.

FOREWORD

THE field work on which this monograph is based was done under the auspices of the National Research Council, which granted me a Fellowship for research in Uganda in 1932-3. Their award was supplemented by a grant from the Anthropology Department at Columbia University. I wish to express my gratitude for this financial support to the institutions involved, and also my deep indebtedness to the late Professor Franz Boas, who made it all possible. I am grateful too to all the others who helped me on the way, as teachers, advisers, consultants—Ruth Benedict and Margaret Mead particularly, and also Audrey Richards, Diedrich Westermann, B. Malinowski, and Lucy Mair —and to those, British and Chiga alike, who gave me their friendship, help, and confidence during my year in Kigezi. I want especially to thank Professor Daryll Forde and Mrs. Beatrice Wyatt of the International African Institute, who have given most generously of their time and effort in editing and preparing my manuscript for publication. To all of these, and to the continued encouragement and helpful advice and criticism of my husband, I owe whatever there may be of value in this study.

Additional matter—in particular a detailed account of Chiga material culture—not included in the present book, has been filed at the Uganda Museum, Kampala, by the courtesy of the Curator, Dr. Wachsmann, where it is available for study and research purposes.

MAY M. EDEL

New York City, 1956.

1

INTRODUCTION

THE western part of Uganda is a land of great contrasts. There are enormous snow-clad peaks, and low steaming valleys; great rolling plains of elephant grass, and forests of tall trees and jungle creepers, where hordes of monkeys chatter and tease at the passers-by. To the south the land rises sharply and there, above a steep escarpment, some 7,000 feet above sea-level, is Kigezi county, home of the Chiga. A few of them live in tiny individual clearings in the Kayonza forest district of the north-west; some have moved north into the grassy plains of Mpororo, where their cattle can grow more sleek and numerous. But most of the Chiga, well over 100,000 by all estimates, live clustered in small hamlets in the eastern half of the province, which is certainly the most densely settled and intensively cultivated part of Uganda.

Little of this Chiga country is level. The hills lie in great chains of ridges, with rounded crests and deeply grooved sides. Between them wind sluggish streams bordered by papyrus swamps. Compounds lie in groups along the top and slopes of the hills, their combined fields stretching in terraced patches of brown and green over the sides of neighbouring hills. Between the cultivated areas are stretches of scrubby bush-land. Slash-and-burn farming, practised for generations, has kept the land denuded of trees, so that one sees very few, except for the groves of Australian black wattle that have begun to crown some of the hill-tops in a government reafforestation programme. This is millet country, too cold for bananas, too hilly for good pasturage. It is here, directly on the Equator, that the Chiga grow their millet and corn and peas, and tend their flocks of sheep and goats, and their few rather scrawny cattle. In good years there is plenty of millet and honey beer, and people may even eat meat from time to time. In bad years, which come all too often, they must tighten their belts and wait for the next harvest.

The Chiga people speak a Bantu dialect which is related to Nyoro. Except for a few simple consonant shifts it is virtually identical with that spoken in Ankole and Mpororo. Their cultural similarities with these neighbours to the north, and with Ruanda to the south, are profound. They live in similar beehive-shaped, grass-thatched huts, arranged in circular compounds with fences of living trees. Songs and dances are borrowed back and forth, as are many fashions in clothing, hair styles—even religion. The women working in the fields with their long-handled hoes; the growing fields of millet and maize and beans; the smooth-cropped polls, little hair tufts, or tight clay-packed curls; the leather skirts and many anklets of the women, and the cowskins slung from the shoulders of the men; the ubiquitous spear, tight-clenched in every man's right hand . . . all these are familiar from many parts of this area. So are many aspects of Chiga social life—the polygynous patriarchal households, the far-flung exogamous patrilineal clans, the bride-price payments, the worship of ancestral spirits. All these are characteristic not only of their neighbours, but of very large areas in East Africa.

But there is also a very important difference between the Chiga and their immediate neighbours. For in both Ankole and Ruanda the population is divided into distinct castes. The peasants, clearly akin to the Chiga, are ruled by pastoral overlords who, in physical type as well as in their mode of life, appear to be just what local legend calls them—a distinct, intrusive, conquering people.

The Chiga have no such overlords. They are an independent farming people. This independence they and their neighbours ascribe to their fierceness in war, their 'disloyalty' and independence of spirit. Undoubtedly their mountain home has also contributed to it—not so much by difficulty of access as in providing no pasturage good enough to support even a limited number of pastoral chiefs.

Like a few other mountain-dwellers in Ruanda, the Chiga must represent a surviving enclave of the original population which elsewhere hereabouts has come under the domination of the 'Hamitic' Hima and Tutsi, the aristocrats who rule the somewhat feudal and centralized states which have long been familiar to us as characteristic of this region. Even the cattle of the Chiga appear to be 'pre-Hamitic'; for most of them are short-horned, as befits the cattle of peasants, rather than the long-horned type to be found in the grassy plains of their pastoral neighbours.

whose peasants are usually denied the privilege of keeping cows at all.

As an independent one-class peasant people in this region of sharp caste differentiation, the Chiga are of particular historical and comparative interest. Naturally, we cannot read their culture as it stands in the twentieth century—even apart from recent European-influenced changes—as representative in detail of the way of life once established here. There have been too many influences, too much contact, for that to be the case. However, I am inclined now to be less sceptical than I was when I did my field study of the time-depth of their basically anarchic structure. At that time it seemed to me necessary to allow a high probability to the possibility that there had been cultural breakdown under the constant pressure of warfare both with Ruanda and Ankole, and the moving about of large groups to escape attempts at subjugation and demands for tribute. However, parallel pictures of structured or ordered anarchy, on a very similar basis of fissioning, segmentary lineages, have now been described and analysed for other peoples of north-east Africa, such as the Nuer, so that what appeared to be a less centralized clan structure by comparison with the south-east emerges as a relatively common pattern of the north-east, and one which therefore may well be of long standing here.

The Chiga are not a united people. There is no tribal organization, and there is much inter-clan fighting. There are minor variations in custom and even in dialect in different parts of the country. But to their neighbours, as well as to themselves, they are a distinct people. To the chiefs of Ruanda who have several times tried to conquer them, to exact tribute, or to dominate them through gifts of cattle and similar patronage, they are 'those rebellious Hima', while to their neighbours of the north they are dangerous sorcerers, referred to by scurrilous epithets and deeply feared. To themselves they are simply the independent people from Chiga.

During the early part of the twentieth century there was open warfare with Ruanda. The Nyabingi cult, of which we shall hear a great deal more later on, was growing into a political force, directed against the rulers of Ruanda. The Chiga were being further harassed by a series of organized raids by Pygmy peoples who were hiding out in the forest country to the north-west and across the border in the Congo. The Pygmy raids seemed particularly terrible to the Chiga because they were entirely destructive. The Pygmies were not interested in stealing live cattle; they slaughtered all they could lay hands on, and burned and destroyed all the villages in their path. Many people fled from their houses at that time, taking refuge in papyrus swamps or crude shelters in the uncleared bush. Some of the people near the lake shore took refuge on the islands, towing their cattle after them, and thus escaped the heaviest brunt of the fighting. In many places homes and families were so broken up that today many young people are ignorant of their relationships. Throughout this period of protracted fighting, many people took advantage of the situation to push their own feuds, in some cases actually siding with the Pygmies against their traditional Chiga enemies.

While the Chiga were being harried in the south, they were successfully pushing their own boundaries out toward the north. This was not a general tribal movement. Portions of clans moved piecemeal into territory which was first claimed by raids. The groups which have moved into the fertile plains north of the mountains have grown more wealthy as their cattle have multiplied in the excellent pasturage. Many have taken on pastoral ways of speech and life to match this; but they and their children are still known as Chiga, nor do they accept the overlordship of the rulers of Mpororo. These northern rulers too from time to time attempted to dominate or conquer them. Many Chiga still boast of family participation in the murder of two sons of Kahaya, a chief of Mpororo, who were sent down to exact tribute from the Chiga and mysteriously disappeared. And many still swear by Kahaya—not as a former overlord, but as their enemy, just as others swear by the lake, which has often drowned their relatives.

At the time when I lived among the Chiga, in 1933, their contacts with European civilization were all very recent and, in superficial ways, not very conspicuous. Kabale station was set up in 1913, and the missions were only a little older. There was little acquaintance with money. Apart from a short, wrapped cotton shirt popular with the young men, few people wore cloth garments or used any kind of store-bought goods. And there were no Europeans in the district other than government officers and missionaries. But far-reaching influences were actually at work, and the less obvious consequences of this official contact were already considerable.

Open feuds had been ruled out, which lessened, though it by no means did away with, 'murders'; this made possible a new freedom of movement within the country, of which increasing advantage was being taken. Local courts under Ganda-trained chiefs were widely resorted to. The head-tax was a first step towards a money economy, which was beginning to have an effect on working habits and exchange. Forced limitation of bride-price payments was influencing marriage arrangements, so that more young men were finding it possible to get brides of their own.

Much more important was the effect of the comprehensive ban on religious practices, introduced as a consequence of the uprisings of the previous two decades. The whole cult of the Nyabingi spirits was deemed a subversive secret society; most of its practitioners were captured and taken as prisoners to Kampala; and many other religious practices were forbidden. The result is that overt religious practices dwindled to nothing. The spirit huts were destroyed, no one wore even ordinary charms, and Christianity flourished.

During the greater part of my year among the Chiga, I lived in the village of Bufuka. This is a hamlet of some sixteen families, linked by close ties to some twenty-odd other related families who lived nearby. Bufuka is a high peninsula, sloping steeply to the papyrus-rimmed shore of a beautiful island-studded lake, Bunyonyi, place of the little birds. The lake plays only a small part in Bufuka living. There is a little fishing, and only a few people trap and smoke frogs. The one aspect of Bufuka life into which the lake does enter to any extent is in the use of the canoe. At that time transportation by water was common; most families owned some sort of canoe, and depended upon it to reach some of their outlying fields. Moreover, ferrying provided some cash income from time to time for many of the men, who ferried the District Officer and native officials on their regular visits of inspection. But apart from this, life in Bufuka was like that of most other Chiga villages. The basic diet was derived from the produce of the fields, as it would be in any other Chiga village. My friends in Bufuka had no greater affection for the water, for all its attractive availability, than any of their less fortunate

fellow Chiga, whose water supply was often a considerable distance away—and a muddy mess at best. Washing was as carefully avoided, and the drinking of plain water as disdainfully
shunned, in Bufuka as anywhere in the region.

The houses in Bufuka are grouped along the peninsula; their
fields lie interspersed with those of their nearest neighbours farther
along the lake shore and a little distance inland. Here the women
spend most of their days from dawn till early afternoon. Often
they take the younger children with them, unless they can arrange
to leave them in the care of an old man or older sibling at home.
The older children may go along to help, or go off separately to
tend the flocks and herds. The six-year-old boys trail along with
the twelve-year-old herders when the latter condescend to tolerate
their presence. Most men also are away by day, fetching materials
for house-building, arranging the purchase of a hoe, or just drinking beer, so that by day the houses and courtyards are often
very quiet.

After four o'clock, when most women come home from the
fields, smoke rises through the straw roof-tops throughout the
village, greetings and messages are called across the courts and
paths, and sometimes quarrels are aired. But after dusk the
village grows very quiet again. As dark comes on and the last of
the cows are herded into the compounds, the entrances are barred,
and soon after house doors are put up and the fires burn low.
There is no artificial lighting—nothing but brief-lived rush
torches—and no one except thieves and witches is likely to go
about on ordinary nights. When the moon is full, girls may
take advantage of its light to dance and visit in the evening. And
when there is a wedding or other festive occasion, people will
gather to feast, to drink beer, and to dance. Otherwise, each
family spends the evening quietly at its own fireside, eating, talking, perhaps telling stories, till children and adults fall off to sleep.

My house in Bufuka was a compound built for me well in the
centre of the hamlet. My living arrangements were those of an
individual of some wealth and position. I had a large compound,
with several houses and numerous retainers. (The problem finally
became one of limiting the number of my retainers' retainers—
they tended to multiply by a system of continuously extending
apprenticeships.) My cook was not a Chiga, but the rest of my
staff were, and many were recruited from Bufuka and nearby

villages. My closest contacts were with members of one network of patrilineal kin, that of a large lineage of the Abayundu clan. However, I had a substantial 'in' with the important and extensive Abasigi, for a local schoolmaster who lived in Bufuka belonged to an important family of that clan. Despite his Christianity, he was well-liked, well-respected and even trusted by his kinsmen, so that his friendship proved invaluable to me. He made it possible for me to speak in confidence to several older men on religious topics which would otherwise have been closed to me. Another valued friend who widened my circle of contacts was Mukombe, a senior chief and a most intelligent and sympathetic man, with genuine intellectual curiosity, who was always interested and helpful. But I owed most, perhaps, to one family in Bufuka, whose womenfolk befriended me as mothers, and one of whose daughters came to live in my compound, to be my companion, my social secretary and special mentor.

My work in Bufuka was conducted entirely in the Chiga language. This was not so much a matter of principle—there were many occasions when I should have been happy to have had the services of an interpreter—but of simple necessity. No one but a chief or two and a few members of my house-staff spoke any Swahili—which in any case would have improved matters very little—and English was known to only a few boys in the higher forms at the government school. One of them worked with me for a while at the beginning of my stay, shortening the period I needed to learn the language enough to be on my own, but he did not come from a nearby village, and his continued presence would have been intrusive rather than helpful.

The account of the Chiga as I present it here is for the most part a picture of life as it was still being lived when I was there in 1933. Where significant changes were already taking place, I tried to get as full a picture as possible of the established older ways, while these were still within most people's memory and many people's practice. The various directions of change that were taking place at that time are discussed in the contexts in which they seemed to me most relevant, and will therefore be found in various chapters throughout the book.

2

SOCIAL STRUCTURE

THE structure of Chiga society is polysegmentary. It is based on a fissioning lineage system similar in many ways to that which has been described for the Nuer and other peoples in northern East Africa. Among the Chiga, the process reaches from the individual household, which contains the dividing lines of future separation within its unity, to the exogamous clans, which are linked segments of larger totemic groups. The individual is thus a member of a whole series of patrilineal groups, each a segment of the next larger unit, each reckoned back to a successively more remote common ancestor. There is the small group of immediate agnatic kinsmen whose mutual social contacts and obligations are extensive and deep; and there are increasingly larger lineage groups whose members' common social responsibilities are correspondingly less intense. The group structure is all patrilineal. Residence is largely within the extended lineage, marriage bonds are limited by clan exogamy, wars and feuds are patterned along lines of clan and lineage cleavage. The individual has links with other, non-agnatic kinsmen through his mother and through his wife; and he has personal bonds with various non-relatives created by formal pacts of blood-brotherhood. But these do not constitute any sort of group structure; they are unique for each individual. There is no formal organized political unity at any level, but such joint responsibility or corporate action as there is, is structured along lineage lines.

HOUSEHOLD

The patriarchal household (*eka*) is the basic social unit. Physically, the household consists of a circle of huts connected by a fence of live bushes. The whole forms an enclosed compound, with only one gateway. The closed circle of the compound symbolizes the unity of the household. Within it are the homes of the living members and the spirit huts of the ancestors; in the centre is the fire where the master of the household sits to warm himself, and where he takes his meals when the weather permits. Here wedding feasts and mourning rites are held, diviners and medicine men practise their skills, beer is brewed and drunk, and guests are entertained. In the courtyard stand the family grain bins, separate ones for all the separate huts, and here the cows are kept safe for the night, guarded by piled-up branches at the gateway and the vigilance of the household head, who gets up many times during the night to look out into his compound and see that all is well.

Outside the compound is another courtyard, a flat, dry place where grain can be spread to dry, or bundles of rushes sewn into mats. Here a casual passer-by may stop to chat; but entering the compound is a formal visit, an intrusion by one who is not invited, unless he be a very trusted friend.

The nucleus of the household is an extended patriarchal family. The head of the household is the oldest male. He may be the father, or the eldest of a group of brothers. His married sons normally live in the same compound, in houses of their own which may be part of the same circle, or in a kind of annexe attached to it. Each wife, and each son's wife, has a house of her own; men have no separate houses for sleeping or entertaining, but spend their time in rotation in the huts of their various wives. Children live in their own mothers' houses until they are grown up. A son stays on in his mother's house for a few months after his marriage, while his bride learns the ways of his family. A daughter leaves her parents' home when she is married, going to take her place in her husband's family, where, if all goes well, she will spend the rest of her days.

A wife is definitely part of her husband's family group. The conclusion of the marriage rites assimilates her to it completely. She remains a part of it even after her husband's death, as a wife to one of his younger sons or, in her later years, as a dowager mother. With respect to her own father's household, her household-of-origin, her status changes sharply when she marries. Although she remains a kinswoman there, it is no longer her home. When she comes there on a visit, or even if she lives there for a while pending a possible divorce, she is an outsider, not a member. All sorts of disabilities and tabus hem her in.

The household may also contain persons who are not kinsmen, but complete outsiders. Slaves, for example, both male and

female, were sometimes kept. They were captured in war or purchased, most often from the neighbouring Nyaruanda. A slave
worked for the master of the household, or for some particular
wife to whom he or she was assigned. A male slave might sometimes be allowed access to a woman, but seldom had a wife of
his own. The status of a female slave varied; in some cases she
remained a handmaiden; in other cases she was actually accepted
as a wife and had a house and fields of her own. The children
of slave women were full members of the household and of the
family. If their mother had no special designated husband, they
counted as the master's children. Male or female slaves who
were acquired as young children were generally treated as children
of the family and exogamous marriages were arranged for them.

There might also be temporary outsiders in a household, mostly
youths come to serve as herdboys or apprentices, or children
being reared for a time by maternal kinsmen. Sometimes such
youngsters were not claimed back by their original patrilineal kin
and became adoptive members of the new household. Such
adoption was entirely informal and was marked by no rites.
Older youths who attached themselves to a household might stay
on and eventually marry into the community, setting up their
own separate households nearby.

Every extended patriarchal household is in most respects a
single social unit, and one which has considerable independence.
It has its own cows, its flocks of sheep and goats, its own fields,
spread among those of its neighbours along the slopes of the
surrounding hillsides. Economically, it is independent and must
support itself, raise the bride-price for the marriages of its male
members, supply the sheep and goats for necessary sacrifices.
The *nyineka*, 'master (or owner) of the household', has full control of everyone and everything in it—wives and children, houses,
fields, cattle, servants, and slaves if any. He parcels out the gardening patches, makes offerings to the spirits, decides when an
animal is to be butchered and how it is to be shared out, both
within the household and to friends and kinsmen. He makes
marriage arrangements for both the sons and the daughters, and
must be treated by all with respect and obedience.

Within the household, however, individuals have many customary separate rights. Each wife, and each son's wife, has her
own hut, and every hut is a separate unit of domestic economy.

Each wife tills her own fields, stores her own crops, feeds her own children, and cooks separately for her husband. A wife has no responsibility whatsoever for the children of her co-wives, and there are even differential property rights among the various houses (see below, pp. 35, 96). Grown sons and their wives maintain their own daily routines quite apart from those of the main household, though they must do certain defined chores and bring specified gifts from time to time. Even quite young children may work their own fields or own some separate property (see below, p. 94).

This separateness which exists within the household's formal unity is an important expression of the segmentary principle upon which the larger social structure is built. Like the series of larger patrilineages of which the household is a part, it is in a state of potential fission, tending to split into component units which will have independent status. In the household, these lines of potential cleavage are the separate sub-households of the various sons, particularly those of different mothers. Even during a father's lifetime, a mature son may become a household head in his own right, with his father's permission. To build for himself without this permission would be a serious offence. No one would help him in such a defiant enterprise. But if his father does give permission, and lends his formal assistance, the son may build a compound of his own, maintain his own herds and fields, arrange his children's marriages, and so on. He will, however, still make offerings to the ancestral spirits through his father, and will carry to his father the customary first-fruit gifts that mark his formal dependence.

After the father's death, sons are expected to remain together as a unit under the authority of the eldest among them, who is the official heir. But in practice the bond is a tenuous one and, as the years pass, the sons become more independent, even to the point of building their own spirit huts. They will still be bound by many ties of mutual obligation. Some of these are largely voluntary. They will help each other in daily chores and in times of crisis, lend each other cattle for a bride-price payment (to be returned in full), go together to beer feasts and sometimes on cattle-raids. In a more formal way, a senior is responsible for the well-being of junior orphaned siblings, and should see to their marriages, as their father would have done. And brothers serve as necessary witnesses at each other's weddings. Most formal and most important of all is the obligation to avenge a brother in the event of his murder. This is more or less independent of any question of cause or provocation; a man's own kinsmen will not lightly agree that his murder was justified, though a persistent thief might be abandoned to the vengeance of his victims (see below, p. 112).

The obligation to exact vengeance falls on the closest kinsman, preferably a full brother. It is he who must perform the ceremonial act which will appease his brother's ghost. This consists, at its most formal best, of offering the murderer or one of his kinsmen to the ghost as a sacrifice. Preferably he will be taken alive, so that he can be shown to the ghost before being speared to death. Afterwards, the victim's body will be thrown out into 'the wilderness', where it will be eaten by beasts or rot away, unless it is rescued by a pact-brother and taken back to its former home for burial.

At the very least, the ghost must be told that the vengeance killing has taken place. Otherwise, it will haunt its brothers, giving them no peace. However, it is not absolutely necessary that they should do the killing. They may accept the favour of a lineage kinsman, who has had, or taken, the opportunity to make a suitable killing. The brother will talk to the ghost, in proper formal fashion, and reward his helpful kinsman with the gift of a goat, the 'reward of the brave man'.

The Chiga make a sharp distinction between the required formal relationships between brothers and the informal acts which are based on friendship. 'The hyaena of your own family', they say in a proverb, 'may eat you, but he will still gather up your bones for burial.' And, indeed, brothers do become embroiled in quarrels, even fratricidal ones, though normally their households remain linked, even after their death.

LINEAGE

Groups of closely related households, brothers and brothers' sons, form the first level of what the Chiga call a *mulyango* or lineage. This is a generic term which applies not only to such a group, but to much larger patrilineages, tracing their common descent from ancestors much farther removed. (It is interesting to note that the Chiga term *mulyango* is not only the same term as that used by other Bantu groups for similar segmentary lineages, but has the same meaning as the corresponding, linguistically unrelated Nuer word for lineage: 'doorway'.) Members of a lineage refer to themselves as the 'sons of so-and-so'. 'So-and-so' may be a great-grandfather in one context or a more remote ancestor in some other context, where reference is to a wider group of agnates.

We can best clarify the structure by illustrating it from some of the actual relations in Bufuka.

Most of the families in Bufuka, as well as on the two neighbouring peninsulas along the lake shore, belong to the Abajura lineage of the Abayundu clan (see diagram, p. 196). The Abajura are all descended from Nkuba, who is said to be a grandson of Kayundu, the clan ancestor. Many lineages take their names directly from that of the clan ancestor, but in this case the connexion is indirect; *enkuba* is thunder, and *enjura* means rain.

The Abajura in turn are divided into a number of segments, the Abazigate, the Abatora, and others, and these in turn into further segments. On Bufuka there are several clusters of houses which belong to groups of brothers and cousins. One of these belongs to the Abahabga lineage, a segment of the Abatora; another belongs to the Abahirane, a segment of the Abazigate. There are several others which belong to different segments of the Abakobga. Any of these levels may be called *mulyango*, and used as a designating reference by a member.

All these lineage segments are distributed in similar small clusters on the neighbouring peninsulas as well. The people of Bufuka and the next peninsula reckon themselves as fairly close relatives, peacefully living together within this general area. Those of the farther peninsula are relatives too, but the amount of social interaction is smaller. They are Abajura, and some are members of the Abazigate or Abatora, but not usually of the same smaller segments (see map, p. 195).

Within the boundaries of this whole area, the houses of brothers and cousins tend to cluster together; otherwise the distribution does not follow lineage lines closely. And the fields of all these families are distributed in still different patterns over the surrounding hillsides. An Omukobga from Bufuka may cultivate a section of a slope which lies next to that of a man whose house is at the end of the next peninsula, and who belongs to a lineage of the Abazigate.

Beyond these peninsulas along the lake shore are hamlets belonging to other Abajura families; a few are segments of the same lineages; some belong to other Abajura lines. There are also Abajura houses and fields out on the islands and across the cove; some belong to people from Bufuka who are moving in that direction; others to a quite distinct but friendly lineage of the Abayundu. Farther along the lake shore lie the houses of people of other Abayundu lineages, some friendly, and some unfriendly, to the Abajura, but none on terms of active social relationships with them. There was more visiting, lending, helping at feasts, and so on with some nearby families of another clan (Abasigi) than with the members of these remoter lineages.

The various members of a lineage such as the Abahirane have a high degree of social integration. Their mutual relations are much the same as those between actual brothers, especially if the group is small. For a larger lineage group like the Abazigate, the mutual interrelations are of a more formal character, consisting principally of required attendance at each other's ceremonial functions. The oldest girl of each household in such a lineage must come to dance at the wedding of any of its members, must welcome a new bride, and go to visit a lineage sister in her new home after her marriage. They are the sisters-in-law of her new husband and are permitted a degree of familiarity with him which exists only in this relationship. Men of the lineage have similar formal roles in relation to weddings. All of them, too, must attend the funeral of anyone in the lineage, and observe the four days of mourning, when no work is permitted.

There is no similar formal relationship between fellow members of such a large lineage as the Abajura. The daughters of an Abakobga household would not dance at the wedding of an Omuhirane girl unless especially invited; they would certainly not visit her at her new home after the marriage, no matter how close their friendship had been as maidens. That would be an unseemly kind of contact with strange people, and strange men particularly. For they are all Abajura, but not of the same lineage segment. On the other hand, they would have to visit the new bride of any Omuzigate man, even if they have no personal kind feelings toward him or his household. This is their duty

as members of the lineage. But girls of the Abakobga households will wait until the bride comes out of her retirement and
becomes a working member of the community.

While at any time the action context which defines each particular level of lineage grouping is clear, there are no formal rules
for marking them off—no fixed number of generations, no specific
size. The Abahabga on Bufuka are closely related, but there is
considerable tension among them. As the diagram (p. 196) indicates, they are all children of one grandfather. But the senior
brother of the group is a harsh and bitter man who treated his
junior orphaned siblings and half-siblings so badly that they built
separate homes for themselves as soon as they were able. One
of these present household heads is not even married yet. He
and a younger brother live in a house he has built for them with
their mother, who does the necessary woman's work. It seems
most likely that this group of 'brothers' will separate as time
passes; if the strained relations continue, their children may come
to consider themselves distinct lineages, involved with each other
only at a very formal level. Meanwhile, they and the Abakobga
are somewhat separated off from the other Abatora.

The Abahirane, on the other hand, have only a common great-
grandfather. They are no closer to each other than the Abahabga
are to the Abakobga, except that their grandfathers were apparently, at least as now reported, full brothers rather than half-
brothers. The Abahirane on Bufuka are a very closely interacting
and friendly group. When 5 hurt his arm, it was his 'brother' 9
who came every day to milk his cow. Their children too reckon
each other as close kinsmen and may continue to do so. As time
passes, and especially if the lineage group involved increases in
size, they may come to limit their social relations more exclusively to each other, attend each other's weddings, but not those
of other Abazigate, and so on. Already there is only one other
household nearby with whom they maintain anything like such
lineage relations. They may, therefore, soon come to constitute
a lineage of the same level as the present Abazigate. Probably,
too, in both these cases, genealogical references, when they are
made at all, will be shifted to fit the new situation more closely.

This is the way the fissioning process works. Individual friendships, quarrels arising between individuals or small groups, the
number of living members of a lineage group, their physical

proximity or distance, which may be a function of some individual quirk or accident—all help to determine lines of cleavage between brothers' households and within lineage groups.

The largest lineages, like the Abajura, are major segments of the exogamous patrilineal clans. Such a lineage is to a considerable extent a local group, though some of its segments may become separated, as has one Abajura lineage, the Abachuchu (see p. 17). The various members of such a major lineage are on the whole a friendly group and, particularly when they are also neighbours, there is much casual visiting, lending and borrowing. Everyone knows everyone else's business pretty well, and their fields are often spread out over the same hillsides, as we have seen. Although it is not marked by any structure of ceremonial or authority within the group, such a lineage does have a kind of unity, particularly in its external relations. This is seen most clearly in relation to the vengeance feud. As we have noted, taking vengeance is the task of a full brother, a co-member of the smallest lineage segment. But the object of vengeance is not so narrowly defined. Vengeance may be exacted on any member of the widest lineage of which the murderer is a member. And since vengeance for the Chiga is not a simple single act of retaliation, but tends to set up a permanent situation of feud, large lineages, even within the same clan, may be in a state of perpetual enmity. This does not imply that the lineage fights as an integrated unit. Those who enjoy raiding and fighting will go off as an attacking party, on some remote pretext of settling a score; the whole community may, however, be the target of some later retaliatory attack by the victims.

Theoretically, such feuding and fighting does not happen within the lineage. Actually, however, fights do flare up, even between close relatives, and sometimes they result in death. This is murder, and a heinous offence. Should the victim, however, be a remote kinsman rather than a close one, his relatives would be likely to turn the occasion into a general fight against the close relatives of the murderer, and thus threaten to precipitate a real feud within the lineage. If a man has no close kinsmen in the lineage, he is in an exposed and dangerous position. My neighbours in Bufuka insisted that one man, who lived at the tip of the peninsula, would never have been able to remain there safely before the *pax Britannica*, for although he was of the Abakobga like many of the others, he did not belong to the same minor segment as anyone else. So, in the old days, one of his remote lineage 'brothers', tempted by his cattle, might have plundered them, or even killed him, with impunity, knowing that there was no one who would be concerned to prevent or avenge the act.

There is a way to avoid continued bloodshed within the lineage, or between two closely related ones. This involves a special peace-making rite (*karabisa*) and the payment of compensation. In the ceremony a sheep is killed and its blood poured over the murderer and the bereaved, thus reuniting them. This sheep is a kind of scapegoat. It is eaten by the ritual specialist, who thereby transfers to himself the curse which forbids friendly relations between the murderer and his victim's family. The two lineages can then safely associate with each other, but not with him. The amount of the compensation is arranged by bargaining. I was told it was usually 'smaller than a proper bride-price'. This is the only way in which the Chiga use wergild. It is never acceptable between members of different clans, but serves only to avert further fighting between related groups. However, even within the lineage there are no authorities to insist upon preventing further bloodshed. The rite can only take place if the respective parties agree to it. Otherwise the feud is on, and instead of two friendly segments within a lineage, there are two separate, enemy lineages.

Although the large lineage is in a sense a local group, it does not own the land which its members occupy. House-plots and garden-plots are owned by the individual households. The relation of the lineage to its land is a matter of safety, of peaceful co-residence rather than of joint ownership. The boundaries of lineage land are not fixed. A group of brothers may move away on to bush land, if they can find any that is unclaimed. Any close kinsman may follow and claim nearby land, because he feels safe where other members of his lineage live. Sometimes a group of brothers moves on to land that some other group already claims, establishing their right by fighting for it. That is what the Abachuchu did only a few generations ago. They fought their way to land much farther north, where the pasturage is much better. They established themselves there, and they and their flocks and herds have flourished. The Abachuchu were

originally a lineage segment of the Abajura; since their separation and subsequent growth they have come to be considered a
separate major lineage of the Abayundu, though they continue
to remember their close bond with the Abajura near the lake.

This whole picture of land use and land rights must be seen
against a background of considerable mobility, rather than fixed
relationship to a particular area of land. Any period of ten to
twenty years will normally see a total redistribution of the people
in any neighbourhood. Household by household, the members
of the village move away, often in different directions. Areas
once cultivated revert to bush. In these circumstances the relationship to the land and the meaning of land-ownership are very
different from what is likely to prevail where settlements are
continuous over many generations (cf. pp. 99-101).

There is some question as to whether there was a greater degree
of lineage cohesion in earlier times. People refer to some individuals as having been 'leaders' or 'elders' of various lineages.
As nearly as I could make out, such leadership was not specific
or institutionalized. A man who happened to be a rain-maker
performed his rites for members of his lineage. And such a body
of power and knowledge tended to be hereditary, setting up a
family line of leading men in a lineage who could make rain.
Individuals known for their fighting prowess also had considerable prestige. Their opinions might be sought and their advice
followed, but they had no power to command obedience or enforce decisions. In at least some areas offerings appear to have
been made to spirits associated with lineage ancestors, rites which
were performed by senior elders. This could have constituted a
structural point with a real stratification potential, but there is
no evidence of such a tendency in the current picture. The term
mukama, 'master' or 'ruler', which is as close as one can come
in Chiga to anything like 'chief', was not applied to any such
lineage elders. It was applied only to the priests of Nyabingi,
officers of a new cult which had swept the land just before the
coming of the British, superseding many other cults and rites.
These priests had arrogated to themselves powers of a political
sort, modelled on the Ruanda chieftainship, which cut right across
the traditional structural lines (see below, p. 155). But there is no
evidence that lineage elders or anyone else had anything like comparable powers before that time.

The lineage is made up of members born into it. One does not permanently sever lineage ties, however inactive they may become. Nor can one, so far as I could discover, become assimilated to another lineage. Even women, although they become members of their husbands' households, do not become members of the lineage; their status is the special one of wives, women married into a lineage rather than members of it. They remain members of their own lineage of origin, though they are no longer parts of their fathers' households. To their own lineage kin they remain 'girl of the clan'; and they owe them friendly hospitality and other tokens of kinship if they come visiting. Some people do live apart from their agnates. Driven by famine, perhaps, or a quarrel at home, a man may take refuge with his wife's brother or his sister's husband, and build a home under his protection. Members of this brother-in-law's lineage may come to accept him, even to respect him, as a friend and neighbour. But he cannot become one of them formally; he and his sons can even marry among them, for they are outsiders. Most communities numbered one or two such alien householders, but they were a very small minority. They were never a large enough group to affect the strictly kinship basis of the community.

In a formal sense, a community really has no official existence. The term *echaro* means occupied, rather than bush, land; it does not mean the people living there. There is a great deal of difference in settlement patterns in various areas. There are places where homesteads are isolated, each set in the midst of its own fields. More commonly, compounds are set in clusters, which may be only 100 feet or so apart from each other over a considerable area, as in Bufuka. Then the fields stretch out over the surrounding hillsides in a neat patchwork of small plots. People thus occupying neighbouring house-sites and field plots are mostly lineage kin, as we have seen, and their associations are primarily determined by degree of kinship. But lineage kin and outsiders alike, who are neighbours, are often friendly and helpful. A woman will stop to help a neighbour shell peas and gossip briefly, or will bring some warm gruel for an invalid. And neighbours will certainly all come to a house-raising, help with food and firewood towards a feast, stop by for a song and dance and some beer at a wedding, regardless of kinship ties. And so will friendly individuals from farther away. Several neighbours with

only a few cows each may herd them together, or build common
watering troughs for their cattle. Beer compacts and hunting
parties are organized on a basis of neighbourliness and friendship,
and not according to strict canons of kinship. And if there is a
blacksmith in your village, you are more likely to turn to him
for a new hoe than to seek one out elsewhere—though you need
not. Village mates usually start their planting together, too, because, they say, no one's fields will then be alone to bear the
brunt of an attack by wild animals or birds. Should a man catch
a thief in his compound, or should a leopard enter the neighbourhood, or someone's house go up in flames, everyone within
hearing distance of the cries would be expected to come running
to the rescue, irrespective of kinship. In fact, failure to assist is
taken to mean probable complicity. And should a witch be
apprehended, and proved by ordeal to be guilty of murder, then
everyone, not just the aggrieved family or the victim's kinsmen,
will turn out to stone her (or him) to death.

Apart from such contexts of emergency joint action, though,
the community as such has no necessary integral unity. Its unity
comes from the lineage bonds and ties of friendship which unite
most of its members; it is these that determine patterns of joint
action. Such bonds all members share with other agnates who
happen to live a little farther away, on the next hill, or the next
peninsula, as well as with particular non-agnates, uterine kinsmen or part-brothers who are different for each family in the
community.

CLAN

Lineages are segments of larger patrilineal groups for which
the Chiga use a district term. This is the *oruganda*, the 'main
branch'; because the official differentiating criterion for this group
is the practice of exogamy, I have called it the clan. This also
corresponds with the usage in the older literature for this area.
The Abajura who live in and around Bufuka are Abayundu; they
trace their ancestry back, in a way that has no doubt long departed from strict genealogical accuracy, to Kayundu, and so do
the members of several other large lineages, most of whom live
farther on along the shores of the lake. With two of these other
Abayundu lineages the people of Bufuka were more or less at
peace when I was there; they did not co-operate with them very

closely, so that a marriage in one of these villages was known in Bufuka only when the echoes of the singing and dancing at the marriage feast could actually be heard. But with one of the other lineages, the Abahanda, they were involved in a feud that had been going on for many years. All hope of peace-making had long since passed. This lineage was considered far more of an enemy than were members of other clans, for there were many specific aggressive acts—on both sides, no doubt—lying between them, and no compensating marriages or pact-friendships, such as would normally involve different individuals with members of other clans.

The clans are not, strictly speaking, local units. That is a function of the larger lineage segments. However, some at least of a clan's lineages will ordinarily occupy lands adjacent to one another. To outsiders, members of other clans, such areas will usually be referred to as 'the lands of the Abayundu'. For when there is any marked social distance between two groups, the clan designation supersedes the lineage as a point of reference. 'We are marrying a girl of the Abakongwe,' a marriage party may announce; though, in point of fact, no close ties of any sort are set up with the other clan by a marriage; the implications of the affinal bonds affect only lineage kinsmen of the bride and groom. In the same way a man's proud war boasts may speak of raids against some other clan, when in fact the target is a particular lineage within it. Similarly, a girl married and living away from home is 'one of ours' or 'a daughter of the Abayundu', and even a remote clan sister, met on one's travels, becomes a relative. People also tend to identify themselves by their own clan membership, and to accept as appropriate certain ascriptions of local habits and even personality. For example, my Abayundu friends had a reputation for being inhospitable, which, to the Chiga, is the virtual equivalent of theft. This reputation they have not only among other people; I have heard them say of themselves, 'If an Omuyundu is not lying, he's stealing.' Other differences, like styles of dancing or a new hair-do, when they spread through a neighbourhood, are often referred to as the ways of such-and-such a clan—for certainly they pertain to the people, not the geographical locality.

Some of these inter-clan differences appear to be a little more significant. For example, one clan has certain customs in relation

to burials and to mother-in-law avoidance which are said to
be like those of the people of Mpororo, the neighbouring kingdom
to the north. And certain clans have a definite inter-clan function. They are known as Abashe and are reported never to have
engaged in warfare. They were never aggressors, and were
apparently also immune from attack. As a result, they were able
to perform a number of distinctive services. A solitary person
when travelling found it safe to go and stay with them, even
though he was a stranger. Sick or wounded persons were left
with them until their relatives were able to fetch them. They
are even said to have acted as intermediaries between warring
clans. They would go and stand between the warring parties on
their own initiative and attempt to separate them—or so I was
told. But I was not told what combination of circumstances
would prompt such unlikely action. In addition, the Abashe had
a special ritual role. They stood as proxies in various ceremonies
for people who were not able to be present in person. For example, should a man die and be buried without handing over his
property to his heirs, the ritual might be gone through later with
the help of the Abashe; or a girl married far from her father's
home might complete some of the later marriage rituals with the
Abashe as proxies for her father, to save the long journey home.

The clans, then, have structural significance, placing an individual in a very wide sense *vis-à-vis* the rest of the Chiga as a
member of a particular exogamous group; their implications for
in-group relations, however, are minimal. Clan members have
no common required participation in any activities, no common
leaders or form of authority, no common lands. They do have
a common ancestor, but this is too far back in time to have any
important implications for living clan members, as an ancestral
ghost has influence only over a stretch of two or three generations, not indefinitely. Sometimes a man in a position of personal leadership in a particular lineage will be well enough known
for others to speak of him as a man of importance, but his position
is not official. Among members of other clans, such a man might
well be called a leader of the Abayundu or Abasigi; within his
own clan, however, his following would not be so inclusive.
There was among the Abasigi, for example, a leader and warrior
named Tomasi, whose quick acceptance of the Europeans was
said to have brought the Abasigi as a whole into a friendly

instead of a rebellious relationship with them. Yet that was due entirely to his personal influence and following. Two of his own brothers chose not to follow his tactics, and there was no one to compel them to do so.

Just as lineages and households subdivide and are replaced by several descendant units of the same order, so may clans. The Chiga do not consider the clan as an essentially fixed and static grouping. Clans may and do subdivide along lines of previous lineage division. A clan is an exogamous patrilineal grouping. When two lineages within a clan intermarry, then they become two separate clans. To judge by recent occurrences, such marriages take place on the initiative of the families involved, and in spite of the possible protests of other people. Just beyond the hills inland from the lake shore near Bufuka lie the lands of a rather small clan called the Abahesi. There were numerous intermarriages between them and the Abayundu. But the Abachuchu lineage, which had moved off to the north, had not heard of this 'fashion'; they still considered, and designated, the Abahesi a separate major lineage segment of the Abayundu.

In line with this fissioning of the clan, we find the clans grouped into larger, non-exogamous, groupings, which refer to themselves as having common *obwonko* or origins; they have a common eponymous ancestor, and share a common totem. The Abayundu, for example, together with the Abahesi, are Abagahe, descendants of Kagahe. There are other Abagahe clans as well, including the extremely large clan of the Abasigi, whose lands extend for many miles to the north. That they are not as closely related as are the Abahesi and Abayundu is indicated in the semi-legendary genealogies in which the latter are called half-brothers, children of one of Kagahe's sons, while the Abasigi are descended from him through another son, by a different mother.

Clans with common origin have no unity beyond their common food tabu, which has little significance in ordinary living. That of the Abagahe is a particular variety of cow. Should such a cow be born into one of their flocks it would be traded away; little interest or attention needs to be devoted to it. There are other food tabus, of far greater importance and concern to people, which arise in other contexts. For example, one must avoid eating of anything that has come into contact with a spear that caused the death of a member of one's family. Such tabus, which strengthen the lines of enmity between feuding groups, are often in people's minds and in their conversation; clan tabus are casual and unstressed. In general, the fact of common descent which relates different clans does not establish any actual kinship among its various members. They do not call each other brother, in even the most remote sense; and no man thinks of himself as one of the Abagahe, in the way he definitely does think of himself as an Omuyundu.

RELATIONSHIPS OUTSIDE THE CLAN

Similarly, there is no tracing of common origin for the Chiga as a whole. Some clan groups tell tales of coming down from the north; others speak of a proud escape from attempts by the kings of Ruanda, their southern neighbours, to make them vassals. There is no formal tribal unity. They are simply 'Chiga, the people who live within a common territory and speak a common language'. Among the Chiga as a whole there is in general a balance between feud relations, which prevail between groups, and friendly relations of uterine kinship, marriage, and pact-brotherhood which link individuals across the lines of feud.

The vengeance-feud pattern has come to dominate the whole pattern of inter-clan relations. Except for truces between small neighbouring communities, where there are so many personal and affinal bonds that a state of temporary friendship can prevail, it is rather the normal thing than the exception.

Fighting may take the form of small sorties or individual ambuscades in pursuance of a particular vengeance feud; or it may reach the level of regular battles, designed to drive some other group away from the land or to take plunder. Men are killed in such battles; cows and goats, hides, hoes, and food, and sometimes children are seized and carried off. Women may be taken captive, but they are never killed, for a woman's death has to be avenged by both her husband and her father, and 'not only once, but many times over, to make up for all her children yet unborn'. Closely intermarried lineages may not involve themselves in such fighting, but the risk of it is present. That is why a man usually straps a dagger under his arm when he goes to a feast. Spears may be left at the gate to maintain a peaceful atmosphere, but caution suggests some protective weapon close at hand.

Blood-brotherhood

Between the independent warring clans marriages have to be negotiated, sometimes over long distances. And occasionally, in times of difficulty or famine, a family has to move to some other part of the country. Sometimes such arrangements are made through uterine and affinal kin bonds (to be discussed in the next chapter). But there is another standard way of establishing individual safety within this general context of inter-clan ambush and fighting. This is the familiar African institution of the pact of blood-brotherhood which follows the usual lines here. Two men take an oath of mutual help; this is accompanied by a ritual in which each swallows some of the other's blood, together with a few grains of small millet or a portion of specially prepared gruel. (The blood is drawn from an incision in the abdomen.) This constitutes a potential curse, believed to be automatically effective and very powerful. It will descend upon either party to the oath if he betrays the other. The whole thing is dramatized; the oath itself contains a long string of formulae defining the relationship: 'If I should kill my pact-brother, may the Little Red One [the blood] destroy my house, and kill my oldest wife, and my best milk cow. If my wife refuses him food, may the blood kill her. If enemies fall upon him and he raises an alarm, if I do not come to save him, may the blood we have drunk kill me,' and so on.

In order that they may not be mistakenly punished for good acts which superficially resemble bad ones, the participants must then act out in advance the obligations and the prerogatives they are assuming. For example, they snatch a bit of grass from the thatch of the house, for 'if a man finds the house of his pact-brother burning, he may tear it apart, and save the materials, and take out the belongings, and this will not be plundering'. And they cut a slip of wood from the fence and put it on the hearth, for 'if one finds no one at home at the home of his pact-brother, he may help himself to wood and build a fire to warm himself'.

Usually gifts are exchanged. This is called 'Something to get the blood out of your mouth.' For the wealthy this might be as much as a goat or even a cow, but it may be a hoe, or even just a small token.

Once the oath has been concluded, it is considered very

binding indeed. For any serious offence against your pact-brother, even if it be an omission, you will surely die. Your abdomen will swell up and burst. (As described, the symptoms sound not unlike the haemorrhages characteristic of a particularly virulent form of dysentery which is occasionally known in this region.) Indeed, whole families are said to have died because of breach of the pact.

The point is constantly made that the bond between pact-brothers is much stronger than that between real brothers, because of the strength of the sanction. You may quarrel with your own brother and refuse ever to have him in your house, but a pact-brother must always be helped and given hospitality. Everyone can cite cases of brother killing brother, but no one could point to an instance of the murder of a pact-brother. The obligation to help him is so strong that you may even kill your own brother for attacking your pact-brother, and not be put to death as a fratricide. In fact, should you be prevented by your relatives from taking this action, they, as well as you, might suffer from the blood of the oath. And should your own brother steal cattle from your pact-brother, you would try to get him to restore them—even fighting with him for that purpose if necessary. On the other hand, it is quite a regular pattern in thieving to work with a pact-brother against your own kin, even spying out the ground for him, or hiding him, and so forth—and taking your share of the spoils, though they are stolen from your own kinsmen. Occasionally one is told with bated breath tales of someone—never the teller, nor anyone he really knows—who dared, not actually to attack but to conspire against a blood-brother, giving information to others by means of which they waylaid and killed him or stole his cattle. Survival after such an act of treachery was ascribed to the unusual powers of some ritual specialist, who was able to counteract the blood of the oath. Such power is not a general attribute of sorcerers.

The pact of brotherhood is not made between kinsmen, where it is regarded as superfluous. I knew two lads within the same clan who commonly addressed each other as 'my pact-brother', but no one knew whether they had actually gone through the ceremony, or whether they were merely using the form of address. Feelings about it were mixed: was it a joke—a rather *risqué* one —or a very ill-advised act?

A man may have a number of pact-brothers in different parts of the country. Some may become close friends, others may be mere casual acquaintances, who swore the oath for some special occasion and never renewed the relationship. The purpose is primarily to establish relationships across clan lines, rather than to strengthen existing bonds.

The pact-brother is not a kinsman, nor equated with one. The relationship has its own particular character. The term used —*omunywani*—means quite simply 'the one I drank with reciprocally'. But there are one or two ways in which the pact-brother is looked upon as a brother. For example, adultery with his wives would not be frowned upon, might even, in some cases, be connived at, but relations with his daughter are forbidden as incestuous. It is, however, permissible for the children of two pact-brothers to marry; it is even said that this is looked upon with particular favour.

Adoption

I have heard of one legalistic device by which the stranger can secure protection through adoption. 'You may grasp a woman's breast, or throw yourself at the mercy of a household head by falling before him and clasping his knees. Such an act establishes you as the child of the person in question, who must give you the favour for which you are asking, and subsequently treat you as a member of the group.' This pattern was reported to me as a possibility; but I heard of no case of its use, and was not able to discover when such an extreme measure was resorted to, or whether the person chosen had the right to extend or withhold protection as he desired. I was told also that the home of the priest of Nyabingi offered a refuge to the stranger, the murderer, and even the witch.

Apart from these purely individual bonds uniting persons from different clans in various interrelationships, there is nothing to tie the Chiga together. Almost all embryonic recognition of other clans' rights, as well as all marriages and other friendly negotiations, are established on the basis of individual ties of the sort we have just examined. And, apart from the nascent power of the Nyabingi priests, there was no authority which crossed clan lines. The Chiga are, in short, a people united only in their common disunity; a group of relatively homogeneous culture, divided into independent exogamous clans, which are related through a network of intermarriage, but are engaged in almost constant feuds. These clans are not static units, but are themselves subject to a fissioning process which characterizes Chiga groups at all levels. Each type of group has a similar pattern, being a segmentary rather than a unitary whole, and itself a segment of a larger, equally segmentary whole. Each level of patrilineal group organization is in a state of temporary equilibrium, with a limited and specific set of interaction patterns operative among its members, according to its particular level within the hierarchy of groups.

3

KINSHIP

ALTHOUGH the patrilineage is the structural basis of Chiga group organization, every individual in the lineage is set in a nexus of other affiliations. Not only the frequent pacts of blood-brotherhood, but also the kinship bonds arising out of the exogamous marriage relations cut across the divisive clan lines, forming a network of inter-personal relations which reach out in all directions. Close kinship bonds, with members of one's mother's lineage and with the families into which one's sisters and father's sisters have married, as well as with one's wife's kinsmen, are an important basis of much social action. Visiting, gift-giving, and certain marriage arrangements are all channelled along these lines. Mother's parents are as close as father's parents, and many children spend years in their households. Even within the patri-lineage, closeness of kinship counts, and the small family is set off against the wider lineage in many contexts. In reckoning kin-ship outside one's own patrilineage, this kind of limitation is even more important. While some recognition is given to affinal bonds beyond the immediate families of the parties involved, this does not reach farther than the small lineages (such as the Abahirane of the previous chapter) in any significant sense.

Chiga kinship terminology is a simple one of the standard Dakota type, though with some fuller use of compound descriptive terms. Modified terms, such as *nyinento* (little mother) for mother's sister, differentiate other kinsmen from the nuclear family, which is set apart in a number of ways throughout the system. Within the close family, relative age and full and half-relationships are also sometimes indicated. There is matrilateral cross-cousin marriage; the mother's brother's daughter is an ap-proved and preferred mate, while father's sister's daughter should never be taken in marriage. However, this difference is reflected only in the niece/nephew terms; for cross-cousins only one term is used. As is so often the case even in strictly unilinear systems, mother's and father's parents are linked in one set of grand-parent terms.

Kinship terms are always used with possessives. In some cases these are incorporated into the words themselves, so that the forms are different with the different persons. In such cases the terms are presented here in their third person forms, with the first and second person forms, in that order, enclosed in parentheses immediately after. Where terms are modifications of some of these primary terms, parallel changes in the derived forms occur, and will not be noted unless there is some important irregularity. So, for *icenkuru*, grandfather (3), from father plus old, the form *tatenkuru* will be understood (cf. 6).

Ascending Generation:

1. *icenkuruza*, male ancestors, and
2. *nyinenkuruza*, female ancestors, beyond the second ascending generation. When alive, addressed simply as 'grandparent' (3, 4).
3. *icenkuru*, 'elder father'; male grandparent in either line, and
4. *nyinenkuru*, 'elder mother'; female grandparent in either line, and their siblings.
5. *mukaka*, own grandmother—actual parent of own father or mother.
6. *ice* (*tata*, *co*), father; actual progenitor, or father's brother who has married mother.
7. *nyina* (*mawe*, *nyoko*), mother.
8. *nyineitcwe*, special respect term for mother.
9. *mukeice*, wife of father; also father's brother's wives. Women may also use this term of father's female cross-cousins (potential wives), but men would use a descriptive compound, *muzara watata*, 'father's cross-cousin'. As a rule, personal names would be preferred in such a relationship.
10. *icento* (the first person form is not used), 'little father'; any male to whom father would use the term for brother or brother-in-law. Not much used in direct address, where names are preferred.
11. *nyinento*, 'little mother'; mother's sister; seldom extended beyond her close kinswomen.
12. *nyinarume* (second person not used), 'male mother'; own mother's brother, and anyone she calls brother.
13. *nyinacendje* (*cwenkazi*, *nyokocendje*), 'female father'; any father's sister; mostly used before her marriage. After

marriage, all but the closest are more often just 'girl of our clan', which is also used for married women of own generation who are not close kinswomen.

Own Generation:

14. *munyanya*, sibling of opposite sex, usually used only of full sibling, or closest next in line.
15. *mweneice*, 'child of father'; all members of own lineage, own generation, more particularly males; sometimes extended very widely to fellow clansmen of same generation of other lineages.
16. *mwenenyina*, 'child of mother'; full sibling and maternal half-sibling; also child of mother's sister by own father.
17. *mwenenyinento*, 'child of little mother', mother's sister's child.
18. *murumona*, next younger full sibling, either sex.
19. *mukuru*, 'elder'; any older sibling; wider than 18 in its application.
20. *muzara*, cross-cousin, either line, either sex; widely extended. This is one of the few kinship terms commonly used as a term of address.

Descending Generation:

21. *omwana*, 'child'; with possessive, almost a generic term for any relative of descending generation; widely extended. Even used for those more correctly designated 22, 23, or 24.
22. *omwihwa*, sister's son, man speaking.
23. *omwicendjezane*, brother's daughter, woman speaking.

These terms have special significance because of the preferred matrilateral cross-cousin marriage, in which mother's brother's daughter is a suitable spouse, but not father's sister's daughter. It is noteworthy that these terms, specific here, are used in a cross-generation sense in related languages.

24. *omuijukuru*, grandchild, either line; also close collateral.
25. *obumira*, great-grandchild.

Affinal Terms:

26. *icezara* (no second person), spouse's father; widely extended to all his 'brothers'. I even heard it used by a girl

of a man who had sued for her, unsuccessfully, on his
son's behalf.

27. *nyinazara*, mother-in-law; any wife of 26.
28. *mukazi*, 'woman'; with possessive, own wife, brother's wife;
    sometimes used of cross-cousin who is potential spouse.
29. *iba* (*ibanye, baro*), husband; extended to his brothers.
30. *muramu*, brother-in-law, both sister's husband and wife's
    brother; extended widely. Also used by a man of his
    wife's sisters. More correct than 28 for wife of remoter
    'brother'.
31. *muramukazi*, brother's wife, husband's sister, woman speak-
    ing.
32. *mukeiba*, 'husband's wife', co-wife; husband's brother's
    wife. A more respectful circumlocution, such as 'daughter-
    in-law of my mother-in-law', is preferred for a very senior
    co-wife.
33. *musanzirane*, wife's sister's husband.
34. *mukwe*, son-in-law (passive form of wife); also his brothers.
35. *mukamwana*, 'wife of child', daughter-in-law; formal, ex-
    tended. 'My child' is oftener used in direct address.

Any combination of these terms may be used descriptively,
both when specific reference happens to be necessary, and also
as a mark of respect. A parent-in-law will be addressed by reference to some remote consanguineal tie rather than as 'mother-
in-law'; a man may also use teknonymy—'mother (or wife) of
so-and-so'. Outside such special respect situations, where personal names are actually forbidden, the more complex terms would
not ordinarily be used very much, as personal names are preferred
both for reference and direct address.

Kinship terms established in childhood tend to be permanent.
When a woman marries one of her husband's sons, outsiders may
speak of him as father to her children, but within the household
his half-brothers and sisters remain his siblings. He is, of course,
their senior in authority in any case. The new husband's children
by a former marriage continue to call their new stepmother
'grandmother' rather than 'mother', and his wives still regard
her as having the superior status of a mother-in-law, rather than
as their equal. On the other hand, if a man's brother marries
his widow, her children, especially if they were quite young at

the time of the marriage, may refer to him as father, though the actual relationship would be remembered and used in certain contexts, especially those referring to inheritance.

ATTITUDES AND OBLIGATIONS

Several kinds of patterned attitudes are used in kinship contexts by the Chiga. One is respect, though this is not limited to kinsmen but is generally due to all elders. In general, when one stands in a relationship of respect (*etcitinisa*, respect, means literally 'cause for fear') to someone one must speak to him 'modestly, in a low voice. Do not attempt to outdo him in argument or contradict him. Speak only seriously. Never be frivolous or attempt to make jokes. Listen quietly when he speaks and agree with him. Sit modestly before him. Do not eat his food, but serve him first and wait for the remains to be passed to you. Offer him your stool or fetch him one, spread a mat for him to sit upon. Fetch fire for his pipe.' Failure in any of these respects is *gaya*, to insult or despise the person whom you should respect as superior. Towards parents-in-law, in particular, this is serious, and will have to be made up for by a special feast-offering, or they will allow no further association. Towards parents-in-law, and also one's own husband and one's deceased parents, respect demands the further observance of name avoidance. This means not only avoiding mention of the name as such, but also not even using an ordinary word in which it occurs. A slip is deeply embarrassing, and flaunting one's husband's name in public is a gesture of extreme defiance, provoking a scandal and possibly divorce.

A more moderate degree of respect is expressed in such ways as initiating a greeting. It is the senior relative who must do this; a mother-in-law to her daughter-in-law, for example, or a father's sister to her status juniors, even if they are her age mates or slightly older. Seniority is primarily a function of relative kinship status, but age implications also enter. If the kinship status is noticeably at variance with the actual age relationship, the terminology will be shifted a little so as to fit the circumstances more appropriately. For example, if a young child is collateral 'grandfather' to a grown man, the latter will be likely to call him 'brother' and to treat him as an equal.

The relationship of permitted familiarity across sex lines is another specific pattern with its own particular limits. Brothers and sisters, and to a lesser degree the children of pact-brothers, are trusted together and allowed casual contacts. But casual friendliness would be most unseemly between strangers or non-relatives of different sexes. The right to jest or tease (*tera etogo*), in particular, is banned between unmarried girls and unrelated men. It is, however, permitted between cross-cousins, particularly those who are potential mates, and also, after payment of a gift, between a man and his wife's younger sisters, some of whom also he may one day marry. This implies a considerable degree of freedom and contact, but it is not as directly sexual in tone as the relationship between a wife and her husband's brothers.

Friendship, trust, and affection are personal rather than kinship attitudes. There are friendly and unfriendly pairs of brothers, cousins and brothers-in-law. In many kin relations there are, however, specific obligations, and these must be carried out irrespective of private feelings and opinions.

Father–Child

The father is full master of his own household, even if he in turn is subordinate to his own father. Young children may get away with impudence—provided father happens to think it cute at the moment—but older children owe him respect and implicit obedience. He eats in dignity from his own bowl or basket, sitting by himself or with honoured male guests. Sometimes, when there is no company, he may relax a little and take his meal by the fireside with his wife and children, but even then he must be served first and more formally than the rest. As the children approach adolescence, they must accept his say in all major matters, especially all plans relating to marriage. Even a boy who has somehow acquired cattle by his own efforts would not go sueing for his own bride; no responsible father of a marriageable girl would accept a young suitor who sent go-betweens in his own name. And even in later years, a son can move out to build a compound of his own, and arrange his own affairs, only with his father's full consent. Even then he marks his continued subordination by sending his father the choicer bits of any animal he kills and first-fruits of his crops, as well as coming to help in tasks like building and herding. These are not just free gifts and services, performed in affection or gratitude. They are required in the relationship, and no serious breach would be tolerated. The father's role continues even after death; the sons' independence can only be established by the performance of a formal inheritance rite, which gives them the right to run their own households (see below, p. 96).

A girl, too, will be severely punished if she gives any signs of disobedience during adolescence—staying out later than she should, talking to a strange boy, or resisting a marriage plan. She may be beaten or tied to a stake in the courtyard if she needs to learn a lesson. No other person may stay a father's hand raised against his own children, though a mother may try to intervene. In many families, as a matter of course, most discipline and decisions about daily details of the child's life are in the mother's hands, but major control is still the father's.

The absoluteness of the father's power is being modified somewhat today. This is partly because the supernatural sanctions involved are less impressive to the younger generation than they were, so that a youth is more likely to risk defiance. I was also told that Ganda chiefs (imported to teach the Chiga to rule themselves) had allowed children to win cases which they brought against their fathers for whipping them. Parents certainly now fear to mete out the former customary severe beatings or other physical punishment. As a result, many of the children go to church and even insist on their own marriage choices, to the scandalized but impotent horror of their fathers.

Although a girl's marriage breaks the tie with her own family, so that she is thereafter under her husband's rule rather than her father's, she may always come home for help and advice. If distance permits, she and her husband will come on frequent visits and exchange gifts with her parents, and she will lend a hand when they are ill. Should she be divorced from her husband, she should return to her father's home and wait for him to arrange a new marriage for her.

Mother–Child

In the Chiga household each mother is separately responsible for her own children. She feeds them, parcels out chores, supervises their manners, cuffs or scolds them when necessary, cares for their persons and clothing. She commands a less formal kind of respect and obedience than does the father; there is often a great deal of loving tenderness, and grown children will make gifts to their mothers and help them in many ways beyond the formal requirements. I have even known cases of wives being jealous of the attentions paid by their husbands to their mothers. A mother has no official say in major decisions affecting her children's lives, such as wedding arrangements, though she must help with the work of brewing, feasting the guests, and so on; but she often makes all the smaller decisions, such as whether an adolescent son should save some pennies he has earned or put them towards the purchase of a family goat.

A mother's special relationship to her children does not end as they grow up. It is to his own mother's house that a son brings his bride for the first months of marriage; the cows paid as a bride-price for her daughter are reckoned as part of the herd of her household, and should be used for a wife for her son. And it is her own son who should 'build' for her after she is widowed.

It is, however, only as a member of the family, through the continuance of her marriage relationship in the patrilineal group to which they belong, that a mother maintains these relations with her children. If a woman leaves to 'marry elsewhere', whether during her husband's lifetime or after his death, she must leave her children behind. A wife is 'stealing' her baby if she tries to run away and take it with her. A widow who has married elsewhere when her children are more grown up may, however, return to visit them, and maintain a close though informal personal bond.

The responsibility of caring for the children and the reciprocal obligation on the part of a son to care for his mother later in life are functions of the real mother-child relationship, and do not apply to other women in the same household. Co-wives are not responsible for feeding or caring for each other's children even when one is short of food. If they do so, it is entirely a matter of rather unusual personal generosity. Nor has a woman any right to order the children of her husband's other wives about. I have seen a woman send the young child of her husband's brother on an errand, but never a co-wife's children; most women are careful to avoid any such incident, as it might give rise to friction.

In turn, a child is not at home in the house or garden of his father's other wives. The only exception is a child officially assigned to some other wife who has no children of her own.

This woman then has the full responsibility of a mother, and is, in turn, entitled to the fulfilment of the obligations and duties a child owes its mother.

If children are left motherless, their father will expect his other wives to feed them, but not to give them any close attention. A child without a mother is an orphan—and so is expected to wear shabby clothes and have no one to remove the jiggers from his toes—unless his father can marry a new wife willing to step into the former wife's place. If she is divorced, that may be possible, but if she is dead it is very difficult, as stepping into her place means stepping into an unlucky house, and even the danger of leprous contagion. Only a woman in some very awkward personal situation is likely to risk it (cf. p. 72).

Grown sons are in a dual position with respect to their fathers' wives. These women fall into two categories. There are junior wives, whom a man may marry after his father's death, and senior wives, old enough to have nursed him as a baby, who have the status of mothers. These older wives he may not marry, but he should 'build' for them—that is, provide them with a house, tools, and so forth. A woman's own sons will undertake this if they are alive; otherwise the responsibility falls on her husband's other sons, whose solicitude and affection are not likely to reach very far (cf. below, p. 78).

Grandparent–Grandchild

The relations between children and grandparents are very close and friendly. Both grandmothers are expected and permitted to be very indulgent. There is no terminological distinction between maternal and paternal grandparents, and little difference in attitude. Some children are brought up by their maternal grandmothers, especially when a second child is born before the former baby has grown up. Only if the paternal grandmother has remarried elsewhere is the relationship more distant. Even so, she will usually come visiting and maintain close relations with her first husband's family. The bond with grandparents is so close that a man will continue relations with his wife's family even after her death or divorce, for the sake of the children.

After the death of a grandparent a great many special tabus come into effect. A grandchild may not mention lightly the name of his deceased grandparent. This is a matter of ordinary respect.

In addition, he must never eat off any plate, basket, &c., previously used by a deceased grandparent, under penalty of leprosy. At a burial, the grindstones are always removed and placed on the grave in order to get them out of the way of grandchildren, who might otherwise come into contact with them and thus be seriously endangered. Usually, too, an especially large spirit house was built for the ghost of the paternal grandmother which had special status (see below, p. 131).

Brothers

We have already seen much of the special character of brothers' relations to each other—informal, as neighbours and friends, who send each other titbits of a sheep that has been slaughtered, and lend each other substantial help, and more formal, as having certain roles to play in marriage arrangements and the responsibility of exacting vengeance for a murder. If brothers 'trust' one another, the relationship is a close one. A man may sit in his brother's seat by his hearth in his absence, may even have a liaison with his brother's wife without provoking serious criticism—or a 'good' brother's jealousy. But loyalty and affection are not taken for granted. 'Do I sit at my brother's hearth?' a man will reply to a question about his own brothers' attitudes or likely behaviour, and tales are often told of deceptions and treachery practised on brothers. And brothers do not in fact owe each other any specific economic assistance. Each, as master of his own household, must amass his own bride-price cattle, and the materials for any sacrifice or feast. Any substantial help rendered in these contexts must be fully repaid. The only exception to all this is the responsibility of seniors to their junior orphaned siblings, especially if the latter have no mother whose new husband can take care of them.

In general, relative age is important between siblings. Older brothers and sisters are expected to have something of a parental attitude towards younger siblings, who in their turn should show their older brothers and sisters something of the respect due to greater age. A 'good' older brother or sister will give gifts to and make things for his younger siblings just as he does for his own children. And it is the eldest brother who becomes head of the household after the death of the father, seeing to the marriage arrangements and the fair partition of the inheritance, and

supervising the disposition of the wives and children. An unmarried younger brother will often live in the house of his older
brother, helping in the work of the household, and in return
being fed from the household granary. A younger brother, old
enough to 'know good customs', will come with his senior when
he goes to feasts, to serve as his right-hand man—'fingers' is the
Chiga term—guarding him if he gets drunk or takes a nap,
bringing him his pipe, and advising him if there is anyone around
to whom he must remember to be respectful. And an older sibling must always be married before the next in line is eligible.

The distinction between full and half-siblings is also important
in many contexts. As children, full siblings share the same house
and are cared for by the same mother. They have a common share
in the special inheritance that belongs to their own mother's
house (see below, p. 96). Often there is a close bond of affection between them, which persists in adulthood. A half-brother
by the same mother (provided that he is also a lineage kinsman
and resident in the same community) is closer than a half-brother
who is 'of the same father'; and lines of cleavage traditionally
fall along the lines of such half-brother/full brother distinctions.

As we have already noted, the patterned relations between
brothers are extended in somewhat limited form to close parallel
cousins. This relationship may, however, sometimes be a very close
one, particularly when there are no full brothers (cf. above, p. 15).

Brother–Sister

Brothers and sisters are allowed to associate with each other
freely. A girl is considered adequately chaperoned by the presence of even collateral relatives of the status of brothers. She
may talk and jest with them and sit on the same log. The Chiga
attitude towards the incest tabu between siblings is rather like
ours—the tabu is thought to be strong enough to make association safe. While siblings are still tiny and unclothed they may
share the same bed, but as they grow older this is unseemly.
They may, however, continue to be alone together in a house
without suspicion of impropriety. At feasts, when the girls of
the lineage who have come to dance are clustered in the back of
the house where no man may enter, a brother may sleep across
the doorway. In a brother's presence a girl is even free to talk
with other men. Brothers have a special interest both in their

sister's chastity and in her marriage. Brothers play an important ceremonial role in their sister's wedding, carrying her through the gateposts of her father's compound to the home of the groom and, in a later ceremony, handing her over officially to the new group, who claim her sexually. But, of course, a brother's special interest in the marriage of his sister, and in adequately chaperoning her before it, is more than a ceremonial one. The bride-price paid for the girl is the property of her father, but if she has a full brother the cows should be used to secure him a wife. This sets up a continuing formal relationship between the brother and sister.

There is no apparent restriction on sexual conversation when brothers and their sisters are together, but brothers do not ordinarily discuss sexual matters with their sisters. They do lecture each other on other aspects of marriage, on how to be obedient as a wife, and not too domineering as a husband.

There are many minor ceremonial relations between a brother and sister, particularly after her marriage. A married sister must obey certain restrictions at the home of her brothers, whether her visit is brief, or whether she is living there more or less permanently when separated from her husband. For example, she must not take off her belt and put it down in his courtyard, or tie up his goats for the night. Any violation of these tabus spoils the goat, food, or whatever was mishandled, and prevents its use by her brother. Since he can then make no further use of the object in question, he is in a sense forced to give it to her for her husband. Intentional violation of these tabus is an extreme measure and not lightly undertaken; its sole probable occasion would be to force the payment of a debt. However, such an act is dangerous and disapproved; it is considered almost equivalent to malicious witchcraft (see below, p. 166).

Incest is not unknown, even though it is not generally considered necessary to chaperone a brother and sister. There is a riddle which goes, 'What is a grass which grows sweet on the housetops?' and the answer is: 'The vulva of your mother's daughter.' That is, it is something desirable, but unattainable. As a matter of fact, when an unmarried girl becomes pregnant it is usually assumed that the man responsible must be a brother —perhaps only a clan brother—since a girl has few opportunities to see anyone else. It is this belief which makes the punishment meted out to her so severe.

Sisters

No special formal relationship exists between sisters; for the most part they will be separated at marriage. When both are married to one man or to brothers, informally they may be closer than other co-wives, but their formal relations will not be different. Before marriage there is some consideration of seniority, the elder being in a position to scold or advise the younger ones and to send them on errands. Furthermore, the order of marriage must always be in the order of seniority. It is the eldest one living at home who represents the family at marriages and other formal occasions; after her marriage the next oldest automatically steps into her place. Half-sisters, like half-brothers, are parts of separate families; each such household line is represented by its own eldest daughter, independently of those in other wives' families.

Father's Brother–Brother's Child

To your father's own brothers and close cousins you are linked by all sorts of important ties. His unmarried younger brother may even live in the same house. Your uncle is your 'little father'. It is he who helps out when your father is ill. He gives you little gifts and calls you his child, and you play freely with his children. You may sit in his house by the fire, and are likely to be fed there. Your uncles will participate in negotiations for your marriage, as witnesses and judges of the cattle. If you are a girl, one of your uncles will come along as an important member of your bridal party. However, your uncle's home is not your own home, and your uncle is not really father to you in affection or solicitude. Should your own father die and you have no grown brothers, he might assume responsibility for you, but only if you are very young will you fit directly into his family. Even if he should marry your mother, distinctions will be maintained within the household. Proverbs testify to the difference between a true and a merely legal father: 'A child who is not your own will not bring you glory,' they say, and, 'The child at the home of its own father will be given another straw if it breaks the one it has,' implying that such extra consideration and kindness will not otherwise be his lot. All this contrasts with the patrilineal phrasing, which permits an uncle to refer to his brother's son as 'my child', and allow a man to wrest his infant nephew from its own mother's arms if she is running away with it. And, of course, it is modified considerably by personal factors of kindness or meanness, the child's age and possible helpfulness, and so on.

Mother's Brother–Sister's Child

There are a number of special obligations and bonds between a man and his mother's brother. The most important of these is that set up in the approved and preferred marriage pattern, matrilateral cross-cousin marriage, in which a man marries his mother's brother's daughter. (The converse form, in which a man marries his father's sister's daughter, is strongly disapproved.) As the Chiga formulate their particular slant on this preferential marriage arrangement: 'It is suitable for a mother's brother to provide a wife for his sister's son.' In any case, a regular bride-price must be paid when such a cross-cousin marriage is arranged, just as it would be for any other marriage. Even when the preferred marriage does not take place, the mother's brother's wife is often addressed as mother-in-law. It is advisable to remember this possible relationship, for if a marriage should take place later on, past lapses in the respect due parents-in-law would have to be made up for by special gifts at the wedding.

I was told that a maternal uncle should give his nephew a cow or two goats toward his bride-price if he did not actually supply him with a wife. (No such gift was made at any marriage I witnessed.) The uncle is said to be giving his nephew the offspring of the bride-price cattle collected at the marriage of his sister, the nephew's mother. This suggests a stress on the line of receivers of bride-price cattle, such as has been noted in other regions. Certainly, the original owner of the bride-price is always kept in mind, and must be given a pot of beer at the wedding ceremony when his cattle are used once more. However, I noted no other formal stress on the relative positions of giver and receiver. The preferred mother's brother's daughter marriage does not take place with enough regularity to establish a clear line of relationships between families. I do not know whether consideration of the relative positions of donor and receiver affects relations at the own-generation level. I met no cases of brother-sister exchange marriages, but I did not explore this implication in the field. The lines as drawn are always relevant only within the small kin group; so a man may have a remotely related mother's brother who is also a father's sister's husband.

The maternal uncle has a role in relation to the marriage of his own sister's daughter. He is supposed to perform special rites, which will secure the assistance of his family spirits in helping the young wife to conceive. For this appeal to the spirits, the mother's brother should receive a cow at the time of his niece's marriage. A bride's maternal uncle should also come to her coming-out party and give her presents (see below, Ch. 4). Although, in the marriages which took place during my stay, the religious role was either omitted or played down and no cows were paid to the maternal uncle, he did participate in the later gift-giving. His role is apparently a modified parental one; he shares, to a lesser degree, bride-price receipts and special responsibilities to the bride, and gives her gifts similar to those properly due to her from her father. He even calls her husband 'son-in-law'; the latter on his part may call him 'father-in-law' or 'maternal uncle'.

This ceremonial role of the maternal uncle in marriage is linked with a more general function of the mother's family. Maternal family spirits continue to be influential, not only to the daughters even after marriage, but also to their children. If the diviner should ascribe a child's illness to the ghost of its mother's mother or some other maternal relative, the mother will take offerings to her brother for him to present to the spirit; she herself cannot make them directly, as offerings must be made by men. After the mother's death, her children may continue to make offerings to the ghosts of her family through her brother or his heirs. However, no permanent parallel lines are set up, as the power of the ghosts does not endure for more than two generations.

There are also various ritual relations between a man and his sister's children. A girl has to obey certain restrictions similar to those affecting her mother. For example, she must not sit upon the grindstone in her mother's brother's home, nor do such ordinary things as putting up the bars across the gate, or gathering gourd-seeds or tobacco from his garden, though with regard to other crops she makes herself quite exceptionally free. And if she or her brother should die while visiting at the home of a maternal uncle, he would have to abandon his house. When a man kills a beast, he must give certain special parts of the meat to his nephew or any fellow clansman of his who happens to be about. And he must avoid cutting the rope binding up a bundle of firewood brought by a nephew; he must undo it carefully for otherwise it would be like hacking at the child himself.

There are many such rules, but they are all set in a general context of friendliness and goodwill. For your mother's brother is, in general, a close and friendly kinsman. Normally, he lives in another village, but is a familiar figure in your own. He comes on visits from time to time, when he is treated as an honoured guest in your mother's house, spending his time lolling about the courtyard with your father. You visit him too, going along with your mother when she visits her old home. Sometimes a boy grows up in his uncle's village, under his grandmother's care, so that this is a second home to him. Even if the distance is too great for casual visiting, greetings and gifts will be sent back and forth through kinsmen and pact-brothers who happen to travel by, and such messages should serve as a passport to friendly welcome and hospitality.

Father's Sister–Brother's Child

A father's sister, unmarried and living at home, should be treated with some respect, though, as a matter of fact, where there is parity of actual age this may be very slight. There is a proverb, 'A person who grows up with his paternal aunt will not know what is making him sick'—that is, when her spirit takes revenge for past inconsiderateness. An aunt must begin any greeting, and expects little favours of respect from niece or nephew. She can send a nephew or a niece on an errand, just like any older woman of the village. A sister of one's own father will always be referred to as an 'aunt' even after marriage, but a more distant relative of this status will be merely 'girl of our clan', a term which is used loosely, without any generation implications.

A father's sister may be sufficiently concerned about her brother's children to take one of them into her own house after her marriage, should circumstances leave him unprovided for or badly provided for at home. Often, however, if she marries far away, there may be few occasions for contact. Some men had lost track of their sisters completely and were not even able to tell me their children's names.

When the preferred type of cross-cousin marriage takes place, the young bride finds her own paternal aunt as her mother-in-law; sometimes a girl may even marry her aunt's own husband and become her junior co-wife. This marriage, while not very usual, is quite acceptable. In either case, the presence of a related older woman in the group of wives in the household to which she must accommodate herself may smooth her path a little. However, this relationship has a formal character of a special sort only if the actual marriage link is within the household. That the potential mother-in-law–daughter-in-law link is stressed at all is suggested only in the term which a woman uses for her brother's daughter, whether or not she is her son's bride. That term, *omuicendjezane*, is associated with the function of taking over the mother-in-law's *emandwa* spirit. But, in fact, responsibility for the spirit cult passes to a woman's own daughter-in-law, not to her brother's daughter (unless they are the same person) (see below, pp. 61, 63).

Mother's Sister

One's mother's sister is treated with varying degrees of affection, depending on personal factors. If she is married to your father or his brother, she is closer than your other stepmothers. A mother's sister in such a relationship is almost a second mother to you; what is more, no matter how much younger than your own mother she may be or how distant in actual kinship, she would be classed as a 'mother' with respect to inheritance. You could never marry her as you might your father's other younger wives.

Your mother's sister's children are closely related to you, but in most cases circumstances keep them remote. If they do live nearby or, as may occur through marriage, in the same village, they are treated as especially close kin. But even in the normal case of very rare contact, every courtesy and hospitality should be shown them, and this should be extended to children of a mother's collateral sister, not only to your very close kinsmen.

Cross-cousins

All cross-cousins are expected to be friendly and may treat each other with some familiarity; their kinship also affords some degree of protection. The general term *buzara*, which means something like kinship, comes from the same root as the word for cross-cousin (*zara* is 'to give birth'). Where one has *buzara* one expects to be greeted in friendly fashion, to be hospitably treated, and to be safe from active hostility. One has *buzara* particularly in one's mother's paternal home. The village of one's own maternal grandparents and maternal uncles often becomes a second childhood home. Even members of that village not closely related, but of mother's lineage, are to some extent kinsmen. I also have *buzara* where my father's sister has married, but this cannot be safely counted on beyond the limits of her husband's own family.

Very important distinctions must be drawn between one's mother's brother's children and one's father's sister's children, although the term *muzara* is used for all. The most important difference is in the potential mating arrangement. As we have already noted, a man may marry his mother's brother's daughter, but marriage with the father's sister's daughter is severely frowned upon. A certain amount of licence is permitted in the casual relations between a man and his mother's brother's daughter which is not found in any other relationship. A bit of flirting, *risqué* allusion, careless touching, and so forth are quite permissible. A man may even call his cross-cousin 'wife', though no marriage has been proposed.

The effects of the two types of cross-cousin marriage would of course be very different. When the approved marriage is arranged, the man is simply taking a wife from his mother's family, thus strengthening existing bonds. Marriage with the father's sister's daughter would, however, have very different implications. The bride would be brought into a community of her own uterine kinfolk; it would be difficult to make up for the innumerable previous familiarities with people suddenly become parents-in-law. The most difficult avoidance relationships would be required towards her own mother's brother, who should instead have a relaxed and fostering relationship to her. The Chiga feeling that the interpersonal relations set up by marriage should be retroactive makes such a situation particularly shocking.

Such marriages may, however, occur. They are not tabu in the strictest sense of the Chiga term (*zira*) which usually carries the threat of leprosy. But this disapproved marriage will bring its own unfortunate consequences such as childlessness, or the birth of deformed or abnormal children. Such marriages are, however, banned only for fairly close relatives. Kinship lines are not extended widely in this context. In fact, when marriages take place, it is assumed that there will be some women of the bridegroom's clan—his classificatory father's sisters—married into the bride's family, who will rejoice with the groom's party rather than wail for the bride when she is carried off from her mother's house to be delivered to her waiting groom.

Affinal Relations

The basic relationship between a wife and husband—one of formal subordination of the woman and considerable actual co-operation—is presented in relation to marriage (see below, pp. 58ff.), as are some of the basic relationships set up between a woman and the other members of her husband's family. Here we shall note only some of the other relationships which are set up by marriage, particularly those between a man and his wife's kin.

Brother-in-law

Apart from the pact of blood-brotherhood, this is the strongest bond between men not of the same patrilineal group, whether or not they are also cross-cousins. Brothers-in-law should trust and help one another—and always ask each other to beer parties. A man seeking a new home, away from his own patrilineage, will most often make it where his sister's husband lives. The sister's husband has some slight seniority and respect advantages in this relationship. This is marked formally by his being the one who initiates greetings between them. This may be related to the fact that very often he—or his family—is the original owner of the bride-price cattle which were used in the second man's marriage, a relationship which, as we have noted, the Chiga always stress as important.

Brother–Sister-in-law

The relationships of brothers and sisters-in-law—one's wife's sisters or husband's brothers (*muramu* of the opposite sex)—are the only ones which are standardized in terms of anything approaching sexual licence. While a man does not have an automatic right to marry his wife's sisters, there is some sororal polygyny. And a man's relations with his brothers' wives include

privileged sexual freedom and some levirate rights, subordinate,
however, to those of a man's sons (cf. pp. 55, 66, 77).

Son-in-law–Mother-in-law

The son-in-law must observe a stringent respect attitude towards his mother-in-law. In some areas he may not even see her
until he has formally presented her with a goat. Until then his
mother-in-law must hide when she hears him coming, or step
off the path with her eyes downcast; any conversations they need
to have must be carried on indirectly. Among other groups,
where this initial complete avoidance is not observed, the remaining formalities are quite strict. Son-in-law and mother-in-law
may never eat together or sit in the same part of the house. When
she is visiting, the mother-in-law must retire to the back room
while he sits at the fireplace. He must never call his mother-in-
law by her name, but must use some roundabout designation.
(She, of course, may use his name freely, as the respect is not
reciprocal.) It is she who greets him, never he her. When she
announces that she is coming on a visit, he must go to meet her.
While she is visiting her daughter, if he has two wives he will
sleep in the house of the other wife; but if there is only one
house, she will use the back room or bed, and great care must be
exercised to maintain privacy.

The basis of all these rules is respect. The Chiga do not consider them tabus; breaches are not spiritually dangerous, but very
embarrassing. To fail in the observance of due respect towards
one's mother-in-law is to despise her and cause great shame.
I heard a man say, laughing shamefacedly as the Chiga always do
in such an embarrassing situation, 'The prison has no shame,'
when he told the story of a man who had been imprisoned while
his mother-in-law was also incarcerated there.

There was at least one ceremonial obligation a son-in-law owed
to his mother-in-law. After her death, he should give her ghost
a live cow, which was to be milked for her spirit. The milk was
used in offerings for her ghost or her spirit familiar, in order to
help her daughter conceive and bear children.

Son-in-law–Father-in-law

A man owes respect to his father-in-law as well, but this is
not very formal. There is no avoidance, except that he may not

use his father-in-law's name. They may converse freely. As is usual in respect relations, the son-in-law may not eat with his father-in-law. He takes his own basket, or whatever food may be given him, behind a partition in the hut. Any remains are given to the children. (These may never go from inferior to superior.) It is particularly bad to gnaw one's father-in-law's corn, and this should be refused even if it is offered. To accept it would be worse than disrespect: it would be an irreparable insult. The relationship is, in a sense, retroactive, for if the groom has previously been guilty of any behaviour towards his father-in-law which is insulting in the new relationship, this must be righted by a ceremony at the wedding. He must present his father-in-law with a sheep at the time when the bride-price is paid, before the bride can be borne away. Any flimsy evidence of his ever having cursed him, or even argued with him, will be used and made the basis of a demand for such payment, so that it is almost a regular feature of marriages where there has been any previous acquaintance.

The relations between a son-in-law and his wife's father involve one special obligation: each is expected to invite the other to drink when he brews beer. The husband should also send his father-in-law a gift of meat when he butchers an animal, if the distance between their homes is not too great. There is also a continuous economic relationship based on the bride-price cattle. When all the cows have borne calves, the son-in-law sends a gift of a sheep and two pots of beer, and in return he is given one of the calves. (This would be returned in case of divorce.) A calf of the next generation should also be given him, but this does not complicate the divorce picture, as by this time the marriage has achieved such stability that divorce is out of the question.

In case of dissolution of the marriage, whether by divorce or by death, if there are children the relationship to the parents-in-law remains a real one. If there are no children, there will be no special observances of gift-giving and so on, but affinal terms will be used, and in case of any encounter the proper respect must still be extended. The parents-in-law terms, and some traces of respect behaviour, are sometimes used even when a marriage has been proposed but has fallen through.

4
MARRIAGE

CHIGA marriage follows a standard African pattern. It is poly-gynous, exogamous, and patrilocal, and based on cattle payments made to the bride's family.

The form of a Chiga wedding symbolically represents the whole social structure of their marriage relations. First comes the bride-price payment, which is, of course, not a sale, but a contract be-tween families. Its payment serves primarily to determine the status of children of the marriage; only if the bride-price has been paid can a father claim the children as his own descendants. It serves also as a bond guaranteeing the proper fulfilment of marri-age obligations on both sides. For should the bride be too lazy, or the husband too mean, the threat of a divorce, involving return of the bride-price, can be used by the aggrieved party in demand-ing improved behaviour. The Chiga distinguish such a marriage sharply from the outright sale of a daughter, which sometimes is resorted to in famine times. When a father sells his daughter, he relinquishes all claim to her and control over her. The cattle or other valuables he receives in such a sale are used up for food. The bride-price cattle, on the other hand, must never be 'eaten'. They should be kept intact and used to negotiate a subsequent marriage, preferably for the bride's own brother.

Negotiations for the marriage are carried on between the fami-lies, not between the bride and groom, who have no say in the matter at all. The negotiations are conducted with great form-ality and deliberation, and are always initiated by a go-between acting for the groom's father, through a pact-brother or other friendly contact who will serve as representative of the bride's father. Visits and discussions go on interminably; sometimes they last more than a year, for they will be interrupted when the rains begin, to start again after the harvest when there is plenty of beer.

No matter how desirable the match, no self-respecting father will consent the first time the suitors come to ask for his daughter. Even after many talks, the suit may 'die' because he has decided that the boy is too young, or has heard a rumour that he has a terrible temper and might prove to be a wife-beater. Or it may come to grief over the size of the bride-price, which is settled only after prolonged bargaining. Its size is important and reflects the status of both families and the general reputation of the bride. Since marriages are often arranged between families who live too far apart to know anything of each other at first hand, the go-betweens play a critical role. They vie with each other in glorifying the virtues of the bride, or the groom, but on the whole these claims are generously discounted. The decisive factor in the ultimate decision is likely to be the size of the bride-price offered or demanded.

During the marriage negotiations, the fathers receive a great deal of advice from their brothers, who must act as witnesses to the transfer of the bride-price cattle. They have no economic stake in the transaction, but are involved in it none the less at many points. One of the bride's father's brothers, for example, goes along with the wedding party when the bride is taken to the groom's home, as representative of her family.

Once the bride-price has been settled, the marriage ceremonies begin and take a long course, which dramatizes the girl's removal from her own family, and underlines ceremonially every stage in her gradual assumption of full wifely status.

The first stage in the wedding is a kind of 'marriage by capture', in which her brothers hand her over to her bridegroom. The girl, who supposedly knows nothing of all the arrangements until this dramatic moment arrives, is whisked off and hidden in the back of her mother's hut when the groom's party arrives to claim her. After some hours of debate over the precise merits and demerits of each animal in the bride-price, and after numerous extra demands have been met—a cow for the bride's maternal uncle, so that he will pray to the spirits of his family to aid the bride in conceiving; and perhaps a sheep or goat to the bride's father to make up for some act of disrespect which the groom may have committed towards his father-in-law before the marriage was arranged—everything is finally ready. Ownership of the bride-price is ceremonially transferred to the bride's father by handing over a hoe and a lead rope, and the festivities can begin. The groom's party will dance, and shout boastfully of their accomplishments; women of his clan who are married to men of the bride's father's clan will break into the women's shrill, triumphal screeching. And the bride, hidden in her mother's house and dressed in her best, will begin the artistic weeping and wailing with which she must now bemoan her sorry lot for several days on end. Sometimes she will just sob rhythmically, but at times she must also 'bring words' to suit the occasion: 'Oh, goodbye! I'm going away from home now. Why is my father, why are my brothers, so cruel to me? I'm going to be so lonesome. My husband will beat me and I shall have no friends.' The pattern is fixed, but the words are her own. A great deal of pride is taken in doing this well, and a girl will be praised for the quality of her weeping.

The festivities go on most of the night. The groom's party are feasted, the girls of the bride's lineage alternately sing the special marriage chorus for the men's dancing, and go into the back room to help the bride with her weeping—and everyone drinks a lot of beer.

After a rest in the morning, it is time to fetch the bride out—against her determined resistance. There is a real fight, in which the girls all help her. One by one, her brothers drag them out of the house; clothing is torn in the tussle, and ornaments not carefully taken off in advance are broken. Finally the bride herself is seized, her head is ritually shaved, and she is carried off on her brother's shoulders. As she passes through the gateway of the compound, a small twig is broken off. This symbolizes the end of her maiden status in her own family. Even if the marriage should proceed no farther she will be a married woman, with all that the change in status implies. She will not dance as a girl dances at the wedding feasts, or be at home in the same way as a girl is in her father's house.

The party sets forth amid much weeping. The bride, her head covered over with a cloak, is carried on the shoulders of her brothers all the way to her groom's home, where, all washed and anointed, he is eagerly—and often nervously—awaiting her arrival. She is set down, crouching, at the gateway, and he taps her with a little twig, announcing, 'You may speak once, but I will speak twice,' thus indicating that he intends to be master in his household. She is led into the house where her mother-in-law greets her ceremonially. Then she stays in the back room and weeps some more, while the groom's relatives and her escorts feast and dance. She may eat a little, daintily—but if she forgets her manners and starts to eat greedily, the married woman who has accompanied her, and who will spend the first night there with her, will pinch her to remind her that she is under observation.

The marriage is not consummated that night. Towards cock-crow a special ceremony takes place. The girls are awakened and begin to sing. The bride's brothers are given beer and then go into the inner compartment and bear forth the wailing bride. Meanwhile, her groom, and such of his brothers as have arranged to share in the ceremony, urinate on a stool. The bridegroom places his hands in this. Then her brothers pull off the girl's skirt and seat her in the hands of her husband on the stool. She struggles all the while. As soon as he has touched her genitals she is released, and the bridegroom and his brothers leap and dance, and break into their best ceremonial boasts. All those who have shared in this ceremony are, in a sense, supplementary husbands and have the right to sleep with her when all the marriage rites are over.

The next day, when her escorts have left, the groom buys off his sisters and his mother with gifts, so that he will at last be left alone with his bride. When he comes into the partitioned-off bed-place where she is lying, her rhythmic weeping becomes more intense. Her mother has instructed her not to cry too loud or too long, lest everyone laugh at her, but at this point she is expected to behave as the unwilling victim of a rape. This is known as 'the fighting'. The girl, who in the circumstances may be genuinely upset, often struggles vehemently to avoid the embrace of her husband. To aid her, the escorting woman has greased her well with butter. Sometimes she actually succeeds in holding him off for a time. This is rare, but much applauded. When her husband has finally succeeded in effecting the consummation, her struggles should cease, and she is expected to be ready to receive him thereafter without protest.

When this bout is over, her husband comes out into the courtyard, proudly victorious. His sister goes in to dress the bride and give her food, but she refuses to eat until her husband has given her gifts. The girls attempt to treat her gently and make her feel at home, but she may remain sulky and silent.

For a few days she stays on as a privileged guest. She is in the home of her mother-in-law or her husband's chief wife, in either case in a separate compartment. Her husband sleeps with her at night. She does no work, and neither does he. Only the gathering and cooking of food is allowed in the household.

After a few days the girl's father sends two children to fetch the newly married couple. They must come home now for the ceremony called 'to finish the butter'. There will be a feast, and all the bride's girl friends come to visit her and spend the night there with her. The women of the village come to say goodbye, and once more the bride is dissolved in tears. When she and her husband leave to go back to their home, she may once more protest against being torn from her friends and her family, but after this she is supposed to give up such longings, and settle down to the wifely status, which she must now gradually assume.

Throughout the ceremonies, there have been charms and herbs administered and innumerable points of ritual to be observed. For example, in preparing porridge for the bride at her new home, the groom's sister must always lay aside her belt. (The woman's skirt belt has a recurrent ritual significance.) The bride is carefully seated upon her mother-in-law's lap when she reaches her new home, just as she was seated on her mother's lap before she left her old one. And bits of grass and twigs must be gathered from the places where the bride's brothers set her down to rest along the way; these are used to cook marrow leaves, symbols of family communion, for the escorting party to eat on their return home. Every one of these points must be scrupulously observed, for any error may endanger the bride's future child-bearing.

Once the bride is back at her husband's home, there is a little rite to symbolize her assumption of a regular place in that household. Her mother-in-law prepares marrow leaves for her to eat with the other women of the household. Then she and one of her sisters-in-law together thrust a stick of wood into the fire, and she smears herself with some earth from her new home, brought in by her sister-in-law. After this she should stop being silent and reserved, and may talk and laugh as much as she likes with her brothers-in-law as well as with the women of the community and the girls who visit her. She will now be called by a new name as a married woman.

However, she will still remain in seclusion—literally, 'nesting'. During this period she does no work in the fields. She may cook, and she works for one day on a little basket, which will then be put aside until her first child is born. She remains indoors as much as possible, preferably in the rear of the house. When she is compelled to leave it, she keeps her head covered, lest she should see or be seen by her father-in-law or others of his status. No penalty is attached to being seen uncovered, but the girl would be very much ashamed. There are various real tabus upon her at this time as well. For example, she should avoid seeing anyone who makes pots, or her skin will not become light as that of a bride in seclusion should.

After a period, which may be one month or several months, her father will finally send for her to *aruka*—come out of her seclusion. This is a very gala event at which there must be plenty of feasting and drinking. Just before she leaves for her visit home, her husband's father and his lineage-kinsmen—all her formal fathers-in-law—give her gifts to end their mutual avoidance. She may then go with her head uncovered for the first time since her marriage.

When they get to her father's home, her husband will give the girls of her lineage gifts, to establish their full status as his sisters-in-law, so that he may joke and drink beer with them.

After a night of steady drinking, a ceremony of giving presents to the bride takes place. A rich man may send one or two of the bride-price animals back with his daughter 'to dress her'. (However, these are not lost track of, and in case of divorce would usually be counted as a portion of the bride-price already returned.) The bride's maternal uncle brings a pot of beer for the feast and gifts of goats and wearing apparel for his niece. He and her father take turns to adorn her with ornaments. Since her marriage she has been allowed only one necklace, but now her father and her uncle, and others too, give her necklaces, wire strands for her legs, and metal bracelets. First her father dresses one side of her—that is, gives her ornaments for one arm and one leg, and then her maternal uncle dresses the other. The total return in gifts may sometimes be as valuable as the original bride-price. She is also given the iron blade of a hoe to start her off in her regular work as a married woman. Small gifts are demanded of all the friends and relatives attending the festival; a basket is passed to collect them, and it is not good form to fail to give some little gift when asked.

Generally two nights are spent at the bride's father's home.

The return to the groom's home is made amid singing and with a very gay escort. The next day the girl goes with her husband to plant gourd-seeds, after which she begins to work in the gardens with her mother-in-law. She and her husband do not usually have a home of their own as yet; for this, and for the full skirts of a married woman, she must normally wait until she is pregnant; only then will she assume the full status of a married woman, beginning to raise a family of her own.

Although the formal marriage was the normal one, elopements did occur, and not infrequently. If they involved running away to a lover, some kind of love magic was usually blamed. More often, it was rather a matter of running away from home. One girl in Bufuka ran off when her widowed father wanted her to stay at home as his housekeeper instead of bothering to get himself a new wife. Her husband did everything he could to establish her status as a true wife and to assure her good reputation. He paid a very high bride-price after the elopement and showered her with clothes and ornaments. Another girl ran away in protest against a proposed marriage. She came back again in a day or so without having 'sat at the hearth' of another family (this would have meant offering herself to them as a wife). Hers was a serious step taken to show her family that her protests were in earnest; her action had the general sympathy of the community, for most people disapproved of the man her father had chosen. Eventually, however, she gave in and was married to him. Sometimes such a step did move the father to modify his plans, but it was a desperate expedient and not one to which a 'proper' modest maiden would normally have recourse.

If a girl who runs away stays away for several nights and at a man's home, the elopement is considered a *de facto* marriage. Her father may—in fact, should—then declare that he will have nothing further to do with her. But the marriage has no legal status and involves complications with respect to the children. It can be legitimized subsequently by the payment of a bride-price if the irate father can be won over; otherwise the children are not members of their father's family. The girl's father has a permanent claim upon them, and may demand the bride-price at the marriage of her daughter, his granddaughter. If the girl should die, an awkward situation arises, since her family will

refuse to have anything to do with the burial. In order to conduct this properly, a bride-price would then have to be paid 'on
the burial mat'.

In light conversation men discuss how ideal it would be to
have a wife who had not been paid for. In addition to the economy involved, the girl's lack of parental protection is also counted
an advantage. For such a girl, since she has no family to back
her in difficulties, is obviously, they say, forced to behave, obey,
never scold, and so forth. This is all pure phantasy. As a matter
of fact, when a man does take advantage of such a situation, beating and bullying his 'wife' unfairly, she may find the situation
intolerable and run away; if her own family will not have her
back, she can run off to another man. Even a slave wife has
this ultimate resource.

The normal age of marriage varies with a number of factors.
Parents can show off their wealth by marrying their sons off even
before puberty, but this is not usual, for the boy would be too
young to assume a husband's economic role. Ordinarily, the
bride-price cannot be scraped together so readily; younger
brothers are often unmarried until quite late in life. On the other
hand, it is desirable to keep daughters at home for some years
after puberty. This postponement is not often possible, however, as brothers' marriages often wait upon their sisters' bride-
price cattle. The resulting actual difference in marriage age allows
for considerable polygyny without any noticeable shortage of
women. In any case, the daughters in a family must always be
married off in order of age; the oldest unmarried daughter has
a recognized formal status, and must always be 'sued for' first.

Sometimes girls are married off while they are quite young,
usually because of economic pressure. It is entirely up to the
father to make such a decision, but the marriage of an immature
girl is considered a misfortune for the child. When a little girl
of about ten was married from a neighbouring village, there was
considerable unfavourable comment. Several women from Bufuka
actually refused to attend the wedding. As they were not of the
same lineage, they were free to stay away if they chose. (On the
other hand, those who were of the same lineage felt themselves
obliged to attend, in spite of their disapproval.)

When a daughter is married or, as sometimes happens, sold,
while very young, she may stay at home for some years before

being sent to live with her husband. On the other hand, a child wife may go to her husband before puberty. One such girl in Bufuka had been given a miserable time. Her husband's older wives took advantage of her youth and of the fact that she had been 'sold', so that her own family had no right to protect her. They used to scold and tease her and force her to do chores for them. When she reached puberty, and was old enough to manage affairs in adult fashion, her husband moved one of his houses to a neighbouring hamlet, so that she would no longer have to live with his other wives.

While marrying off a daughter before puberty is disapproved, it is considered inadvisable to delay too long after puberty before making marriage arrangements. Delay of a year or two after suitors come for your daughter's hand is enough indication that you are not in unseemly haste to marry her off. Beyond that you are interfering with her best marriage chances. There is a proverb which goes, 'Vegetables are sweet to eat while they are still young.' Husbands prefer young wives. An older woman, I was told, 'would not have a bride's ways. She would not play with her husband, or have as many children.' It is awkward to bring into the family a new wife who is older than the women already in a compound, for her age should entitle her to respect which does not accord well with her junior position.

In the unlikely event that a girl grows old without having been married, a marriage of some sort must be gone through, as it is dangerous for her to die 'with grey hair' and still unmarried. A poor stranger would be asked to marry her and be paid by her family, for he is doing them a special service. If they cannot do this, charms will be used when she dies to avert the evil consequences of this dangerous situation, which might involve the death of all her relatives. (It is not necessary that the girl should lose her virginity, only that the marriage be technically consummated by her being carried out of her father's house past the gateway.)

THE WIFE'S ROLE IN MARRIAGE

After marriage, a woman becomes a participating member of her husband's household. Although her husband may be subordinate to his father or elder brother, from her point of view he is her lord and master. She owes him obedience and respect.

A woman should never address her husband or refer to him by name, but always indirectly or by some locution, such as 'my master', or even 'the master'. Any breach of the name tabu always provokes ridicule, which reflects unfavourably on both wife and husband. However, I have occasionally heard an older woman, in a private conversation, use her husband's name rather casually; this is a reflection of the formal rather than actual sub-ordination of an older wife after a long period of stable marriage.

There are other tokens of the respect relationship. A wife should not eat with her husband. While they may occasionally eat together when there is no company, the husband normally takes his meals first, often outside in the court. His wife must cook for him and serve his food as nicely as she is able. If he is not in her house that day, she sends his portion of food to him, usually by one of the children, or she may take it to him herself. If the food is ready and the husband is not around to eat, I have known women feed their children and even eat themselves, but first they carefully took out a full portion for the husband and set it aside. It must always be the others, never he, who has the leavings.

A wife owes her husband not only respect, but also proper performance of her wifely duties and complete obedience. It is her job to see to the family's food supply, and in most cases the husband does not interfere with his wife in her fulfilment of the daily routine towards this end. She works in the fields, gathers and cooks the food, without any special direction or interference from him, except that he may ask her to bring out food for a special guest, or to prepare beer for him for a feast or a sacrifice. Often she may even be allowed to use her own discretion about arranging the exchange of surplus crops or other products. Only if a woman is lazy about such major things will a husband normally intervene. He may overlook carelessness in her dress or in her tending of the house, or indifference about other types of work, but should she neglect her food-getting job he will beat her or, if she persists, seek a divorce.

A husband is quite free to beat his wife, as well as to scold her. She, however, is behaving badly if she scolds back or even nags, though such behaviour does occur, and rare cases do happen when a wife takes even more drastic steps or flares up dramatically in anger. One man in Bufuka found his wife in bed with a knife after he had beaten her; the next step in punishing her was tying her in the papyrus swamp near his house. However, such episodes were not everyday occurrences in most households, and most men claimed that 'one good beating should be enough for any woman'.

The husband must pay careful attention to each of his wives. He has no separate sleeping-hut of his own, but sleeps with each wife in turn, usually spending two nights in each hut, and he must divide any gifts, such as hides for clothing, ornaments, or meat, with scrupulous equality, so as to allow no jealousy to develop. Usually co-wives go about their ways separately, on good or at least neutral terms with each other; but serious difficulties are sure to arise over any partiality on the husband's part. The senior wife, the one longest married, has a position slightly superior to that of the others. Hers is the duty and the privilege of dispensing hospitality to the most important guests. She shelters new wives in her home during their first months of marriage, and advises them about the tabus, preferences, and any peculiarities of the household that they need to know. Her husband must make her a gift before taking another wife, 'because he will no longer keep her warm at night'. In the absence of the husband's mother, she is head of the household under her husband. Her hut is in the place of honour immediately opposite the gateway. She should attempt to settle any quarrels that may arise, and is entitled to respect from the junior wives. They must not call her by name, though she may so address them. However, she has no actual authority, and is entitled to no special attentions from their joint husband. Many households are on very amicable terms, at least on the surface. In others, quarrels go on interminably. In any case, wives usually take care to keep their disputes behind their husband's back. When feelings run very deep, serious difficulties may arise, culminating in such breaches as accusations of witchcraft.

A wife owes her parents-in-law respect and obedience. For a short period after marriage, she must maintain a ceremonial avoidance relationship towards her father-in-law, as we have already noted. And she must also recognize him as head of the household, accepting his decisions even in matters involving relations with her own husband, so that quarrels are often reconciled by the father-in-law. She must also carry first-fruit offerings to him, as her husband does. Should she fail to bring her parents-in-law beer of the new crop when she brews, the insult is so serious that she must make ceremonial amends. If she and her parents-in-law are on good terms, they may give her gifts in return, but this is not required.

A woman has special responsibilities to her own particular mother-in-law. This may be her husband's own mother, or the woman whose household provided the cows used in contracting the marriage. Sometimes, of course, it is her own father's sister. In any case, this is the woman whose house she lives in when she is first married. After coming out of seclusion, she works for this mother-in-law until her husband has built his own house. Even after that she owes her a certain amount of economic assistance. When she goes out to the fields for the beginning of work each season, she must first do a little gardening for her mother-in-law. A mother-in-law also has the right to mark off a little patch in her daughter-in-law's fields for her own harvesting. Similarly, while a woman should speak respectfully to her mother-in-law, and accept her guidance, cases do occur where they habitually shriek at each other.

Whether all this assistance is merely a formal gesture or amounts to real economic help depends on personal factors, including the character of the daughter-in-law. Some helpful and friendly women make every effort to show respect by working very hard for their mothers-in-law, while others are content with the minimum necessary performance. There was one household where a vixenish mother-in-law met another woman of the same calibre in her eldest daughter-in-law. Scarcely an evening passed without the sound of their voices raised in mutual animosity. They managed to have one common ground—both turned together against the meeker, lazy, and submissive younger wife. Everyone considered this behaviour very wrong, but—it was none of their business. In more normal households, a girl who scolded at her mother-in-law in this way would be treated as an outcast until she performed ceremonial amends by inviting her mother-in-law and her friends to a feast (*honga*) which only they, and none of the friends of the younger woman, might share.

Some of the other households shed light on the interplay of varying personal relations in a context of formal requirements. One woman, for example, is sufficiently jealous of her husband's attention to his widowed mother to have taken the matter to the informal court of village elders, claiming that he takes his mother (who has 'married elsewhere') too many gifts and denies her a fair share. None the less, she carries her regular share of first-fruits of crops and beer-brewings to her mother-in-law, and receives her with good manners when she comes visiting.

In another case, a daughter-in-law is openly disliked by the two wives of her husband's father, neither of whom is her real mother-in-law. They consider her sullen, lazy, inhospitable and dirty. They never speak to her, and she is never to be found in either of their houses. When she carries first-fruits to them, they merely make a formal gesture of eating them, doing only what is absolutely required by tradition and no more. Even her children share the disfavour, partly because she has trained them to cling to her skirts and avoid the other people in the compound. This situation persists despite the fact that her husband is on friendly terms with them all. Were it not for economic factors, there would long since have been a divorce; but there are children in need of a mother's care, the wife's family is not in a position to make immediate return of the bride-price, and the husband has no cows with which to take another wife.

The arrangements in another household were considered very suitable though certainly not typical. This is the household of the man who is supposed to be the schoolteacher in Bufuka. He has a compound of his own back in his native village, where his widowed mother lives. She has not remarried, and lives in the chief house in this compound. He and his wife share her house when they are there, which is not often because of his duties at Bufuka. There are several other women in the compound, all of them stepdaughters-in-law of his mother by her husband's other sons, all deceased. The schoolteacher inherited all these wives and was master of the whole compound. However, as he is a Christian, he is not living with them. Each is more or less openly living with some other man of the lineage. These men would come and fix the grain bins and help in other ways, but had not moved the women to their houses, as this would involve legal complications. The mother is queen of this little domain. All the other women owe her respect and also the other little duties which we have described. She has all her grandchildren about her, some of whom she obviously 'spoiled', and she does not need to do much work. She is particularly devoted to the schoolteacher's wife—both because she is wife to her own son, and because she is her own niece, at least in a classificatory sense.

A daughter-in-law used to inherit a very important ceremonial position from her mother-in-law. This was a ritual role involving the worship of the spirits called *emandwa* 'of the women' (see Ch. 7, p. 146). Only 'old' women—that is, ones who were eldest in their household—took part in this ceremony. Each such woman had a particular spirit or set of spirits in her charge. When she died, this function was handed on to her son's senior wife (see above, p. 45).

SEX ATTITUDES

Chiga marriage obviously dramatizes a girl's virgin reluctance to submit to a husband's embraces. The Chiga view of sex is rather a formal Latin one. It is based on a distinct double standard. The *jeune fille* must be kept pure, but after her marriage she may be mistress of many lovers, provided only that she is properly discreet. On the other hand, a boy's experience of sex begins as early as he likes. The wives of his elder brothers are not inaccessible to him, and other girls may with luck be seduced. Such affairs may even be the subject of proud boasts when a man has been drinking.

Although a girl is allowed no sex relations before marriage, she is completely aware of all the facts about sex from early childhood. It was considered merely touching that a child of six wept bitterly when she heard the crying of her father's girl-bride as the latter's marriage was being consummated in the traditional pattern of virtual rape. No attempt at all had been made to keep the child out of the house, although no outsider would be present at such a time. Young children share the bed of their parents, and later sleep nearby, separated only by a thin woven partition.

As a girl approaches puberty she must begin to conduct herself in ladylike fashion. She dons a skirt and gives up eating goat meat. Such tomboyish tricks as whistling or climbing would be very unseemly, and she would be chided and nagged if she persisted in them. She must prepare herself for matrimony by manipulating her *labia minora* so that they will be properly large: in this she is instructed by friends a little older than herself. Menstruation is generally kept secret because it is rather embarrassing, but a girl will tell her mother and friends that it has begun. There are some things which are dangerous for a menstruating woman, and some things to which she is a danger, but these tabus are slight enough, so that their observance need not be conspicuous. In fact, a young girl may be so unaware of the phenomenon as to be unprepared for it and frightened by it.

An adolescent girl is supposed to develop great modesty in her relations with the opposite sex. She should act shy with strange boys, and although she is allowed to laugh and joke with boys and men who are of her own clan, she should allow no physical intimacy, such as tickling or wrestling. Being caught in such unseemly behaviour, however childishly innocent, would overwhelm her with shame. Only her brothers-in-law (sisters' husbands) are allowed any such freedom (cf. above, p. 46). With strangers, her behaviour must be very circumspect.

Chiga girls accept the convention of modest reluctance, and consider quite shocking the tales they hear of girls in our country being quite willing to be married off without even a bride-price payment. This modesty and reluctance cause quite a complication in carrying out the marriage regulations the British have introduced, which require a licence in advance of marriage. This poses an ordeal for the girl, who, covered with confusion, must state openly at the registry office that she is willing to be married to the man in question. This important breach in customary modesty has combined with other modern innovations, such as the mission's teaching, to develop an unwonted independence in the girls. Many threaten not to go through with the marriages arranged for them, though most of them eventually yield. Girls are trying to exercise some choice, since they are legally required to consent. This, in a number of cases I noted, took the form of preference for marriage as a first wife to a young man, rather than to an older more established man chosen by her parents. (This direction of choice is no doubt influenced to some extent by mission teaching—but with respect to soap and European clothes as much as to polygyny.)

'All girls are soft,' the Chiga say, and, they imply, may easily be seduced by anyone who sets himself to it and has the opportunity. The girls are therefore carefully supervised. On all public occasions, such as weddings, when a girl is likely to meet strange men, her father and brothers keep a careful eye upon her. A girl must always be at home by dark unless there is a regular dance or ceremony at which her presence is required. If she is late in coming home, she may even be beaten. And she is never allowed private converse with a man other than a brother, cross-cousin or other relative who may be fully 'trusted'.

If a girl should be caught in a sexual misdemeanour, treatment will depend in part on the gravity of the offence, its publicity, and the identity of the man. If the offending pair are guilty of incest, they are both likely to be put to death on the spot. If she is caught in a compromising situation with a man from another group, she will be severely beaten and then married off as quickly as possible. The man, if caught, may be beaten, even killed. Sometimes he will be expected to marry the girl, but there is no effective way of compelling him to do so.

If the man who is the offender does not marry the girl, her family will usually make immediate efforts to complete other marriage arrangements for her. The husband who finds that his wife is not a virgin will probably not bother to make any fuss about it—it is as much of a disgrace to him as to her family. He may take the occasion of the 'butter-finishing feast' to complain privately to her father, showing him the handle of a hoe pierced for the blade as a symbol of her condition. The father may then hush things up by giving some of the bride-price back as a gift, and nothing further will be heard of the matter, except possibly in husband-wife quarrels.

If an unmarried girl should become pregnant, the matter is more serious. Attempts at abortion will be made by pressure on the abdomen, but they are not usually successful. A mother may try to help her daughter conceal her condition, but once the men learn of it they take drastic action. They will beat her, insisting that she name the man. There is a strong tabu on a girl's revealing the name of the man who first had intercourse with her. This is apparently even more effective than the sanctions which require a girl to preserve her chastity, for girls do get pregnant, but they rarely confess the name of the lover. If the girl, once pregnant, neither runs away nor tells the name of her partner in guilt, her family is likely to assume that her fault must have been the particularly heinous one of incest rather than mere unchastity, and her father will take the only course open to him—he will put her to death with his own hands, usually by throwing her over a cliff.

If her parents do manage to marry off a pregnant girl to her lover, when the child is about to be born she must retire to a secluded place in the bush, bear it there, and strangle it. She must then be purified by a ritual specialist before her husband can receive her. To restore normal relations with her own family another rite is necessary in which her brothers are involved.

After marriage a woman's status changes in all respects—she becomes a member of a new household, with new responsibilities, and a new name. And the whole picture of her sex life changes completely. Until her first child is conceived she is expected to sleep only with her husband—unless his brothers have been specifically assigned the privilege at her marriage, in which case they have access to her from the time when she comes back from 'finishing the butter'.

When a woman is newly married, living in her mother-in-law's house or in the house of one of her husband's older wives, she is definitely under surveillance. But by the time she conceives, if not before, her husband will build a hut for her, where she will be more nearly her own mistress and, if her husband has other wives, alone on regular sets of nights. If she occasionally consoles herself in her loneliness with some other man—well, no one will care, especially if no one is the wiser. Indeed, no man should be jealous if he does find out, provided his wife confines her favours to his own brothers and lineage kinsmen and observes due decorum—such as conducting her liaisons quietly in her own house and never immodestly 'in the bush'. Only a man of very bad habits would beat his wife for adultery quietly kept within the family.

The sexual freedom in the relations between a woman and her brothers-in-law is at once apparent. I was present when one young man came to see his brother's bride during her seclusion. She had been married only about a week. Although the conversation was innocent enough, his manner was proprietary, and there was an air of leering teasing which would have been unthinkable between any other relatives, or between a bride and any other male.

Sometimes, if a man has many wives, he may assign the house of one of them to a visiting pact-brother to sleep in. This means that the latter will have the opportunity to sleep with the wife who lives there. However, the Chiga do not refer to this in terms of wife-lending. It is merely *arulira*—to spread a bed for the visitor. It would not be decent to refer openly to any other implications of the situation. This is the only case in which a husband might connive at adultery between his wife and a man of another clan or gens. In any other case, should he discover a liaison between his wife and a man not his own relative, he might divorce the woman and would certainly be free to kill the man. The exception which is sometimes made of the pact-brother is phrased in terms of trust. That is, a man can be sure that a pact-brother will not break up his home by stealing or bewitching his wife.

Women are said to be more jealous than men, but this takes a very institutionalized form. A good wife should be pleased when her husband takes another wife, though she will not actually urge him to do so. It brings her reflected prestige and some help. But she is justified in her jealousy if her husband pays more attention to another wife; so that a husband who wishes to keep peace in his home must be scrupulously careful to divide his time and gifts equally among his wives. If he really prefers one wife to the others, he would have to be just as secret about it as though he were having an affair with one of his sisters-in-law or some strange woman.

There is jealousy should a husband fail to be impartial in his attentions, but much greater jealousy should he transfer his attentions to any woman not a wife. This the wives jointly resent. One offence in particular is very serious. No man may ever have sexual relations with another woman in the house of any of his wives.

A woman must never sleep with her own father-in-law or his age mates. Their first relationship is based on extreme avoidance, as we have already noted. But even when that has been ceremonially ended, she must still show him respect, not familiarity.

When there is gossip about a man and his son's wives, it is in terms of serious scandal. It does, however, occur, especially where a man shows off by taking a bride for his son while the latter is still a child.

A young wife and her husband's sons are in a different position. Although such a relationship is not approved, it is condoned if it is not too open. And, of course, after the father's death, such younger wives are appropriately taken care of by marriage to the senior sons. It is only wives whose status is parallel to that of a man's own mother—women who were already married to his father when he was born, and who may have nursed or even suckled him as an infant, with whom the relationship is considered shocking.

As a woman grows older, continued open sexual activity is not looked upon with favour. When her husband dies, an older woman should not marry again, but should settle down to a peaceful old age, enjoying her grandchildren, and a position of respect as a dowager mother in her son's household. To become the actual wife of a younger man in her husband's family, under guise of such a 'building for' relationship, is unseemly, and may even endanger the well-being of her daughters-in-law and their children. A widow who has remarried may, on the other hand, with propriety, leave her second husband and go to live as a widow with her own son when he grows up.

CHILD-BEARING

Birth, even conception, of the first child makes a considerable difference in the status of a married woman, as we have already seen. That is the point at which she should move into her own house and start cultivating her own fields. If he has not already done so, her husband should certainly give her hides to make the proper, full-length woman's skirts, and buy her as many wire anklets as he can afford, so that she will no longer look like a young girl.

A pregnant woman must observe all sorts of tabus if her child is to thrive. Because there has been no systematic training for this important part of her life, she is likely to make many little mistakes, for which the senior women in her husband's compound will call her sharply to task. For example, she may forget that she must no longer lick salt, for that would keep her baby's hair from growing properly. Her husband has his part to do, too. He has tabus to observe and many evil omens to watch out for. If any of them should occur, he must be sure to purify himself immediately.

Although the mother is constantly aware and reminded of the child that is to be born, she must make no formal preparations for its coming. She may not even prepare the little leather sling in which she will carry it for many months after its birth. She just goes on with her regular work, right up to and after the time when the labour pains start. She should not even try to stay at home to bear the child. Brave women bear their children wherever they chance to be at the time, and many children's names, such as 'cornfield', commemorate their birthplaces. Birth takes place squatting or kneeling. A woman tries to bear her child alone, but if she is 'afraid of the bearing' she can call other women to help her, her co-wives and even her mother-in-law (who, however must leave the house immediately after, for there are many tabus upon her there). No man may be present, except a ritual specialist who may be called in a real emergency. Attempts may be made to manipulate the baby into a more suitable position, or herbs may be administered to ease the mother in a difficult case; more often, magic causes are assumed to be standing in her way and every attempt will be made to correct these. For example, it is well to remove a bit of thatch from the roof, in case the trouble comes from her husband having climbed on the roof and neglected some of the required precautions; or to break a stick from the fence, to counteract the bad effect of the occasion when she helped her husband with the masculine task of fence-building.

After the baby is born and the mother has cut the cord and bound it up, she carries the baby home carefully wrapped in the top of her skirt, where no stranger's dangerous glance may fall on it. At home, she washes and massages and anoints it, and then at last she may lie down to rest by the fire, give the baby some water from her hand, and put it to the breast.

For about four days, until the stump of the umbilical cord drops off, mother and child remain in seclusion. She may go out only as far as into the courtyard to lie in the sun for a little while. Her husband stays with her, neighbours bring food and firewood, and all the husband's family observe various tabus. His other wives must be careful in their behaviour, for that, too, will affect the new-born child. It will be especially dangerous for the baby if they should sleep with some other man now in their husband's absence. And all the members of the household 'take time off from planting for the little one who was born'.

Meanwhile, a number of minor rites are performed. The father has announced the birth of a son by pulling up the gateway posts and building a fire with them in the courtyard. He has also made a little bow and put it proudly in the baby's hand. And the mother has uttered a ceremonial protective 'curse', which is a kind of magical vaccination. Striking the baby with the umbilical cord, she says, 'I curse you in bearing you. Now the curse of being struck by lightning will never harm you; the curse of falling in battle will never make you fall in battle, for I have cursed you in bearing you, and I am your mother. Now, though anyone curse you, you will not die.'

When the stump of the umbilical cord drops off, the placenta is thrown away (usually it is buried at the gateway with no special fuss), and the baby is ready for its first public appearance. The mother has made the leather sling by now; she carries it out into the courtyard and sets the baby down on it. Now for the first time other people are allowed to touch the baby. Its head is shaved, a spear is thrust into the ground above its arm if it is a boy—to make him brave—and then, when it is taken back into the house, the mother and father share some gruel which has been ceremonially prepared.

Once this ceremony of 'bearing out the child' is over, everyone, including the mother, may resume his or her normal activities. She ties the child on her back in its little sling and goes to work in the fields as usual. And one day, when she has time, she may go home to visit, taking a little gruel in her child's cup to offer to the ghost or spirit of her own paternal grandmother, who helped her conceive. Until the baby teethes, she will keep it always with her, and especially never sleep elsewhere, leaving the baby at home.

A great many of the usual African beliefs about babyhood and normal child development are found here. For example, if the child's upper teeth should come in first, it is a very bad sign; the offending teeth would be pulled out immediately, and purifying medicines given to the child to avoid the danger of someone dying. Twins are considered very special. Their afterbirth is dangerous and must be well buried, and the spot carefully marked, lest someone get leprosy from sitting on it. They must always be treated exactly alike, given gifts at the same time, even punished together. Girl twins will even go through the first steps of a marriage together, though later one will remain at home, to be married off to someone else, but as a previously married woman, not a girl. When one of a pair of twins dies, the grave is especially tabu, but the remaining twin can go on to lead a normal life. Many special tabus and ceremonial restrictions of a minor sort are laid upon the parents of twins, some of which last all their lives.

Although barrenness is not quite as drastically regarded here as in some parts of the world, and is certainly no cause for divorce, if a woman does fail to conceive serious efforts will be made to help her. The cures vary with the diagnoses. The diviner may find her barrenness is due to the breaking of some tabu. There are many dangerous acts of omission which she or someone else may have committed either accidentally or maliciously since her marriage, or even before, which would stand in the way of her conceiving. Some such 'binders' are tabus through which run obvious symbolic threads. For example, a girl must not eat honey from a hive with no hole pierced in it; and a woman must not put on her father's cloak. Once such a lapse is discovered, a ritual specialist will try to purge her of the evil effects, using techniques specific to each particular offence.

Sometimes a woman's barrenness is due to special medicines which were administered to 'tie' her (that is, to prevent conception). If she thinks that some such charm is operative, she will go to her old lover secretly in an effort to have him 'release her womb'. She may have to buy him off with presents or promises of presents.

Another common cause to which barrenness is ascribed is some error in the performance of the marriage ceremonies. One of the participants expressly forbidden to sleep with his spouse for a designated four-day period may have had sexual relations too soon, or some woman or girl may have worn a belt during some part of the rites when she should have removed it. If this is the case, the essential rites of the marriage must be repeated. The girl will go back to her father's home and be fetched away again, and the whole set of rites at the groom's home must be repeated, including the 'fight' with her husband and the drinking of the gruel. The participants must then carefully observe all the required rules regarding their own behaviour for the four days following the wedding. This is *shubuza* (to begin over again), and is a regular technique employed in many different contexts to avert the consequences of wrong behaviour (cf. p. 169).

A more vigorous appeal may also be made to the spirits, particularly to the spirit of the girl's paternal grandmother. The anxious husband may even provide a bull for his father-in-law to sacrifice to his mother's spirit. But if all this fails, the husband can only hope to marry another wife who will bear him children, or the woman that some luckier co-wife of her husband's may allow her one of her own children to bring up. A woman will treat such a child as her own. If it is a son, she will have some-one to bring her a daughter-in-law and grandchildren, and to build for her in her later years. A childless woman loses all these advantages, as well as having a lower status in everyone's eyes for her failure to give her husband children.

It is important, both for a father and a mother, to have sons to be their heirs and help them when they grow old. A father without sons may have to adopt a 'herd-boy' to fill his need. Daughters are good and important, too, for with them the bride-price cattle come into the family, with which wives can be got to work the fields and produce more children.

Miscarriages, infant mortality, and childhood illnesses bring a heavy toll of loss. One of my neighbours had lost all of seven, and had no child left of her own. Fortunately a co-wife, bearing two children in rapid succession, had found it mutually advan-tageous to let her adopt the elder of them so that she was not alone. One woman in Bufuka had six children and had only lost one; this was considered quite exceptional.

When a mother dies in childbed the father is in a very difficult position. The only solution is to find a foster-mother who can nurse the child. The Chiga insist that even a grandmother can do this; any woman who has borne a child in the past can produce milk again if a child is set to her breast earnestly enough. Cases were pointed out to me of people who had been rescued in this way in their infancy. I did meet one poor father who was making an effort to save his motherless baby himself, feeding it pap from his hand and giving it soaked cloths to suck. Many people were sympathetically interested, but not actively concerned in any way. Some found the idea ridiculous rather than touching, and almost all assumed it was hopeless.

Of course, if a child is left motherless a little later on, the problem is an entirely different one. It may be sent to live with its mother's relatives or even boarded out with someone else for the payment of a goat or two. It is hard to get another wife to step into the place of a wife who has died and take over the care of her children, as her home will seem too unlucky. Certainly no father will willingly marry off an eligible daughter under such circumstances, and only a girl with some special counts against her is likely to be available.

DIVORCE

Marriages are on the whole fairly permanent. Divorce can and does occur, but many attempts are made to resolve difficulties by other means. In Bufuka, for example, all the married women were living with their first husbands, or with men who had inherited them after that husband's death.

If a man and woman quarrel the elders of the village may act as the first court of arbitration, or the woman may go away in anger to her own father's home. This is a frequent occurrence and in most cases is without serious consequences. A woman may return voluntarily, having got only as far as one of her neighbour's houses, where she took shelter for the night until her anger cooled. Or her husband may come after her and fetch her back. This arrangement is definitely a formal pattern of protest rather than the initiation of divorce proceedings. There are in fact formal rules for doing it with proper regard for the proprieties. For example, no woman should ever go off like this when one of the other wives of her husband is also away! It is also important that she should take none of her personal possessions with her, for if she should later bring them back and use them, her husband would die. Such an action might be the desperate, or the spiteful, expedient resorted to by a girl forced to return to her husband against her wishes. Its threat might be used to prevent just that outcome. Such behaviour is, however, regarded as virtually equivalent to witchcraft.

In the normal course of events, when a wife goes off to her father's house, her husband will follow in an attempt to negotiate matters and start afresh. He may be able to prove that the quarrel which caused her to leave was due to her own misconduct. If so, he expects her father to scold her and order her to behave better. If her ways have been seriously wrong, as in the case of one Bufuka wife, who was shiftless and lazy and finally accused of stealing food from her co-wives and defecating in the house, the husband may demand, and get, a sheep—or, as in this case, even a cow—to postpone divorce action. This animal is both a recompense for her past misconduct and a pledge of her better behaviour in the future.

If, on the other hand, the husband finds that the wife's family sides with her, it will be up to him to promise to reform, or they will allow her to stay on at home and proceed with divorce negotiations.

Normally, after some years of marriage, relations settle down to some kind of acceptable state. Some marriages are extremely peaceful; others involve frequent noisy quarrels, magic and countermagic, runnings-away and returnings, wife-beatings and, as in one exceptional case mentioned earlier, even attacks, or threatened attacks, by the wife on the husband.

In some cases, however, quarrels eventually result in divorce. There are no formal 'causes' that are legally sufficient. It is entirely a matter of negotiation between the families. Divorce proceedings can only start with a woman's going home to her family. If she does not do this, there is nothing her husband can do. He cannot send her away, though he can make life extremely uncomfortable for her. If he is anxious to get back his bride-price and marry again, the husband may resort to all sorts of trickery and inducements, but if the wife is willing to put up with rough treatment, there is little more that he can do. On the other hand, if a woman's family will not consent to a divorce which she very much wants, she may simply run off. Her husband will probably pursue her with magic to get her new husband to return her to him; or else to pay a bride-price for her, which her family can then give to him to settle the case.

If a divorce is finally agreed upon as the only way out, the son-in-law is entitled to the return of all the cows which he paid as bride-price. Sometimes, however, he will settle for less in recognition of the fact that the bride is no longer a virgin, and the bride-price given for her remarriage will probably be a much smaller one. (Any cows given to the bridegroom as gifts are counted as already returned.) If the girl has had no children, the calves borne by the bride-price cows must be returned to the husband, but if she has had a child not more than half the calves need be handed over. Questions concerning such problems as the exact number of cows and the particular cows to be returned are settled by a joint council of the bride's and groom's paternal uncles, who were witnesses to the original marriage. Obviously, the negotiations are bound to be long and complicated.

Special complications are caused by the fact that the proper arrangements call for the return, not of equivalents, but of the same cows that were originally paid. If these have died, special arrangements will have to be made. Certain established rules exist that cover some cases, but they are subject to interpretation and argument. For example, a cow which died soon after the marriage is the groom's responsibility and would not be returned. (In fact, in the normal course of a marriage, such a cow would have had to be replaced by the groom.) Furthermore, if the cows have been used for a subsequent marriage, as is usually the case, it will be necessary to go to the father of the second bride and ask him to return the 'other people's cows'. The possibility of such a future claim is always recognized at a wedding: a pot of beer is formally set aside for the previous owner of the cattle, to keep the line of connection perfectly clear. Although the claim must be recognized as valid, it is not always easy to collect it. Even if the cows are returned, this does not necessarily dissolve the second marriage. If the girl's father likes, he may allow her to stay on, with an understanding that her husband will pay a new bride-price as soon as possible.

Both the husband and the girl's father will usually take precautions to avert any malicious magical acts the other may be provoked to after the divorce. Such hard feelings are commonly anticipated. However, if there are children, the parents-in-law will try to remain on friendly terms with the divorced husband, so that they may continue to visit their grandchildren.

The presence of children, particularly infants, makes for special complications in divorce. A woman is not allowed to take her baby with her; it belongs to her husband's family and she has no rights to it except as a member of that family. None the less, women normally do take their babies with them when they run off. In the past this meant subjecting them to great risk. The new husband might kill the baby, particularly if it were a boy. One quite mild old man of my acquaintance is reported to have killed two children who came to his household in this fashion.

He had dashed them against the floor so that they died of broken bones and other injuries, and then insisted that it was merely an accident. Such a 'thing that came along', as the child would be dubbed, might be tolerated if it were a girl, since that would mean a bride-price later on. However, at that point the true father would probably claim it back. In any case, its lack of status would be emphasized on every possible occasion. The same dangers beset a baby borne by a woman after elopement if she was already pregnant when she ran away, except that if she could succeed in concealing the time of its birth, the new husband might try to claim it for his own. There was rather a tense moment in our village when a stranger coming by tried to find out from one of my housemen whether his former wife, who had eloped to one of my man's kinsmen, had been pregnant at the time. Of course, he got no answer: both duty to a kinsman and a wish not to get mixed up in the affair would guarantee that! But it was perfectly clear that the former husband's claim to the child was recognized as valid, if the child had been conceived before the wife ran away. Sometimes, however, a husband, willing to agree to a divorce, will let his wife take an infant with her and arrange to pay a fostering fee to her new husband when he comes to claim his child later on.

When a woman is married again after a divorce, there is none of the attendant fuss and fighting at the wedding. She is expected to walk to her husband's house rather than to be carried, and her wedding party is smaller; there is no feasting at the bridegroom's house, and the only rite performed is the eating of the marrow leaves, which makes her part of the new household. She sleeps with her husband the very same night. In many cases of second marriage, it is very important that the affair be conducted quickly and the bride-price paid at once, as it must be used to pay back the bride-price due to the first husband. If this need does not exist, a second marriage may sometimes be arranged on credit—the sheep and goats given at once and a cow promised should the bride bear a child. In any case, a father would be anxious to have his daughter remarried, as his house is no proper permanent home for a daughter who has once been married. On the whole, all sorts of pressures operate to minimize the incidence of divorce, including a woman's pride in *not* being a twice-married woman.

LEVIRATE AND SORORATE

As we have already seen, once a woman is married her husband's family is responsible for providing for her after his death. If she is a young woman, she should marry one of his sons, or at least one of the other members of the lineage: some personal choice may be exercised. But should she refuse all of them and leave, procedures would follow as for any other divorce. If she is an older woman, she will probably not remarry at all, but simply remain as a dowager mother. If she has a grown son of her own, she may have an excellent life, for he will take good care of her. But the position of an old woman with no sons of her own may be one of hardship, unless one of her husband's brothers marries her. When a man marries his brother's wife, especially if she is not yet an old woman, he must make sure that the ghost of the dead husband will permit it. A purificatory ceremony is necessary before he can safely sleep with her, and he must make at least a token payment to her family, as a son would not have to do.

Should a wife die young and childless, having failed to perform her expected functions, her family has some obligation to make it up to the husband by giving him her sister in marriage— but only if she dies at her father's home. The widowed husband would have to pay a bride-price for his new bride, but the payment would be relatively small. All the clothes and other belongings of the deceased would be kept for her. If the father does not supply a second wife, the bereaved husband may return all the clothing and other gifts and demand at least a partial return of the bride-price. However, if the young wife dies at her new husband's home, her father will recognize no further responsibility. He may even charge the husband with witchcraft against his daughter. One of my friends in Bufuka nearly got into this kind of trouble. He was in an especially difficult position, for he was not in fact regularly married to the girl who was living with him. He was saving up to pay the bride-price when his wife died; fortunately for him, she was visiting at her father's home at the time. This absolved him from responsibility, and also relieved him of any obligation to pay the bride-price. Had she died at his home, he would have had to pay 'on the burial mat', or her family would have refused to attend the burial.

There were other complications in this case as well. The girl in question was a young widow who had eloped to him instead of being married to one of her brothers-in-law. The affair had just been straightened out. He had agreed to pay a bride-price, and the father had returned the original bride-price to the family of the deceased husband. The girl was on her first visit home after affairs had been amicably arranged when she fell ill. Had her illness occurred earlier, it would probably have been contended that it was the first husband's family who were magically causing it, and she would have been sent back to them to prevent her death. Modern conditions make open accusations rather difficult, but suspicion may still rest upon the husband's family.

Except that one of them may be given to him in lieu of the return of the bride-price if his wife dies soon after marriage, a husband has no special claim on his wife's sisters. He may be freer with them (after the payment of a special gift) than he would be with other unmarried girls, but if he wants to marry one of them, he must pay a regular bride-price and make all the usual arrangements. Such marriages of pairs of sisters are said to occur only when the husband is particularly well satisfied with his wife. I knew of no cases of marriage to two sisters in or around Bufuka; marriages of pairs of brothers to women of the same patrilineage were, however, quite common.

5

ECONOMICS

PRODUCTION AND EXCHANGE

DESPITE the obvious importance of cattle in their social system, the Chiga are primarily not herders but farmers. Vegetable food is the mainstay of their diet, and the rhythm of their lives is set by the seasonal round of planting and harvesting, its times of waiting and of working, its times of fast and of plenty.

The heavy work of the year begins with the light rains in September and October. That is when peas, beans, and corn are planted, and the fields are prepared for 'small millet' (eleusine). This is sweet for porridge, but needs a great deal of careful work —weeding by hand, rather than by hoeing and, at harvest time, slow cutting, stalk by stalk, with a small knife. By the time these crops are started and the heavy work of preparing the large fields for millet has begun, belts may have to be tightened, for last year's crops are beginning to run low.

Millet is planted by preference in fields which have not been used for a while, so that they are beginning to grow back into bush. This overgrowth must be cut, piled into long bundles, and burnt; then the fields must be dug and harrowed. By this time the first planting of peas has ripened and provided a welcome fresh relish; beans and corn are beginning to be picked and soon will be dried and stored, yielding a supply which may last till the millet harvest if luck holds out. Meanwhile, more of these crops may be planted to ripen along with the millet. Only potatoes are planted and gathered without a specific seasonal schedule; they are not stored, but dug as needed. The prudent housewife plants potatoes as extensively as possible so as to have something to fall back on when the stored crops of grain and peas and beans are running low.

The full harvest comes with the beginning of the dry season in July or August. This is a time of relative leisure, of beer drinks and wedding feasts. Before it is over, and the next year's work begins, belts will probably have to be tightened again, as remaining supplies are husbanded for seed.

All this represents long, hard work for a relatively low yield, and a none-too-ample food supply. There is little wild vegetation to supplement the regular crops. No fruits, nuts or berries are to be had; only some greens and a few mushrooms can be gathered. The country is too high and too cold for the bananas and sugar-cane which provide so well for many of their neighbours, nor are groundnuts grown. The Chiga know nothing of manuring, and the shallow hoeing just scratches the top-soil, depleting the overworked land still further. Fields are rotated to some extent; but the land is very heavily settled and new fields, extravagantly cleared of all cover every few years, quickly wear out again. Hailstorms and locusts, droughts, or unseasonable rains may wipe out an entire crop and cause severe local famines, sending men forth with their families to seek new homes with pact-brothers or kinsmen, or even driving them to sell their daughters in exchange for food.

The determination of planting times is rather a hit-or-miss affair. The Chiga calendar is lunar, but very vague. Most people name the month by observing what the seasonal occupation or state of the crops is at the time, and often disagree in their reckoning. In a community such as Bufuka all the people follow roughly the same planting schedule, but it need not be the same as their neighbours'. I noted a difference of a month and a half at one time between the beginning of the planting time for a particular crop on two neighbouring hills. When one man decided to go against tradition and started a late millet field independently, the village laughed at him for a fool, and displayed great satisfaction when his fields dried up—despite the fact that the drought was general and other people lost their corn, beans, and peas. The explanation they gave of this synchronized activity, so unusual in the general context of Chiga disinterest in other people's actions, was that the risk to a solitary field from marauders, particularly birds, would be too great. I think, however, that the root of the matter probably lies in the defunct institution of the rain-maker. In the old days rites were performed to bring the right weather at the right time; clearly there was no point in individuals starting separately, or in being much concerned with the behaviour of people on a neighbouring hillside, who had their own rain-maker (see p. 139). Certainly some people did risk pushing out into new areas, clearing lonely patches of new land for themselves.

The demands of herding have no comparable effect on the rhythm of Chiga life. There are no seasonal migrations; there are not even designated grazing grounds. The cattle feed on whatever lands happen to be unused for gardening, eating the grass or the stalks of the previous season's corn or millet. The heavily cultivated and cropped-over hillsides provide thin pasturage. Cows are few, scrawny, and yield little milk. Most households have only a cow or two, and a few sheep and goats. This is scarcely enough to provide an adequate supply of hides for clothing, and of butter, which is essential as an unguent rather than as a food item. And it means that most families depend on a daughter's bride-price to provide the cattle for a son's wife. Milk is seldom plentiful enough to be used regularly for food, and only the wealthy eat much meat. Mutton (which women may not eat) is usually available for a feast or sacrifice, but the beef supply depends almost entirely on the occasional death of a cow, whether by accident or illness. Instead of having to divide their herds for pasturing, as so many of their pastoral neighbours do, the Chiga more often pool them, one herd-boy collecting the cows of several neighbours from their separate compounds each morning, after the milking, and bringing them back to their homes again each night. The cows are tended together with the sheep and goats, and very little of the lore and ritual of cattle-care, as practised by the Hima, is known or followed by the Chiga.

The Chiga practise all the techniques which are known in this area for which the materials are available, including iron-working and pottery. They use all the local resources and, at least in the case of the rather scarce wood supply, husband them carefully. Houses are grass-thatched over wattle and daub, needing large poles only for the major roof supports; baskets and wooden trays serve more often than wooden bowls to eat and drink from; firewood is fed carefully, stick by tiny stick, on to the hearth. Bark-cloth cannot be grown up here in the mountains; clothing is made of hides, worn with the fur inside. A toga-like garment of two cowskins, knotted at the shoulder, is the men's dress. At work, one skin may be wrapped about the waist. Modesty is not an issue for the men, as it is for the women, who wear a long cut and sewn skirt, and a short cape when it is cold. Grasses and reeds, bark of reeds, pliable vines, animal sinews, are used for weaving, tying, and sewing. All tools and materials for their production are local, made in the individual household or by a neighbourhood craftsman. Only a few luxuries—beautiful black clay pipes and bamboo trays made by the Pygmies, some salt, and the cloth, soap, and tobacco that are bought in Indian shops—are imported, and for all these there are local substitutes.

But despite the range of techniques and use of materials, one is forcibly impressed both with the real poverty of the Chiga, and with their poor craftsmanship. Possessions are few; clothing is often patched, and some people do not own an extra cloak for a bed cover or a change, or ornaments to wear on festive occasions. Few people have surplus tools, and some not even essential ones. The finished products are rougher and cruder than those of their neighbours, and far less decoration is used. Doors for the houses are usually neatly woven, but the partitions inside are crude and roughly plastered. A woman who makes pots will only bother to run the stippling or braiding press around the neck of one or two pots in a baking; and one girl in my village who bothered to dye the grass strips she was going to use in a sewn mat was considered unusually industrious and even a little odd. The Chiga themselves formulate this lack of artistic interest and pride in special skills quite clearly. 'A decorated basket is very pretty', they will say, 'but you can drink beer just as well from a plain one.'

The larger share of all Chiga work tends to fall upon the women. Theirs particularly is the steady, unremitting daily routine of food-getting. Except for the initial clearing of the fields, they do almost all the gardening—from the first turning of the soil to bringing home the harvest; they not only keep the house clean, tend the fire and do the cooking, but they also do the concomitant heavy chores of gathering the wood and fetching the water. They prepare the materials for and make the baskets and mats, sew and mend the hide clothing and make all but the largest beer-pots.

As a result, women have very little leisure. During all but about two months of the year, work in the fields occupies a good deal of every woman's time. During the busiest seasons, the more energetic women are in the fields by daybreak, leaving a little of the last evening's food, cooked but cold, for the father and children to eat when they get hungry. A woman may take a day off every few days, or come home occasionally about noon instead of late in the afternoon, but there are usually chores connected with food awaiting her attention at home—trays of grain or beans to flail and winnow or set to dry, or flour to grind, and so on. Some utensils and clothing may be mended from time to time when absolutely necessary, but most such tasks must wait for the brief respite of the dry season. Then, when she has her crops dried and stored and is not brewing beer, a woman can find time to weave baskets and twine mats, to make pots if she knows how, or to cut out and sew a new skirt.

Men do a good deal of heavy work too, but it is more varied and less exacting than women's work. The steady chore of cattle-tending is regularly delegated to the children, who take the animals out to pasture, guard them, keep them from straying and raise an alarm if danger threatens, water them, and even take them from time to time to the salt licks. Grown men need only do the milking, any necessary doctoring, and occasionally extra tasks such as bleeding the cows—undertaken both for the cows' health and for the blood itself, which is relished as a delicacy. They do the butchering and cooking of all the meat; this is outside the women's department. Women do not even eat it, for the most part, as they may eat only beef, not any form of sheep or goat meat.

Men build all the storage bins and keep them in repair; these are huge baskets or miniature huts set up on stilts in the court-yard. They clear the fields and, if they feel like it, may even help in the gardening from time to time. They tan the hides, when these are available, make simple wooden products, including handles for the metal hoes, sickles, and knives; and they make any special equipment they need, such as hunting snares or fish-ing weirs, and so on. Men who have special skills, such as a knowledge of carpentry or iron-working, may spend considerable time at these specialized tasks. Their heaviest task is house-building, which is exclusively men's work. Women may not even help to prepare the materials—except the beer which is used to feast the people who come to the house-raising. But unless a son and his new wife need a house of their own, or there are deaths in the family which necessitate moving, new houses are not built very often, and a good thatching job should last five years or so without major repairs. So that on the whole men have much more leisure than women, and much more freedom in arranging their time. Some of the leisure used to be spent in hunting and fighting, both of which were checked by the British; but a great deal of it was always available for loafing and for drinking beer.

Most men and women have a rough knowledge of the basic techniques for all the important tasks appropriate to their own sex, so that on the whole each household can and does take care of most of its own needs. However, a few tasks require co-operative work, for which members of different households pool their resources. And there are also specialized tasks which need special tools or knowledge, or at which people are not all equally adept. Pottery-making, for example, is a skill that only a few people in any community are really good at, though others may try their hands at it fumblingly. Some women are much better than others at cutting out skirts; and there are men who are specially good at tanning hides or butchering sheep, though any man can make a stab at either. There are even women who cannot make a satisfactory basket of the simplest sort, but rely on the help of their co-wives or neighbours. Anyone with a reputation for special proficiency in doing or making something is often called upon to help his friends and kinsmen.

There are other skills, however, which are more formally specialized. The smith and the carpenter, for example—the real carpenter who can carve a canoe or a fine stool, not just whittle a hoe handle or point a stake—have to serve a long apprenticeship, and own valuable special tools—hammer and anvil and leather bellows for the one, whole sets of axes and adzes of various sizes and shapes for the other. Bee-keeping too is a valued skill not known to everyone, handed down from father to son, and requiring much knowledge, not only of how to build a hive and smoke out the bees, but also of powerful magical lore. There are medical craftsmen too, herbalists who know a charm or two, or cures for specific diseases; and there were in the past powerful sorcerers who used spirit aids in their work and diviners of many different sorts with varying degrees of power and skill.

There were specialists of most of these kinds in and around Bufuka. Not every hamlet boasted a smith, as Bufuka did, so people came from quite a distance to get him to make a knife or some new anklets. There was no carpenter in Bufuka proper, but there were two in nearby Abayundu hamlets, one on the next peninsula. In addition, one woman was a noted potter. However, when skins were to be tanned, Abasigi friends were called upon rather than anyone closer by. I knew at least three former diviners among my close acquaintance, and there were others among the friendly nearby Abasigi.

Although people from many households may engage the services of these special craftsman and reward them for their work, none of them is a full-time specialist, dependent for his livelihood on the products of his special skills. Their households, like anyone else's, are essentially independent subsistence units. Their wives grow grain and make beer, their sons herd and help them keep the houses in repair. This is the kind of household economy on which all Chiga production is essentially based.

As Chiga work is organized, the various men in a household, father and grown sons, share the men's work and the responsibilities of the household to some extent; they take turns in herding and milking, work together in building, and so forth. But the women do not ordinarily work together at all. Each woman, wife or son's wife, who has her own hut, has her own fields and granaries, for which she alone is responsible. Daughters and daughters-in-law do a certain amount of work in the mother's fields, but not necessarily together. A woman normally has various plots under cultivation at one time. She can therefore send her grown daughter off to hoe in the cornfield while she herself goes to the top of a different hill to plant potatoes, and a small child sets off to spend the day shooing the birds away from a third patch where grain is maturing. An adolescent girl may prefer to have a field assigned to her which she works by herself. Only rarely will several members of the family be seen working side by side in the fields. Habits are not attuned to it, so that when people do work together they are sometimes hurt by each other's hoes. There are no work songs or other rhythmic helps. There is no large-scale co-operative job that women do, except brewing beer. Even that is often done separately by each wife; the guests at a common household party will then come to the various huts in turn to drink.

Men's co-operation sometimes extends beyond the limits of the household. House-building, for example, is a task calling for organized group work on a far larger scale. The man who wants a new house will dig the site and prepare the materials. He will also need lots of beer, which his wives will have to supply. When all is ready, friends and neighbours will come together to help him. A house-raising is a gala event to which dozens of people come, anxious to share in the drinking, feasting, and general merry-making which follow the work. The house was always put up all in one day. There was no apportionment of reward in terms of services rendered. Everyone who came did as much or as little work as he liked, and then drank and ate as much as he liked. The wives of friends helped out with gifts of food or firewood, and came to help with the cooking, but as women they had no share at all in putting up the house.

Although the economic responsibility of each man is limited to his own household, there are a number of tasks which men normally do on a co-operative basis. Hunting, for example, when it did occur, was usually a joint enterprise, arranged on a voluntary basis among several men, who shared the proceeds according to strict rules, based on the irrespective contributions to the actual kill. A specific share would go to the owner of the dogs responsible for a particular catch, a smaller share to a man whose dog had started the animal, and regular parts to the people who wounded the animal, and so forth. Neighbours also build watering-troughs together (needed to avoid the danger of the cows swallowing leeches). When they do, such a watering-place is for their exclusive joint use, access being allowed to others only with their express permission. Men often band together also to bleed their cows, a rather exciting task, undertaken about once a month. One skilled man will open the veins by shooting arrows into the side of the cows' necks, others hold the animals and lead them off afterwards, or carry and care for the buckets of blood. The rest just come along to watch and add to the noise.

Surpluses and shortages in different households, and the distribution of the special products of craft skills, are taken care of through informal gift-giving and reciprocity, in terms of friendship rather than along strict kinship lines. One woman in Bufuka, noted for her skill as a potter, always had most of her batch of pots promised before the clay was dry. In return, her neighbours helped her fetch the clay or the grass for the firing, and they always brought her gifts when they asked for the pots or soon after. A man who comes to help his friends butcher an animal will be given certain parts of the meat in return, and so forth. Similarly, a woman may beg a bit of butter from her brother's wife in order to dress up for a feast and will send her some mushrooms soon after. A man may send every second or third day's milking to various friends and relatives whose cows are not yielding any milk at the moment, and when a man kills a sheep a considerable part of it is immediately distributed in gifts. There are no fixed rules for distributing such goods, except for certain regular gifts from a son to his father and fixed obligations about invitations to beer feasts. But reciprocity is expected, and though there is no check on equivalence of values, making quick return for gifts is a point of pride. I constantly received chickens, eggs, and milk in return for my gifts of tobacco and salt. And those who failed to make such return gifts were unfavourably commented upon by my Chiga household.

It is permissible to beg for what one wants, though doing this habitually would give one a bad name. I have seen a girl ask for—and receive—a bracelet she admired from a girl in another village who was just a distant maternal cousin. A return gift in the near future was, of course, necessary, though it meant making a special trip to take it to her. It is not really good form to ask anything of a non-relative, other than a very close friend, unless one is ready to acknowledge the giver as a patron, and give him a heavy return in services (see below, p. 106).

Hospitality in the form of serving food and, if possible, beer is a required gesture towards any honoured visitor, and is the basis for further informal exchanges. Such hospitality, together with provision of shelter for the night, is an obligation of kinship and of pact-brotherhood. It is also customary to give gifts, as many as possible, to the departing guest, while he in turn should bring something with him. Sometimes people go to visit their relatives primarily with some specific exchange of articles in mind. The routine of bargaining and trading would not, however, be used. A gift would be given, the desirability of something else hinted at—that was as far as one could go.

There is a good deal of both formal and informal sharing of beer. To make beer takes about two weeks of intermittent, fairly hard work. And after it is ready to drink it cannot be kept for more than a day or so without spoiling. Because of the work involved, no family can be constantly and adequately supplied with beer by its own resources alone. As a result, beer is usually made in large rather than small quantities, the major working-time of the household being concentrated on that task during the process. Neighbours are then invited in to the drinking, and the household expects its own beer wants to be supplied by these neighbours when they brew. And one must invite a brother-in-law or father-in-law even to an informal beer drink. In addition, of course, beer is an indispensable part of any feast, whether it be a ceremonial occasion, a wedding, or a house-building.

Men often enter into regular beer-making compacts. The participants of such a compact jointly pledge to take turns in making beer for the entire group. Such an arrangement is quite formal and has fixed rules, assuring to each a full return for his efforts and excluding outsiders so far as possible. (In general, manners allow anyone to stop for a drink when passing by 'where there is beer', but to sit down at the pot requires an invitation.)

Products and services requiring a higher degree of specialized skill are handled on a more formal basis than are simple reciprocal gifts. One does not just go and buy a hoe, or a stool, or a canoe. Rather, one has to engage the services of the blacksmith or the carpenter, just as one might those of a ritual specialist or diviner. A smith does not ordinarily have hoes or knife-blades and ornaments on hand; he makes them up when they are ordered. Often the client supplies his own material, old scrap-iron, or even charcoal for the fire, and then waits around, lending a hand at the forge, while the smith does the job.

The arrangements for such transactions are standardized. First one must make an advance payment; for most services, a basket of food, but a powerful diviner will expect as much as a hoe, and certain ritual specialists, a sheep or a goat. Paying a blacksmith in advance is considered a particularly annoying requirement, for blacksmiths commonly have the reputation of being cheats, who agree to do a task for you and then put it off indefinitely, or who return a hoe lighter in weight than the broken one they were given to repair. But there is no other recognized way of going about it; all you can do is to stay around and bring fuel or work the bellows, while you see that he fulfils his contract! There are also further payments, in most cases, to be made when the job in question is done. Although the specialist does not live by the practice of his skills, he does have an opportunity to accumulate extra food, sheep, clothing, and so on.

It has always been possible to engage workers for unspecialized tasks. This used to be done preferably by taking an extra worker into the household; there were, as we noted earlier, occasional male slaves and quite a number of female slaves; there were also youths who came to serve as apprentices or herd-boys, who were not paid but were clothed and fed like any other member of the family. But it was also possible to hire workers for a limited time and task even before money began to come into use. Women were not usually available, as their own home chores were too burdensome. But girls liked to come in a group to weed or harvest, satisfied with a good meal at noon, when they could take the occasion for gossip and horse-play, and a small payment at the end of the day's work. Men had more time free, but apparently did not use much of it in this way in earlier days. When I was in Bufuka several men were away working for Europeans. In turn, they hired more extensive field help for their wives, so that they would not have to resort to the despised expedient of buying their food. There are obviously great potentials for change implicit in this situation of possible wage-work, especially as the need for money grows. Already, one woman—the wife of a notorious skinflint—had found time to do a whole week's paid work for another; and the blacksmith in Bufuka had decided to build a large new house, in the Ganda style, with overhanging eaves and a veranda, and was using hired help to get it done. However, wage-labour had made only a very small dent as yet in the independent household economy.

Some direct barter and sale, and rudimentary markets, did exist even in older days, but they were resorts for emergencies rather than part of the regular order of everyday life. These markets consisted merely of a designated place and a customary time. Because of the inter-clan feuds, they were dangerous places. There were no middlemen. Everyone in the market was a buyer or seller in his own right; and everyone had come because of a condition of very special need. More usual than resort to markets in time of need was the practice known as *shaka* by which people went to distant places to attempt to obtain basic necessities as gifts or by begging. The danger of such an undertaking was reduced to some extent by pact friendships and visiting of maternal kin and other relatives, but it was none the less enough to deter anyone from such a venture except as an extreme expedient. Sometimes people who went to *shaka* were never heard of again.

Goods taken along on such an expedition might be anything

at all which the family possessed—animals to be given in exchange for larger quantities of other food, especially grain; bracelets and other ornaments; new or old cow- or goat-skins, and so forth. Sometimes one hoped by giving a small gift to obtain a larger gift in return to be considered more or less as a loan against better times. Sometimes the procedure was more direct bargaining and purchase.

Today this picture has changed a great deal. To carry goods for trading purposes or to go seeking food and other commodities by exchange is still called *shaka*; but markets under British supervision have become the standard, though not the only, places for such efforts. Their recognized safety, together with the wealth of objects of foreign manufacture to be obtained there, are making them increasingly popular. There is a growing demand for tobacco and salt and certain other imported products—especially clothing, soap, lamp-oil, copper bracelets, and bead necklaces. When I was in Bufuka, people were beginning to go to market to trade goods made for that very purpose—long sticks of dried fish, for example, which are prepared exclusively for export to the Ganda. Women also occasionally sold surplus products in the market—extra grain or beer, perhaps a basket or some pots. The money might be used to pay the family's head-tax or to buy a knife or a lamb. There was a strong feeling against using it for food. On the whole, while markets were all very well for selling things, they were an inferior place in which to buy. And to be dependent on the market, especially for food, was still considered both improvident and indecent.

The presence of markets, even if only sporadically utilized, and the practice of direct exchange of commodities, raises the question of standards of value. Apart from British colonial money, the Chiga have no regular medium of exchange, or even a consistent system of relative values. There are some fairly standardized values, but these tend to form independent sets. The Chiga do not think of such things as cows, hoes, and baskets of grain as forming a single scale; as a matter of fact, they would not add up in a reasonable arithmetical fashion if the attempt were made. One can never buy cows directly for grain; and there is no way of reckoning accurately how many bushels of grain would be required to buy the hoes which, together with more grain, might buy the sheep which might be exchanged for a cow.

The hoe is the closest approach to a unit for purposes of calculating exchange; its value might be used roughly in computing other exchanges. But the hoe is not a medium of exchange in the established sense. Hoes were never used purely as counters, nor stored against possible future exchange needs. The older trade arrangements are based on the idea that the individual who promotes a transaction, whether buyer or seller, must have the greater need and is less able to hold out in bargaining. In the actual transaction, the commodities exchanged are the ones specifically of interest to the parties to the deal; one accepts a hoe only if one needs a hoe.

While the rough outlines of relative value are fixed by custom, the details of prices are subject to bargaining. In general, the price depends on the demand rather than on the working time involved; nor is there any consideration of such values as transport, since that is the obvious responsibility of the more interested party. A day's ordinary labour brings from 15 to 20 shilling-cents. But I have seen large, exquisite baskets, which must have been over a month in the making, go for less than a shilling, because 'many people can make baskets'—though certainly not such beautiful ones. On the other hand, a large gourd for churning might fetch three times as much, for most gourds tend to grow rather small. The bargaining technique is the typical oriental one in which a much greater demand is made than there is hope of satisfying. There is much debate first as to who shall make the opening bid, as this is a point of great strategic importance, limiting as it does the range of the operation.

It is always understood that there will be a small 'extra' thrown in with a purchase. This system works admirably in the Indian-run shops today, but puts Europeans at an amusing disadvantage. It is hard to feel that one has been 'soft', as one's 'boys' declare. when one has only paid 1s. for an article for which 4s. were asked. A boy who had been to Kampala and was continually trying to impress his friends with the wonders he had seen, was considered to have stretched his imagination a bit too far when he spoke of shops where there were price tags which were really equivalent to the prices finally given for the articles.

When I was in Bufuka, a goat could be bought for approximately 4s. or 5s. It would once have fetched that number of hoes. A leg of beef cost as much as two hoes, a foreleg one;

a fairly large pot was worth a basket of food, while the largest ones, the kind used for beer brewing, commanded a whole hoe. Shillings—the regular British East African coinage, which includes also smaller coins based on shilling-cents (i.e. 100 to the shilling)—were coming into increasing use; but not all people were habituated to this coinage or to its implications. To many people the shilling still represented a commodity, roughly equivalent to an Indian hoe and half the value of a native hoe, which is bargained with and used much as any other commodity would be. The fact that a shilling can be conveniently divided into parts as a hoe cannot, and that these parts can be dealt with by certain simple arithmetical procedures, was not always grasped. Trying to make change, or to pay a group of workers with a single coin to be divided among them, involved enormous difficulties, and often resulted in gross inequalities for the more naïve if not carefully supervised. There was a growing sophistication about other aspects of the new conditions. For example, many people had come to realize that the seasonal need for money for poll-tax payments creates a seasonal supply of sheep, available as a result of forced sales at tax time.

Such forced sales had not affected cow transfers, however. The sale of a cow has always been a highly formal, almost ceremonial event. The techniques for the sale and exchange of cows will be described later (see p. 105). The difference in value between cows and sheep or goats is reflected in the treatment of their meat. When a sheep or a goat is butchered, it is ordinarily divided up quite informally. A man may send a leg to his eldest brother, give a side to a neighbour who is not even a member of the same clan but who did him a favour, and divide a foreleg between two of his lineage kinsmen. Various bits of the gut and assorted oddments are handed out to the children, who are standing around watching the process. Only a father or a father-in-law, if one happened to live nearby, would be formally entitled to a share. A cow's meat, on the other hand, is not distributed freely.

When a cow broke its leg in Bufuka and had to be killed, none of the meat was given away, except for a small piece the owner gave his brother. The rest of the meat was divided into small chunks which sold for ten-cent pieces. If you take beef on credit and then find you are not able to pay, you must not merely return the meat, but put it on top of some millet in a basket and bring it to the original owner as a gift of millet. Otherwise his animals might all die and you would be responsible. It is absolutely necessary to pay for beef from a cow struck by lightning. The owner must not discuss price with you, lest he be punished for his presumption in assuming that he rather than the lightning is the donor of the meat, but you must pay him none the less.

PROPERTY

Many Chiga concepts and patterns concerning ownership are implicit in what we have already seen of their economy and their social institutions. Ownership, for the Chiga, is primarily a function of the individual household; and there is some separate ownership even within that unit.

Practically all material things are owned by individuals or by the simple family—clothes and ornaments; products of the soil and of the chase; tools and weapons, including some, such as boats, which represent quite a large investment of time; cows, sheep, and goats, with their produce; houses and the materials from which they are made; and even agricultural land and land used for building.

A definite terminology is employed with regard to owning: *natcine*, 'I have it' (literally, 'I am with it'), and *nitcandje*, 'It is mine', are expressions commonly heard in ordinary discourse, in boasts, in lawsuits, and in answer to questions. There is an occasional use of plural possessive pronouns, but this is a loose extension. To say 'ours' does not really imply shared rights of control. A girl might speak of 'our fields', referring to those of any of her father's wives, but she would have no right to work in, or share the crops of, any except her own mother's.

There is another way of indicating ownership besides the use of the possessive pronouns. The term *nyina* itself means 'master of'. It may be used, not only in its most important context of *nyineka*, 'master of the household', but also for the owner of any other material thing. This term is never extended beyond the individual to a group.

Chattel property is held in fairly absolute right and may be freely disposed of, in accordance with customary procedures, by each household in its own right. Brothers cannot pre-empt each other's goods without permission; doing so brands one a thief.

A man will ordinarily give permission to his brother or neighbour to use an axe or a canoe he is not using himself, but he does not always do so. If this refusal inflicts hardship it is considered undue stinginess, a character blemish ranked about equal with a tendency to steal! And, of course, all borrowed goods must be repaid in full even to a brother. Only a carefree herd-boy may help himself to a yam or an ear of corn growing in another's garden, and he is limited to what he can roast and eat on the spot. Brothers have no economic responsibility for or stake in each others' households or marriage arrangements, except on a voluntary basis.

There is some differentiation of property rights even within the household. Although to some extent the overall ownership of all the household's belongings is in the hands of the *nyineka*, the master of the household, other individuals do have some degree of separate control over various things in it—clothing, sometimes small tools, usually a basket to hold ornaments. The unmarried sisters in one house have their own separate working materials; each will, for example, keep her basketry supplies on a separate peg or in her personal basket. Even tiny children have some personal property—clothing, ornaments, perhaps a drinking cup or a toy bow. Over these the child has a considerable measure of independent control. A child of three could alone decide who might use his cup and was allowed to spend some coins I had given him on the purchase of a wholly useless small winnowing tray, though the money was enough to make a real purchase for the family. His mother kept his coins for him and kept strict watch to see that none were used by anyone else. If the family can spare them, an older child may be allowed to keep the products of a field he has cultivated by himself and use them towards the purchase of a hoe, ornaments or even a sheep or goat. A girl who worked for me bought a sheep with her earnings. Animals, however, are in the province of things that men control, so that this was in no way hers to dispose of. But when a lamb which her sheep bore was killed to make a garment it was for one of her own full brothers. Had there been other lambs, her father would have given at least some of them to her husband as a gift when she married, 'to dress her'. (Had she been a boy, it would, if possible, have been saved for the bride-price.) Some of her earnings were set aside towards her father's head-tax and to buy certain necessary things for the family, but she herself was permitted to buy materials for a leather skirt and was consulted over the other purchases. In similar fashion, though to a lesser degree, a youngster might have worked for someone even in the old days, receiving a wage, such as butter, for a day's work. He would have brought it home, but his mother would normally have allowed him a special share in it. In short, the child participates in the family's economic arrangements; his ownership of goods is definite, but limited; it is subject to final parental control. A married son's economy is more distinct. He may own his own cows; he and his wife grow their own crops, and have their own utensils and tools.

Although a wife has considerable independent control of the products of her own work—the crops she grows in 'her' fields, baskets or pots which she makes, and so forth—this is only in terms of subordination to her husband, who is the only real master or owner (cf. Ch. 4, p. 58). Although in most families he does not intervene to tell her what to cook and what to store, what to give away and what to keep, he has the right to do so. There are very significant limitations upon a woman's ownership rights, which are sharply underlined in language use. She may not say 'This is mine' of anything in the household but her own clothes or, in a very limited informal way, of a few of the things like cooking pots which she alone uses. But of major articles, even if they were gifts to her from her family, she should more correctly say, 'This is ours'; and a really respectful wife would say, 'This is his' or 'This is my master's', of a hoe or a knife and so on. She must be very careful about any livestock, even the dog which lives in her hut or the baby lamb she is sheltering. To say 'mine' of such things is to commit an act equivalent to evil magic, for it may cause the death of her husband should he thereafter sleep with her (see below, p. 106).

There was one widely known and very unusual case of a woman reported to be so powerful, supernaturally, that she was wealthy in her own right. She did not live with a husband, but with her brother. Talking of her, my neighbours would always make the point that, though she had amassed, and was known to control, the wealth, it was more correct to call it her brother's, for she being a woman could not be the *nyina* of cattle.

The conditional nature of a woman's relationship to property is clear in another significant fact. In case of divorce, a woman may take nothing at all away with her except her own clothing. So long as she is married, however, she has a right to tools and utensils for her own use, and to a fair share of any food, ornaments or other goods her husband may have or acquire. She also has some special rights even with regard to the major wealth of the household, including the cattle. Animals which were gifts from her father, or were the bride-price given for her daughter; sheep bought through her own sale of goods, are all assigned to her. They are the 'animals of her hut' and should go towards the bride-price of her own son. If they are used for the marriage of one of her husband's other sons, he assumes the position of son to her and will bring his bride to her house. She is entitled to a larger share of the milk from these cows than are the other wives; should one of their calves be sold, the proceeds would go to her house. The milk of a cow belonging to a woman, or rather to a particular wife's household, may be used by the husband for hoes, beer, or the service of labourers, but he would not be free to give it to another wife. Such factors of differential household rights are always very carefully weighed. If one boy does the herding, his mother's house is entitled to more milk than are the other wives; and so on. And when the property of a household is divided after the father's death, a woman's own children have a special claim to the cows assigned to her household.

Inheritance

When the head of the household dies, all his property is divided among the sons under the supervision of the eldest son, who is the official heir and administrator of the estate. As heir he must go through certain rites by which he officially takes over his father's position. These rites take place before the body is prepared for burial. A few gourd-seeds, a grain or two of eleusine and corn, and the rope used when milking the cows are placed in the hands of the dead man and then given to the eldest son. An earthen receptacle is moulded and a little ground millet stirred in it with water. This is symbolical beer and must be drunk by all the sons. If the father kept bees, then a miniature hive must be carved. After the mourning, the heir will bury all these things ritually. He must go through these rites even if he is very young and his uncle is to be his guardian and trustee for some time,

If they are omitted, his cattle-keeping and planting, bee-keeping, and so forth cannot succeed any more than they would have done during his life if they were undertaken without his father's approval. The omission of the rites can be corrected only by having the Abashe officiate in a proxy ceremony in which a small figure of earth is made to represent the father, and the forms of transfer are gone through with it. However, if there are no sons and the property goes to the brothers of the deceased, these rites are not necessary.

As administrator the eldest son supervises the property division, sees to it that all the wives and children are properly provided for, and thereafter acts as head of the household, making offerings, arranging marriages, and so forth. He is not himself entitled to any special share of the property; it is divided equally among the sons, except for the specific shares that belong to the houses of particular wives.

There is no right of disposal by testament. The only approach to this is a very oblique one. A father may disinherit a son by laying upon him a powerful death-bed curse (see p. 122). Normally the rules for the division of property are fixed and have to be followed in all cases. Nevertheless, there were instances of older brothers cheating younger ones out of their proper share. For example, one man in Bufuka had used cows, which properly belonged to the orphaned younger siblings whom he was sheltering, to get himself a wife, instead of saving them to get a wife for one of his younger half-brothers. This was one case in which community disapproval, though impotent, was perfectly clear.

Houses do not count in inheritance, for the house in which a man dies must be torn down and rebuilt some distance away. Certain small articles of adornment are not inherited but must be destroyed at death. This is particularly true of wire bracelets. The clothing of the deceased and various other personal articles must not be used by his own family, but may be given away or sold to outsiders. Only livestock, tools, and weapons are significant property in the inheritance and, of course, the wives. Widows are taken care of by their deceased husband's sons with the status of dowager mothers or as wives, and their separate goods go with them. If a woman has no grown son and is married by her husband's brother, he has no permanent claim to any of 'her' goods, but holds them in trust for her sons until they grow up. Ordinarily a woman continues to work the same fields she has been using, and to provide for her children by her own labours in the fields, no matter who her new husband may be.

When a woman dies the property which was in a limited sense 'hers' remains in her household. Her children should have its use, subject only to the control of the father or household head. The house and the crops stored in her bins should not be given to another wife. Sometimes, however, a new wife may be married to become mother to her children. There is no formal handing over of a woman's property as there is of a man's, since hers is not full ownership, nor do all her things go to her children. Her clothes are sold and her personal storage basket is either thrown away or degraded to some unimportant use, such as gathering greens.

There are several technical terms in use in connexion with inheritance which help to make clear the concepts involved. *Emigabo* describes the equal shares into which the basic inheritance is divided. *Emianza* are the special shares of particular sons which must be taken out before the distribution of the *emigabo*. Besides the things that were specifically associated with their mother's household, sons may have other special claims. For example, a son who had helped his father to purchase a cow should inherit it himself. A man who builds for a childless widow would also claim the special goods of her household. The term *emyandu* is used of the significant property left at a person's death, whether man or woman. *Omuchuju*, however, are small personal belongings, such as those of a child, and they are not formally said to be inherited at all. They merely continue to be used by the other children of the family. Should a child's possessions include anything so valuable as a goat (which he may have received as a gift) this either goes to a full brother or will be part of his mother's household goods.

The debts of a dead man are supposed to be paid by his heirs, and those of which there are adequate witnesses usually are. Any claim must be presented immediately after the death and before the division of the inheritance; otherwise there will be delays and litigation or refusal to pay—just as may happen to debts in any case.

If a man dies childless, his brothers, or even the servants who were permanent members of the household, will inherit the property and take care of the wives. But the appropriate inheritance rites cannot be performed if there is no son; nor can a daughter take his place, because of her disabilities with regard to property and religion.

Land Rights

Land rights among the Chiga are essentially individual household rights. The lineage whose members live in a particular area guarantees their common security by defining the locus of probable good relations and peaceful settlement of most disputes. But it does not assign or regulate the land, which is acquired by its different component segments on the basis of individual claims staked out when the area in question was first settled. The limits of cultivation of a village are always pushing out into any uncultivated 'wilderness' land that lies nearby. Sometimes the people move their houses as well, so that in course of time the location of the hamlet itself may shift, or it may divide up. In addition, settled land may be taken from other groups, by simple force, by a group of brothers or cousins (cf. pp. 17-18).

When new lands are being settled, any individual may appropriate a house-site or garden plot for his own use and that of his household, by simply marking off a few boundary points with a hoe. It is not necessary to work all the land or even to clear it right away. Naturally, having witnesses makes one's claim a little safer, but there is no procedure for establishing title such as attaches to cattle. As a result, there are interminable arguments about boundaries, claims to bush land which once was worked by a different family, and so on.

When I was in Bufuka the village was in process of expansion towards the other shore of the cove. Along the shore lived related Abayundu families, but beyond there was a long uninhabited stretch covered with tangled bush. As all the slopes nearby were claimed or actually under cultivation, several families which wanted new fields for millet were clearing land in this unoccupied area. And it is significant, in relation to questions of land rights, to note that, since the fear of feud killings has diminished, one large stretch was being jointly 'developed' by three Abayundu men and two friends from a nearby Abasigi lineage. One of the men had already built a house in the new area. The others had just staked claims and cleared some of the fields. Women from their households would go out for a day in canoes to start work on these fields.

The household land, like its other property, belongs to the master of the household. He controls its distribution among the various women who will work the fields. Usually a family has several different large patches, a few near the houses, others along the slopes and ridges of nearby hills, some as much as half an hour's walking distance away. The plots belonging to one family will be scattered in all directions, lying next to the holdings of many different neighbours and kinsmen, depending on how initial claims and inheritance rights happen to have worked out (see map, p. 195).

The pattern of distribution within the household is that of assigning a section of each field to each of the women. The size of each woman's plot need not be the same as that of another wife. It will vary according to the amount of the crop suitable to that particular field which she wants to cultivate. But every woman is entitled to part of every field. This avoids hard feelings that would arise because of inequalities in the desirability of different fields, which are in different states of use and disuse, at different distances from the compound, and so on. A woman ordinarily continues to work her 'own' fields from one season to the next, but her husband may redistribute them if he chooses, and he always does so when he marries a new wife. It would not do to assign her a new field. Instead, she gets a portion of each of the old ones; and any new area he clears is divided among all his wives. This is true whether the new clearing is newly claimed land or a patch he had once worked but which has been lying fallow for a while. It is customary to refer to the wife or the son who does the work and claims the produce of a particular field, as its owner, but only in casual discourse; speaking more correctly, the term *nyina* would not be used for anyone except the master of the household.

Once a man has staked his claim to a field or a house-site, it belongs to him and, after his death, to his heirs, so long as precise memory remains. He may rent it to someone else and, under some circumstances, may even transfer it altogether, but no one else may use it without his permission.

Ownership rights, in the absence of surveys and title deeds, are rather difficult to keep clear in a situation in which people are constantly shifting their house-sites and letting their fields lie fallow. And there may be subtler points of right involved. For example, a man may not build his house where his cows, passing to and from pasture through his front gate, will trespass on someone else's fields. A case of this sort arose while I was in Bufuka. A man, moving his house because his mother had died in the old one, chose a site on unoccupied land and, with the assistance of two other men, began to level the ground for the building. At that point another man, who had been away at work, returned and halted the proceedings. He claimed that the new house-site, though not on his land, was too near a garden plot he often planted with peas. There was no appeal from this decision; a new house-site was chosen and the work already put in was wasted.

If a person moves away from the village permanently, his land becomes unclaimed property and is simply taken over by the people who live nearby. There is no mystical bond between a person and his land. If you are going to move away from fields already planted before the end of a season, you may sell the growing crops. A whole field of potatoes will be worth about a goat. The purchaser will harvest the crops and may then use the field for the next season. If you do not return, he may continue to use the fields; but you are still the owner and may reclaim them if you do come back. However, you could not in that case claim any share in the crops.

A case somewhat along these lines arose in Bufuka. A family had moved to Bufuka from a place a little farther along the lake-shore some years before. Later they decided that they wanted to use the fields back there once more, as they needed more land. Meanwhile, however, another man had built a house there. Many protests were made on both sides. In the end it was settled that they had to ask permission to use the fields, and permission was granted. Furthermore, as everyone knew the land had really been theirs, they were not expected to pay anything for its use. People agreed that all this would not have happened 'in the old days', as the other man would not have dared to build at that spot if a modern (British-appointed) 'local chief' who was his cousin had not said he might consider the land abandoned.

While permanent transfer of land did not happen very often, it was possible. One man told me how he and his uncle, who shared a common plot of land, had sold it to another man for a goat; this gave the purchaser full and permanent rights to it. Another man is said to have bought a field among the Abayundu in the same way. There was some disagreement as to whether such outright transfer of land was a standard traditional form, though no one doubts its present validity. Transfers on a more temporary basis were more usual. If an individual needs more land and there is someone else who has a surplus, he may rent some of it or borrow it for a season or two. The amount to be paid may be agreed upon or the loan may be described as a gift, for which of course some return would be expected. People sometimes gave the use of land on a kind of patronage basis. In that case, you must do a day's work for the owner and, when the crops are ripe, carry him a basketful of the harvested produce. You must also allow him to share your beer when you brew. There is always the risk that he may ask for the land to be returned. This sort of relationship is most usual for a man who is living away from his own kinsmen in a semi-dependent status.

In the most usual form of lending, the borrower acquires the right to plant for two seasons—the length of time after which it is considered desirable to let a field lie fallow. The borrower will pay a small fee, such as a hoe. Lending the use of a field for a short-time crop, such as peas, is also common. In fact, such short 'borrowing' sometimes takes place without the permission of the owner and can lead to bitter disputes. Usually a man will be allowed to harvest the peas once he has planted them, but he may be forbidden to use the land again. If a man is foolish enough to put his labour into planting one of the slower growing more work-consuming crops on your land without permission, you may drive him off it with full public approval, but you will be expected to reimburse him for work already put into it.

Ordinarily, the locus of ownership is quite clear. People may say of a certain field, 'Those are the beans of Rwebitara.' But should it be someone else's field which has been lent to Rwebitara for the season, they will add, 'But it is the land of Kabaka.' And unused land will be referred to as 'the bush of so-and-so' if the original claimant is known. Sometimes there will be serious ownership disputes that are not easy to resolve, particularly over land in the 'bush', where reliable witnesses are not always available. One man may start to clear land he claims is his, and another claimant may move in ahead of him and start clearing too. These issues may lead to serious fights unless they are submitted to mediation (see Ch. 6, pp. 117-21).

More typical disputes arise, not over large fields, but over the exact location of the boundaries between the holdings of A and B. The arrangement of the fields, with the holdings of different families and different women in a family lying next to each other in a tight patchwork, makes this kind of problem particularly common. The separate holdings are usually marked off at their upper and lower limits by steps which provide a slight terrace on the sloping fields. Ditches are dug to bound the limits of their width. But at the beginning of the planting season the trenches may be obscured, or some sly person seeking to widen his field may have dug another unobserved. Everyone is on the look-out for encroachment, not only upon his own, but also upon everyone else's fields, so that for some days there is a great deal of noisy dispute and much calling of names, until finally everyone settles down peacefully to the cultivation of his own plot.

It is only the right to build and the right to plant which are claimed as individual privileges. Grazing land is no one's property, nor is unclaimed land about the village parcelled off in any way. I may even allow my cattle to feed where my neighbour habitually plants but has this year left the ground fallow, though I must respect his rights to any stalks of last year's grain left standing. Free access to hunting, grazing, and other un-owned rights about the village is, however, limited, not precisely to the members of the community, but to individuals who, through kinship or through pact bonds, have some rights of access and safety.

It is very important to watch one's sheep or cattle closely while grazing, for trespass on planted fields or growing crops is a serious offence. To trespass (*ona*) with my herds makes me liable at first only to a warning, on the presumption that my cows have strayed by accident; repetition, however, entitles the crop-owner to full restitution. He may either allow his cows to graze over a comparable portion of my field or harvest a portion of my field equal in size to the part damaged by my cows. Everyone is always on the look-out for straying cows; for the youngsters who do the herding are frequently guilty of carelessness. Towards evening one often hears shouts: 'There are cows grazing on the fields of so-and-so'; it might be the cows' owner calling his herder's attention, or just anyone who happened to notice and wanted to alert the boys before any real damage was done. Trespass of this sort, as well as boundary-jumping, is the source of many lawsuits.

The right to gather firewood is restricted to the land-owner only in the immediate neighbourhood of his own house and the papyrus or bushes about it, and in the remains of his own crops after cutting. Otherwise firewood is common or unowned; you may take wood from bushes on the fields of another man where you would not have planting rights. Certain large trees, however, are owned. The right to cut firewood does not extend to the privilege of cutting trees large enough for carpentry from your neighbours' fields. Trees large enough for canoe-building are sometimes planted; a tree so planted belongs to the planter even if it is not on his land, but in wild land.

Watering-places are common property if they are parts of a river or lake. The whole village may share one and keep it in repair. Wells and watering-troughs, which are more satisfactory ways of watering cows, and pits dug near the houses are the property of the builders, who may be individuals or groups. Salt-licks are now owned, but, like wood-gathering and hunting rights, their use is controlled to some extent by clan feuds. You cannot hunt or take your herds to a salt-lick in the territory of an alien clan except under the protection of a pact-brother. Whereas formerly members of the neighbouring Abahesi clan would have come to the tip of Bufuka for salt armed against attack or under special arrangements, they now come regularly under the shelter of British peace and their right to do so goes unchallenged.

WEALTH

In the Chiga view of worldly goods, cattle-ownership has values of its own; it alone constitutes wealth. *Tunga* is the term for having wealth in cattle and it can be applied to nothing else. (The noun derived from this verb—*amatunga*—refers specifically to sheep and goats; this may be of historical significance, but it misrepresents the present picture. For *tunga* means to have cows rather than other livestock.) Having cows is quite distinct from having a good store of anything else. It is different from having grain-fields which have ripened well, or plenty of beer, or a goodly number of wives, excellent and indeed desirable though all these may be.

Subsistence, as we have seen, depends more upon agriculture than upon cattle-keeping. But ordinary food and its acquisition play no part in the Chiga reckoning of wealth. 'Grain supplies are quickly consumed, while cattle endure. Furthermore, grain supplies are easily stolen. Cattle, with luck, multiply themselves. It is not the same thing at all,' they will tell you.

Of course, the two domains do overlap in an important way. While it is possible to have plenty of food and beer through luck and hard work, the best way to be sure of this is by having a large household with a number of wives. And having several wives usually means having, or having had, the cattle necessary for the bride-price. However, this does not mean that wives are counted as property; I never heard such an equation explicitly made. A daughter's services are valued in the household, but the bride-price is not exactly a payment for their loss. Rather it is seen as a means of replacing her by another woman, a medium through which another marriage is negotiated. This is explicitly differentiated from the sale of a daughter, for then cattle or sheep are in fact a payment and will be used to purchase food and other necessities. A family takes pride in the size of the bride-price given for its daughters. And, if they are able to afford it, they give nearly equivalent return gifts to the groom and to the girl herself after her marriage.

Conversion of other kinds of goods into cattle is not thought of as a free process. You cannot just go to market and buy a cow. You must first find someone able and willing to part with one. This may be easy in a time of famine or other emergency, but ordinarily it takes many gifts and much persuading, for a wealthy man has no need to sell his cows.

If you do succeed in finding a cow or a calf you can buy outright (this is to buy *burundu*), the price has to be settled by bargaining. (It would be something like ten sheep or goats.) Today, a licence is required; in the past such a sale was surrounded with the prescribed ritual, including formal gifts. This was always carried out before witnesses, to avoid any later question about the exact nature of the transaction. Any error in the proceedings, such as failure to hand over the lead rope in the proper manner, might lay the basis for a future suit. And it is well to bribe the children who will guard the goats in their new home too, for should one of these goats wander off and return to your flock, the former owner of the cow would be entitled to claim back a calf when the cow had borne one.

Another form of purchase (*omukwato*) is more usual. This is buying a cow before it is born. That is, you borrow a cow, for a fee, herd it yourself and have the use of its milk; then, when it has borne a female calf or two bulls, you keep them and return the cow to the original owner. A man is often glad to make such an arrangement in order to have his cow taken care of, especially if he has only one, as this avoids his having to pay a fee to a herder. Such 'herding-out' arrangements are the source of end-less litigation and quarrels, so that the Chiga often say it is not worth having cows at all if you have no one 'of your own' to herd them.

It is also possible to get a cow from a wealthy man by a kind of client-patron relationship. This method (*omunywana*) is less expensive initially, but it entails long-term obligations; the client has to bring his patron gifts for a long time afterwards—food, beer whenever he brews, and eventually, to terminate the obliga-tion, one or more of the cow's calves.

There are, of course, other ways of getting cows. One is through a favourable bride-price balance. Another is by inheritance. Then there was cattle-raiding, which was tied up with the vengeance-feud pattern and was highly respectable. And finally, there is outright theft—entering a man's compound secretly at night and stealthily driving out his cows. This is dishonourable, dangerous, and without glory, but it was often a successful means of acquir-ing a large herd of cattle. Thieving is virtually a professional specialization, with its own lore and skills and especially its own magic. Thieves work alone or with the help of pact-brothers, who may deceive and betray their own relatives, reporting, for example, when they are to be away on beer drinks, so that the thief can come in relative safety. A pact-brother could not, of course, be given a share of the stolen cattle, as these would be recognized by his kinsmen. However, he would get his reward later in gifts or reciprocal favours. People are afraid of theft and try to guard their compounds carefully. But they also admire the ingenuity with which successful thieves must operate, and tales of famous forays are repeated with great relish.

Though all these methods of getting cattle existed, little consistent effort was made to exploit them. People did not work to get rich. Even the expanded earning power based on working for Europeans was seldom used to buy a cow, except under the immediate spur of need for a wife. One young man of my acquaintance conceived the brilliant idea of growing tobacco for sale, since so many people are fond of smoking and too lazy to grow an adequate supply of tobacco. His scheme was very successful and he had soon made enough from the sale of his tobacco to purchase a calf. This had been his goal, since he owed it as a debt for a bride-price payment. Once this had been realized, he lost all interest in the project and abandoned it. The house-boy saves for a cow only if his family is not in a position to get him a wife. Otherwise he is more likely to spend his earnings on the European goods which confer a social status of their own. A smith in Bufuka put his extra earnings into the building of a new-style house. And of the two men who worked for the Government away from the village, one at least spent the bulk of his earnings on beer and presents for his family and friends.

From the point of view of the ordinary Chiga, a household of several wives is a good thing, but there is no need for these to number more than two or three; four wives at one time is a great number indeed. For comfort and security, a man wants two or three wives to labour in the fields and ensure a good food supply and beer; a balance of daughters to provide bride-price cattle for his sons as they grow up; a few cows for butter and hides; and enough sons to herd the cows and take over other heavy chores as he himself grows older. Greater wealth might mean more meat, more butter, or more hides; but these can also come to the industrious man who is not wealthy through trade or occasional work for others. A slave or handmaiden to lighten work is a comfortable privilege of wealth, but hardly a necessity. The total effect of all these differences is not very great. Without them a man can still enjoy leisure, food, and the respect of his fellows. What possible point then can there be in bothering to work, plan and worry to amass anything more?

There are various other factors which enter this picture of the high theoretical value set on cows and cow-ownership, coupled with little apparent effort at accumulation. For one thing, the

Chiga are convinced that luck plays a primary role in the accumulation of wealth. To 'have a lucky court' is to prosper. There cows thrive and bear female calves; wives bear sons, but even greater numbers of daughters, so that bride-price cattle accumulate. Under such circumstances herds may mount to considerable proportions. But without this gift of luck, of what use would effort be? If cows die or yield few heifers, if you have more sons than daughters, so that bride-price payments deplete your herds, if herders cheat you, the results of years of effort to get an extra cow or two would hardly be noticeable. And there is nothing you have it in your power to do to get a lucky court.

In the wider culture area in which the Chiga form a specialized enclave, wealth in cattle plays an important role. While cows are always too valuable to be killed for meat, their milk provides a major food for the neighbouring pastoralists. And all the counters of importance in life are organized around cattle wealth. Herds play an important part in caste differentiation and also in the maintenance of power within it. The wealthy Ruanda noble maintains his entourage with gifts of cattle and lives in lavish fashion in an enormous household with many wives and the means for splendid hospitality. He can hire peasants to brew him beer, build his well-ornamented home, and make him tools, weapons, and utensils. But among the Chiga there is but an echo of this. The term *omukungu*, which implies general wealth, is known but as a foreign word. While proverbs and stories recognize this special role of wealth and wealth differences, the everyday Chiga perspective is a more limited and strictly practical one. It is true that 'the poor man must sew while the rich man can cut fresh clothes'; but none of the wider implications of wealth difference are possible here. A man with a larger herd of cattle and more wives has a larger compound. But no one lives in splendid style and there is no class differentiation. Most important is the absence of any feudal power structure and of any political significance in the patronage relationships. In Ruanda, giving a cow to a poorer man is one of the standard techniques by which the wealthy overlords stabilize their power. The recipient works for his patron and, if he is a pastoral aristocrat by birth, he fights for him as well if need be. Among the Chiga, even if a man was wealthy enough to make such a gesture, he would not have been powerful enough to benefit by it. For the recipient would be likely to default and even boast of his failure to make the required return. Ruanda chiefs who tried to bribe the rebellious 'Bahima', as they called them, to fealty, found this out to their sorrow. And this would have been even more sharply the case for an ordinary Chiga.

The rise in power of the Nyabingi priests (see below, p. 151) changed the entire balance of this picture. To the priests a special channel for the acquisition of wealth was open. A priest had merely to demand cows or other goods in the name of his spirit master. And this added wealth could be used in patronage, for the priests had enough power through their spirit familiars to guarantee the safety of such investments. The priests had actually begun to use this procedure to build a retinue of retainers like those of the courts of Ruanda, an entourage of young men who not only danced at their courts and tended their cows, but added a temporal threat to supplement the priests' ghostly power against anyone who failed to meet their demands.

Apart from such priests, whose rise to wealth and power was a recent phenomenon, it is doubtful whether any Chiga was ever really wealthy by Hima standards. I heard of no one who had so many cows that he had to have a special compound in the countryside away from his own dwelling to house his surplus cattle. This is due partly to the depredations of the Pygmies and the Nyaruanda, partly to epidemics of cattle diseases, partly to the poor pasturage the land affords. As a matter of fact, Chiga who moved north into the grassy plains which formerly belonged to the Hororo are growing much wealthier very rapidly.

The wealthiest man I knew did not live in Bufuka. He was not even an Omuyundu. A great many factors had contributed to his wealth. He was sole survivor of all his generation; the wealth which might have been divided among brothers and cousins had instead all come to be concentrated in his hands. In addition, he had been a ritual specialist of wide repute and had received payments in that capacity. He had also the relationship of special assistant or delegate to some important priest somehow associated with the Nyabingi cult—a relationship important enough to surround him with a halo of special prestige amounting almost to fear, and which must have meant a great deal of wealth-collecting at its height. Furthermore, he was for many years a small chief under the British administration, receiving a salary in that capacity. He had a household of eighteen living wives when I was there. No one in or near Bufuka had more than four. He had more sons than anyone had accurate count of and a great herd of cattle—so great that, though he had not found it necessary to build more than one compound, the daily tending of the animals was done in several separate small herds. I heard of only one other man whose wealth was reported to be comparable, though I did not meet him or visit his household. This man, who lived some distance away on the lake-shore, was supposed to have been quite an important priest at one time, but had somehow escaped the British dragnet (see below, p. 156).

In the village of Bufuka proper there was no comparable wealth. The blacksmith was much the wealthiest man there, and he had less than a dozen head of cattle and only two wives, one of whom was too old and ailing to keep herself, let alone contribute to the household. His wealth had not all come from his blacksmith work, however. He had also practised divination previously and had one married daughter for whom a considerable bride-price had been paid.

There were several men of parallel wealth in other neighbouring villages. One was a carpenter and a powerful medicine man, descendant of the last of the local Nyabingi priests, who is still considered to have special magical powers. He too had served for a few years as a chief under the British, and is reported to have received presents of cattle from Ruanda chieftains for a pledge of fealty—an obligation which was never fulfilled. He had a thriving household with four relatively young wives.

Another large herd was reported to have come from large-scale thieving. The owner was looked upon askance as a sorcerer as well as a bad-tempered and mean man. He was forced, despite his wealth, to live a bachelor's existence in his later years, because no girl would stay with him for more than six months and the wives of his youth had all died.

The other household heads in Bufuka had at most a few cows apiece, and none of them had more than two wives. The two young men who were poorest of all were a man who had originally been a herd-boy for one of the families and was staying on there, married to a girl whose father had washed his hands of her; and a very young man, with one cow, who was unmarried as yet and had no immediate prospect of getting a bride-price together. His widowed mother lived with him and kept house for him and his younger brother. The household was so poor that, when his married sister came home after her divorce, not only was there no way in which the bride-price could be repaid except by her remarriage, but there was not even the means to buy a hoe for her to work with during the interval.

All of these people, however, lived in similar houses, varying only slightly in size. European clothing was an indication of youth rather than of wealth. None owned such appliances as lamps, the mark of the townsman rather than the wealthy. No Bufuka household could boast of meat or beer as more than an occasional luxury. The smith's household had more butter and more good clothing than some of the others, but there was nothing more to eat from day to day and the margin was a very slight one. Each household, in short, was on a similar plane of fundamental independence and basic reliance upon its own resources, with very little outside resources. Stratification was a Ruanda (and Ankole) phenomenon; there it was associated with an existent class of pastoral chiefs. For the Chiga, apart from the Nyabingi cult, such wealth differences were not set in a structured power context and were nothing more than a daydream.

6

SOCIAL CONTROL

WE have seen that Chiga social organization is based on what Evans-Pritchard has called 'ordered anarchy'. There is no formal authority beyond that exercised by the father over his immediate household. The social groups operate in a state of unstable equilibrium. They serve to define some of the basic areas of individual loyalties, but do not enforce or limit them. Sanctions are, on the whole, imposed on the principle of self-help by the individual or the group directly affected by some misconduct or failure to meet obligations, rather than by the kin group of the offender or by any neutral authority. A high degree of nonconformity to many of the established standards of good behaviour is tolerated, and 'collective responsibility' operates rather to establish and perpetuate vengeance feuds than to limit possible disruptive behaviour. The ancestral spirits play no positive moral role; supernatural sanctions, except those related to purely ritual errors, do not operate directly, but have to be called into play by offended individuals. And there is no structure of government, no individuals or groups with authority over others; even the newly-emergent power of the Nyabingi priests had to be backed by constant threats of supernatural or physical violence.

In this chapter we shall examine the operation of such social controls as did function among the Chiga. While some reference to types of offences and obligations will naturally be involved, the emphasis here will be essentially on procedure, rather than on substantive law; most of the latter appears in other contexts in this account, as part of the picture of required behaviour in the family, among kinsmen, in relation to economics, and so on.

The essence of Chiga legal procedure (using that term in the widest possible, rather than the narrow, technical sense) is the action of the offended party, whether to right an injury by retaliation, or to compel payment of an obligation. In such a society as this, structured strongly along patrilineal kin lines,

there is, of course, considerable difference between offences committed within the lineage and those affecting outsiders. And corresponding with the fissioning tendency, we find special procedures
operative at critical points of potential cleavage. However, there
is neither automatic group cohesion nor total failure to recognize
and deal with obligations and rights falling outside the limits of
the patrilineage.

Offences within the group have to be settled right there. No
person external to it can have any other than a conciliatory role.
A household in particular stands united and independent. So
long as problems remain entirely within the family, no one else
has the right to intervene. If a bad-tempered old man picks a
quarrel with his son and drives him out of the house, everyone
may agree that his behaviour is wicked and unjustified, but there
is nothing they can do about it. When a neglected wife appeals
to her husband's senior relatives, complaining that he buys gifts
for his mother but never any for her, they can point out the error
of his ways and urge him to correct them, but they cannot compel him to do so. If a junior member of a household commits
some offence that involves an injury to a neighbour or kinsman—
for example, if a herd-boy allows his goats to damage someone's
crops—the head of the household is responsible and will be
called upon to make good the damage by paying reparation; but
whether he also punishes the erring boy will be his own concern.
(Of course, getting him to make the payment is another matter,
and sometimes a difficult one.)

Much the same pattern is followed even for very serious offences.
Fratricide and incest, for example, are problems affecting only
the close kin-group, who are the ones actually injured. A man who
has killed his brother is supposed to be put to death by his own
father or brothers; traditionally he was buried alive with the
corpse of his victim. A girl who is guilty of incest will be put to
death at her own father's hands, and the man will also be killed
if he stays to have this punishment inflicted on him. However,
such punishment is the immediate concern only of close relatives,
so that the offending party is very likely to evade it. Indeed, if
the fratricide or person guilty of incest does not take to his heels
soon enough, many of his friends and relatives, who have no
quarrel with him, will prod him into leaving, and help him make
good his escape. When my neighbours and I visited among the

Abachuchu (see Ch. 2), we met a man who had fled from Bufuka in this way because he had been caught in an incestuous liaison with a girl of a related lineage. My friends from Bufuka had no hesitation about greeting him amicably, for they were not close lineage kin of the girl in question and so had no personal grievance against him.

Theft, trespass, or other economic injury, an accusation of malicious gossip, a question of adultery, of abuse of respect relations, of rape, when they happen within the community, are of concern only to the parties immediately affected. Relatives of the offender are not directly involved unless they are the injured parties. They may either wash their hands of the whole affair or take the part of their kinsman. Only rarely, when public opinion is united, are they likely to intervene even to the point of trying to persuade him to take the proper course of action: pay reparations that have been claimed, for example. But their intervention can only take the form of persuasion. For those who choose to be thick-skinned, there is nothing that ridicule, gossip or comment can do, no pressure that kinsmen can exert even when they do intervene. The bully or thief, the man who cheats his junior siblings or gets drunk or never pays his debts, may be criticized and disliked, but when it comes to a show-down he remains a full participant in group affairs (cf. Ch. 2). This does not mean that everyone is equally insensitive to criticism. Feelings of pride, of shame and so forth are strong in many people. There are those who stand high in the eyes of their fellows and take great pride in it. But there are also many who just don't care, who shrug off criticism and gossip. And against these people, ridicule and open adverse comment may be dangerous weapons to use, for if they should take the matter amiss, they might retaliate in some act of overt or secret malice.

The only thing that excites community action against one of its members, beyond the limits of the close kin-group directly affected, is a case of murder by witchcraft.

There are some forms of magic which are acceptable; these are performed by established practitioners and serve very effectively to implement some of the requirements of law and order (cf. p. 142, below). But there is also unlicensed witchcraft, undertaken in malice by wicked individuals. Such witches are general enemies. Having once stooped to dabble in dark and dangerous ways which normal persons shun, a witch has shown an abnormal streak which may develop into a profound menace. Witchcraft is very different from straightforward murder. A murderer is merely acting as anyone might under similar circumstances: that's human nature. The murderer may be made to pay for his misdeed— often, as we have seen, he does not—but society does not need to protect itself against him. Witchcraft, on the other hand, is a total character defect, not just a wrong action. Like our own detective story murderers, a witch has begun what may become an habitual career of evil, and so the whole community, irrespective of closeness of kinship or personal injury, is menaced.

If a witch's guilt is established by divination or ordeal (see below, p. 162), everyone will join in the mob action of stoning him or her to death. But this would happen only if the witch directed his or her evil actions fairly close to home. A witch, however suspect, who had been accused of evil only against total outsiders would be feared and shunned in daily contacts, but not molested, or formally ostracized. One man in Bufuka had such a reputation. He was noted for his malice and was famous as a thief who used powerful charms and spells to protect himself when he went out on forays and bewitched the people whose cattle he intended to steal so they would not awake to hear him. Girls of the village hesitated to step into his courtyard. But their brothers could not refuse to be members of his wedding party.

When an offender is a member of another group, the whole kin-group of the person who is injured may enter the fray. If a man is caught with a girl in suspicious circumstances, all her brothers and cousins will chase him and try to spear him. If a thief is caught in the act, everyone will join the attack on him. If, however, no direct act of aggression has been committed, but a man is claiming damages or the repayment of a debt from an outsider, then the support of his kin-group is conditional upon many factors, some of which are personal. A man is less likely to rush to the support of a distant kinsman or one whom he personally dislikes. He is less likely to support a kinsman who is always getting into trouble. For example, if a man caught as a thief has been tied up and held for ransom, his kinsmen, instead of hastening to his help, may simply abandon him to his fate. In such cases they may not even bother to avenge his death. Moreover, what happens may depend on other bonds of kinship or pact-friendship with persons outside the lineage who are involved in the quarrel. A man may try to persuade his brother to return stolen goods to his pact-brother, for example, or may look the other way if the latter comes to seize a forfeit to keep against the payment of an overdue debt.

Offences within the community also tend to be handled according to the circumstances. When an offender is caught in a serious offence, his close kinsmen will not always rush to his support, especially if he already has a bad reputation. A man beaten up by a jealous husband may simply be ridiculed by his brothers; though, of course, they may make an issue of the matter if they want to. A woman caught stealing potatoes in someone's garden patch may have her skirt snatched off and used as evidence in claiming damages from her husband. Meanwhile, she is publicly disgraced. Thieving women have even been killed on the spot, though this was likely to precipitate an open fight. And a man who caught a woman stealing might risk raping her, feeling safe from the danger of her making any public outcry or complaint.

In all such cases kinsmen may intervene, especially if they feel the accusation is false. This will, of course, quickly line the community up along kinship lines. But they are more likely to keep out of the matter if they can. And for 'disinterested' persons not closely related to either of the parties to the dispute or injury, staying out of things is much the better part of wisdom. Of course, you can report theft or cheating or the like if you want to. But you had better have very good evidence first, or your intervention will simply get you into trouble with both sides. I have heard a man who merely reported having seen a stray sheep accused and held responsible by its owner for not having captured and brought it back. On the whole, informing is a bad thing, about the same as lying, and you had far better not bother to do it except in strict privacy and to someone you can 'really trust'.

Of course, keeping silence has its dangers too. If you do not raise an alarm when you see some act of petty theft or trespass, you are likely to be accused of complicity or negligence! And if a fight of any sort is going on, it is hard to remain aloof from all the excitement. In fact, a good deal of the energy of most intra-lineage or intra-community disputes is dissipated in argument, and difficulties tend to blow over in time, even when they are

not settled by agreement or some mild show of force. If, however, they rankle or reach the point of open fighting, the kinship
lines tend to form. And if anyone is killed, the rules of vengeance
come into play and precipitate a feud. As we have already seen,
the slaughter which may result can only be averted by a special
peace-making rite. Elders not too closely related to either side
may be concerned enough to intervene in such a case and try to
persuade the disputants to settle the matter peaceably. But it is
the brothers of the murderer and the victim who have the final
say. If they do not agree to settle the feud through compensation, there is no way of avoiding a split within the larger kin-
group. That, as we have noted above, is the precipitating cause
of some lineage fissions.

It would seem that with no police force and no community
authority, and with so many sources for quarrels, accusations,
and suspicions, pitched battles would be the constant order of
the day. Not all quarrels did come to blows, though. Many
people were willing to settle matters peaceably and allow issues
to be adjudicated by a kind of arbitration that followed a typical
African procedure—a hearing before a tribunal of respected
'elders' that was almost a regular court trial, though one in which
the court had no power to enforce its decisions. There were no
regularly constituted judges. Respected men of the community
who were acceptable to both parties would be sought out and
asked to hear the case. If the litigants were from distinct kin
or local groups, the judge selected might be a priest related to
neither party or a council representing both. Appeals were possible from neighbouring 'old people of wisdom' to more powerful
leaders, if the parties chose to carry the dispute further or the
case was a 'difficult one to cut'. But all this was contingent on
the voluntary co-operation of the parties to the dispute. Only
close relatives would risk intervening, unasked, even to urge such
arbitration.

Although the decisions reached at such a hearing were certainly not binding, people most often did yield to them, partly
because their own self-righteousness was undermined by an adverse decision, and also because the judge's opinion would tend
to crystallize public opinion and thus influence others in deciding
whether or not to aid either of the parties. When a priest or
ritual specialist served as judge, as might be the case where the

parties thought the issue important enough, fear of his super-natural power added weight to his decision.

Reconstructing the details of the old procedure for hearings is difficult because the popularity of the modern court has led to the widespread adoption of many of its forms. For example, even in a tipsy village quarrel over one man's having failed to do a minor promised chore, witnesses were separated so that they could not hear each other's testimony. This is probably a new point in Chiga rules of evidence, but apparently highly congenial. (Some of the newly introduced forms may come from Ganda rather than British sources, since Ganda chiefs were imported to teach the Chiga how to rule themselves.)

The general outline of the old procedure is, however, clear, and is very much like that used in informal hearings while I was there. Whether the 'court' is an informal gathering of two or three men of the village selected more or less at random, or a more formal and impressive conclave presided over by a priest or other leader, the pattern followed is the same. One person acts as judge, with the final responsibility for making the decision. He has an advisory council who form a sort of jury, help-ing to question disputants and witnesses and making suggestions. These persons are usually recruited by the judge, sometimes casually from people who happen to be around or, in the case of a leader frequently called upon to settle disputes, from ex-perienced 'cutters of cases' whom he regularly calls upon to help him. Judges are never paid for their services, nor are there any fines accruing to the court. I met with no suggestion of bribery or other methods of influencing the decision, but people did quarrel with some decisions as unfair, as 'decided in a biassed fashion'. Probable impartiality was given as a reason for consult-ing priests as judges. 'Are we not all equally their children?'

Once the judge and jury undertake to hear the case and help 'unravel' it, the plaintiff delivers a lengthy monologue stating the issue and presents all the relevant—and quantities of irrelevant—material. Then the defendant speaks at length in his own defence. Each party also brings witnesses, to corroborate the particular stories and to vouch for the disputants. It is hard to estimate the exact function of the witnesses. The major emphasis appears to be on quantity rather than quality. The Chiga moral code does not particularly underscore the virtue of truth-telling,

but it does censure giving information against a friend or relative. Further, it is good to come to the defence of a friend, however little you may know of the particular case in hand. As a
result, the side with a perfectly straightforward case is as likely
as the other to have witnesses who become enmeshed in fanciful
elaborations.

The 'jury' discusses the case as it progresses. All voice their
opinions and ask questions. Even bystanders may participate.
Many people will rehearse the case from time to time, each in
the light in which he sees it. This continues until the judge is
satisfied that he has got to the bottom of things. Then he gives
his decision. Sometimes it is a question of fact which is at issue:
Did the calf my cow bore really die as the herdsman alleges?
Had the bride's father returned the full value of a particular
bride-cow to the groom as a gift before the divorce? Was it my
cow who strayed on to my neighbour's grain crops, or is this a
malicious accusation? Sometimes, however, there will also be
questions of the rights in the case to be determined, and the
judges have to have the wisdom of Solomon to reach a decision
which is likely to satisfy anyone. For example, an old widow
alleges that her husband's brother has deserted her and she wants
him to take her back. The case is very complicated, since she
should really not have been living with him in the first place.
She has a grown son of her own who could have built for her.
Perhaps if she had remained a widow, her daughter-in-law would
not have been childless! However, her husband's brother did
take her for a wife and live with her for two years; many agreed
it was therefore wrong for him to leave her behind when he moved
his household out on to one of the islands. No decision was
reached in this fascinating case, however, for before it went beyond the local elders and some preliminary trial skirmishes, it
had changed its character. The old widow and the man's other
wives became involved instead in mutual accusations of witchcraft, and it was these, rather than the original problem, which
eventually reached the modern courts.

Another case which I heard debated in an initial hearing outside the formal courts had to do with an accusation of house-
burning. This was treated skilfully by an intelligent district chief
who was acting as judge; he had had a great deal of experience
in British-instituted courts. The accusation rested largely on the

fact that the accused had been in a village where he did not belong on the afternoon of the evening on which the fire started, and that he had a motive in that he had asked for a piece of meat and had been refused. Spite of this sort is considered a perfectly plausible reaction, and quite enough cause for such behaviour. His defence was that he had returned home at dusk and had been asleep before the fire started; that he had had to be awakened in order to rush to the scene along with the rest of the neighbours. The examiner tried to trip him up on the timing of his alibi. Had he had to remove the gate-posts when he entered the house? Were the family still at supper? And so forth. The case was eventually taken to the British court, where it was dismissed on the grounds of insufficient evidence. This is exactly what I was told old style Chiga hearings would have done. Indirect evidence was on the whole considered inadmissible, and only the culprit caught in the act was sure of conviction. Other types of cases dragged out and might be settled by ordeal.

Problems of many different sorts were tackled by such court proceedings. Most of the litigation centred around marriage and divorce and cattle transactions arising therefrom. There were also accusations of malicious gossip and witchcraft, cases arising out of loans or trespass and other economic injuries, and so on.

Family affairs and problems of personal relations may be considered in informal hearings, though they can scarcely be settled there. A woman may accuse her husband of beating her or of allowing his younger brother to scold her. In one complex case, a younger brother accused his senior of neglecting the orphaned siblings who had been in his charge; he succeeded in transferring custody to himself, which meant that he would collect the bride-price for the girls. Most people felt that this upshot would not have been possible under earlier conditions. One unusual case that was taken directly to the British court involved a charge by one young girl that another had derided her for dressing neatly, saying she was doing it to attract the boys! (Needless to say, the court was profoundly uninterested and dismissed the case.)

A number of cases which arose while I was at Bufuka concerned purely modern problems. Some were arrests for offences under new codes. Once a waterbuck was captured after a very exciting chase in the water and around the hills. A local sub-sub-chief confiscated it because its capture had been a violation of the

British hunting restrictions. Everyone was very indignant at his excessive zeal, especially as they had been very careful not to spear the animal, but just to club and drown it. (Resulting malicious gossip had it that the animal was eventually eaten by the chief at whose court the case was finally considered!) One particularly interesting case concerned two men, who were not Christians, who claimed payment of a cow from the heir of a local priest in return for one they had earlier given his father. For had not his father cheated them, promising that he would cure their father, and then not succeeding?

If the parties to a hearing are not satisfied with the verdict, they may have recourse to a special oath or ordeal. Oaths are supposed to be very effective, though certainly none was really strong enough to overcome the established tradition of lying in a good cause. The demand 'Swear it to me' is supposed to be answered by an oath upon some instrument—or person—which had once killed a member of the family of the person swearing. Usually the demand is made rather casually in conversation, with no profounder significance than the query, 'Honestly?' in English. Some of the answers also apparently tend to become stylized and casual. For example, 'The lake' was very commonly used as an exclamation when I was in Bufuka, although most of the people using it had lost more than one relative by drowning and might have been expected to use it seriously.

There are more impressive devices for attesting the truth of an utterance which are closer in form to the ordeal. A man accused of setting fire to a house may prove his innocence by eating of its ashes, which would surely kill him if he were guilty. A woman's complicity in the death of her husband may be demonstrated by making her jump over the open grave dug to receive his body. Falling in would be absolute proof of her guilt. There used also to be a practice of licking earth from a place where a priest's drum was kept. And sometimes, as in witchcraft accusations, a diviner would also be called in to use his arts (see below, p. 162).

As in many other societies, action by other persons covers only part of the field of possible punishment for offences. Direct supernatural sanctions also play a role in supporting rules of conduct, particularly those expressed as absolute proscriptions and prescriptions. They also serve an interesting purpose as bulwarks of parental authority and instigators of direct human action.

For the most part supernatural forces impinge on moral relationships and interpersonal obligations indirectly. The spirits do not themselves directly censor, reward, or punish human behaviour. Instead, they are used by people to control other people's behaviour in various ways. For example, a father may curse a disobedient son by a very powerful death-bed oath, contagious in its effect, which makes a pariah of the cursed son.

The death-bed oath is greatly feared. If a son refuses to pay a father the respect which is his due and acts independently instead of obeying him in major things, the father may threaten to invoke this. The curse itself is uttered when the father is ill and near to death. He will say to his other sons: 'Don't have anything to do with your brother. Don't let him share in the inheritance. May all his belongings "disappear as smoke".' After his death his ghost, it is believed, will help to carry out this threat. It will cause people to fall ill if they have anything to do with the delinquent. The cursed son will be an outcast, quite literally. If there is beer in the village, he will not be permitted to partake of it, unless he steals in and takes some without talking to anyone. Sometimes milk may be put by the doorway for him to steal, but nothing may be given to him directly. Any active association with him would be punished with an epidemic. Should even a young child speak to him or remark on his presence, some calamity would befall the group. At the least, a cow would die. Once a curse of this sort is pronounced it can never be removed.

There are other indirect supernatural supports for parental authority. For one thing, there is the bond constituted by the fact that the only proper approach to the spirits is through the head of the family. No son, during the lifetime of his father, can himself make offerings to the spirits of his ancestors, who may be causing trouble. The son alienated from his family would be cut off from this necessary channel of approach to the spirits. Similarly, a father holds a powerful magical weapon in his relationship to the first-fruits of the son's crops. A man may not eat of the first-fruits of any of the major crops before his father has tasted a portion. This gift is required of all grown sons. If a man should sleep with a woman after eating of his crops and before his father had done so, some great calamity, possibly his own death or that of his wife, would follow. This not only serves as a sanction upon the son, ensuring his making the offerings, but also gives the father a weapon to compel his general obedience. For if a son should offend his father in any way, the latter might refuse to eat the offerings brought to him. This would leave the son with the equally unpleasant alternatives of not using the crop in question, or not having relations with his wives. He could right this situation only by formally making peace with his father, through a ceremony which involves preparing a feast for the father and his friends (*honga*) (see also p. 61).

There are also other types of situation in which supernatural action is called forth by human intervention. One of these employs the official practitioner of magic (*omufumu wesiriba*). He practises magic for socially approved ends and under prescribed conditions, without incurring the odium of being classed as a witch (see below, p. 141). His services may be engaged by any aggrieved individual, especially by one who cannot force an offender to make amends because he does not know his identity or his whereabouts. It is used most often against thieves who have escaped without being seen, or wives who have eloped to some unknown stranger. The sorcerer called upon to help in such a case sends his spirit familiars out with a kind of John Doe warrant—to cause the sickness of, or even to kill, the person or persons unknown who are responsible for the offence. It is quite public, so that the intended victim is very likely to hear of the dangers which threaten him. In any case he can take it for granted that such proceedings will be instituted against him. With the aid of his guilty conscience, the victim is in fact often brought to account, for any illness which befalls either the offender himself or any member of his family, is likely to be interpreted as the result of such magic and the harbinger of worse to come. The first signs that his own protective magic is not strong enough to shield him are normally enough to send the guilty person rushing to make restitution and to ward off any further evils that may come from such magical penalties sent after him. So confident are the sorcerers in the efficacy of their methods that they wait to collect their major fees till after the hoped for restitution has been made.

Another important way in which supernatural forces set up by human agencies affect interpersonal relations is the oath of blood-brotherhood. This oath and its uses have already been described (see above, pp. 25-6), where we noted that the Chiga firmly believe in its automatic efficacy, and consider the pact-brotherhood to be the safest and most trustworthy of all relationships because of it.

Supernatural forces enter the system of sanctions in another indirect form. There are numerous supernatural penalties which hang as threats over the head, not of the offender, but of the one who ought to take action against him. This is similar in its logical implications to some points in modern criminal codes, which are phrased as injunctions and instructions to the authorities rather than as prohibitions upon the malefactor. The Chiga have a number of these special enforcement-enforcing sanctions. An important one is that which forces a man to take the usual vengeance if his brother is murdered. As we have seen, whenever a murder is committed, the brother of the victim must perform a placatory rite, for which the killing of a member of the guilty person's clan is a requisite. Otherwise, his murdered brother's ghost will haunt him and may drive him mad.

On the whole, vengeance tends to be its own reward, for it is the greatest single source of glory. Nevertheless, there are some who do not like to fight, and there were certainly cases where new enmities might have been avoided. The need for placating the ghost does serve to stimulate action in such cases. It bolsters the courage of the timid and guarantees that vengeance will be taken if not by, then for, the peace-loving individual.

The danger of leprosy which arises from contact with a fratricide serves similarly to enforce at least minimal action against him. Not only eating with such an offender, but eating from dishes he has used, or eating animals killed with the spear that did the murderous act, and other such long-distance contagions, all carry this threat. While this does not actually force the kinsmen to bury their fratricidal brother alive—we have already noted that this was often evaded—it does at least guarantee his being driven into exile, lest the dangers entailed by his presence impel his brothers to take the severer course.

Direct automatic supernatural penalties also occur, but they are for the most part associated, not with major ethical rules, but with very special ritual ones. These are mainly proscriptions rather than prescriptions—the familiar type of rules we know as tabus. The Chiga have a special term for this—*zira*—which means to be forbidden, usually under penalty of leprosy at some unspecified future date, to commit some specific act. It is, for example, *zira* to step over your grandfather's grave, or to eat from food-trays which he had used before his death. There are food tabus associated with the various clans and with things which were instrumental in causing deaths in a family. All these carry the penalty of leprosy if they are broken. These tabus seldom seem to refer to or to regulate relations between people. For example, the rule that you must not marry a member of your own clan is apparently not so sanctioned, as we have already seen.

In recent years this whole picture has been considerably modified. British rule, while technically 'indirect', involves a new type of coercion of the individual through formally constituted authorities which are under British control. The form of government is modelled upon that set up in Uganda. At first administered by Ganda chiefs (imported to teach the Chiga to govern themselves), the major posts are now largely in native hands. The country is divided into four large districts (*saza*), each with its high chief, who tours the country like the British administrator, interviewing and supervising the local chiefs and hearing appeals. Courts of law and registry offices are established in each sub-district, which has a chief with a number of local chiefs as his assistants. These latter may hear disputes, but only in order to refer them to the proper courts for action. They also have the task of supervising tax collection and public works. In these functions they are assisted by village headmen, who act more or less as policemen and foremen. All these functionaries are appointed by the central Government, and all but the last are paid for their work and understood to be occupying full-time posts. There is also an army, or rather a body of soldiers, but these are all members of other tribes and are directly under British control.

All sorts of specific injunctions and prohibitions have been introduced and most are carefully followed. Inter-clan fighting has disappeared except in a surreptitious form, though murders are still a problem. Births and deaths, marriages and divorces, and all cattle transactions must be licensed and registered. Head-tax and work on the roads and other public works are required of all men, and each woman must contribute a bushel of millet to the public store, to be used in case of famine due to crop failure. Honey beer may not be brewed at all and other beer only upon payment of a licence fee. Attending a feast spear in hand, failing to report a fight, hunting out of season are all serious offences, and such breaches of regulation are now exceptional. Five sheep and one cow are all that may be paid as bride-price. Many still paid a little more while I was in Bufuka, but they were learning that this had its dangers—particularly should there be a desire to retain the illegal extra cows in case of divorce. There are strict bans on the observance of the old religious rites, and arrests are made for divining or attempting a cure with herbs, as well as for practising witchcraft or sacrificing a calf. Almost all the ghost huts have really disappeared; in the whole territory with which I was familiar I heard of only one still standing. And practically no one wears even the most innocent of charms or amulets.

The acceptance of British authority has a quality of sullen resignation before superior strength. In this connexion it is worth noting the opinion of Mukombe, high chief of one district and an exceptionally intelligent man. He holds that it is necessary to continue the religious suppression because otherwise 'the people would quickly spoil', and rebel actively against the Government. Only those who, like himself, have government positions gain from the present arrangement. Other people, he feels, would prefer to return to the old ways if they had any opportunity or encouragement. Resumption of power by native priests might be a key factor in such a situation.

The role of religion in this acceptance of British authority is a curious and important one. To the Chiga British rule is not a system of responsible centralized authority working in terms of a body of intelligible principles and for the maintenance of peace and justice; nor is it merely the force of armed strength, though the *askaris* are a visible factor. They see it rather as an extension —on a more powerful and more integrated scale—of the kind of arbitrary power formerly exercised by the spirits, working through the priests who represented them. Now it is the Government officers and police who represent the mysterious and remote 'govamenti'. As more than one man explained it to me: 'The ghosts of our ancestors are powerful. Spirits which come in snake form [*emandwa*] are powerful. The Nyabingi spirits which inspired the oracular priests are much more powerful than any others. And now the British have driven out Nyabingi and all the priests. The govamenti is much more powerful than Nyabingi.'

It is not merely the driving out of the spirits which testifies to the great supernatural power of 'govamenti'. It is also the interesting fact that its functions are in so many ways neatly analogous to those of the spirits. Taxes are levied mysteriously for ends unimportant or unimaginable to the taxpayer, just as previously demands were made suddenly and arbitrarily for beer and sheep and grain. People are forced to work for the Government, building roads and camps, as they were sometimes compelled to work for the priests. On the other hand, some receive largesse in wages from the Government, just as individuals who curried priestly favour received gifts from time to time. Furthermore, some of the priests who had gone farthest along the road to political power had actually reached the point of using their court followers as a weapon, sending bands of young men to seize the goods of recalcitrants. Does not 'govamenti' use its armed force and its jails, its whole machinery of compulsion, in exactly the same way?

Under these circumstances, some aspects of the modern procedures are an obvious source of puzzled confusion. The priest never extended his power over people to the point of interfering in their private affairs in matters which did not immediately and directly concern him. On the other hand, 'govamenti' is constantly and incomprehensibly interfering in private lives and affairs. The Chiga are very suspicious of the motivation of all the new rules, whether they be limitations on the size of the bride-price or requirements that cattle exchanges of all sorts be registered. Why should a man be clapped into jail because an oar is missing from a lake boat? These demands are all arbitrary, and must obviously be of direct private advantage somehow to the Government or the governors, else why should they have been ordered? As to the grain being stored by contributions from each household, clearly its real purpose could not be the avowed one of insurance against famine, as people were not allowed to dip into it in the hungry period before the harvest. Obviously it is being put aside against needs that might arise if the Europeans should take to fighting one another again!

The effect of the new ways is of course much more pervasive. The imposition of the *pax Britannica* favours mobility and some disregard of rigid clan barriers. The dissolution of the religious bonds, which had already been weakening, is a further impetus to the loosening of kinship ties. Most striking is the cumulative effect on the family itself. The autocratic position of the *pater-familias* has already been undermined. For one thing, children flaunt a growing independence, based upon a belief that the courts will support them in a show-down. Certainly the courts will side with the child against a parent who attempts to use such a stringent old method for enforcing obedience as tying him to a courtyard post. To get a licence for his daughter's marriage a father must obtain at least her verbal, even though unwilling, consent in advance, since she must make the application in person. Smaller marriage fees make it possible for many a young man to earn his own bride-price payment, making his dependence on his father purely moral rather than economic. The father's role is further reduced by the fact that his son is no longer dependent on him for intervention with the spirits, while his prestige is weakened by the diminishing role of the elders in general, especially as official posts and jobs tend to go to the young men who can 'read'. While most of these influences were still new and their effects only beginning to be felt when I was in Bufuka, there is no question of their general tendency to augment the individualism which is such a basic and clearly marked a feature of Chiga society, despite its formal kinship basis.

7

RELIGION

BECAUSE religion has undergone drastic suppression in recent years, this aspect of Chiga life will have to be described in rather bare outline. Although the British ban was actually directed against one particular cult, the cult of Nyabingi, the Chiga have interpreted it as a general one (see below, p. 157). The result is that no one dares to wear the most ordinary charms; ghost huts have disappeared; diviners are no longer openly consulted; and religious and magical practitioners have laid aside their spirit 'horns'—though they may continue to cherish and even to feed them in private. My information had therefore to be dug piecemeal from informants who were either poorly informed or reluctant and suspicious. Ceremonies I witnessed were versions put on for my benefit, just to show me 'how we used to do it'. The basic formal features are, I think, fairly clear; but their functional significance is not always so evident.

The general picture that emerges from the information I was able to obtain is a familiar African one, but, like Chiga institutions generally, rather less formalized. For the Chiga, the universe normally goes on in a more or less smooth routine way. It is vaguely conceived of as ordered by a remote high god. But it is also infested with a great many different types of spirits who interfere with its normal functioning—and always for the worse. There are ghosts of recently departed ancestors who trouble their own descendants and make them ill, and there are various other malevolent spirits which work through human familiars, smiting them, their kinsmen, and even strangers with all sorts of horrid afflictions. All these spirits are arbitrary and cannot be kept in order by systematic ritual. They must constantly be placated by offerings which are made whenever they start to cause trouble. It is the function of the diviner to determine which of these various powers is causing or threatening evil, so that appropriate offerings can be made. There are also evil powers exercised directly by human beings through magic. Some of these can be controlled by counter-magic or by protective spells and charms of varying degrees of potency, which form a general first line of defence and safety in many situations.

Offerings to the ancestral ghosts were made by the heads of the households directly; but more powerful spirits could be approached only through their own personal intermediaries. These religious specialists did not form a hierarchy of priests, although some were more powerful than others. Practitioners of various categories had no systematic relations with each other. Diviners, who were in a sense the warp strands running across all the others and supporting them, were the least organized and least professional of the lot. Family heads were free to choose among diviners and sorcerers, who had no more fixed and systematic relations with their 'followers' than with each other. Only where formal ritual cults existed was there any indication of linked common practices, and even here there is no evidence of close organization, though there may have been some in connexion with the Nyabingi cult.

SPIRITS OF THE DEAD

Belief in the continued power of recently deceased relatives— *abazimu*—was a basic element in Chiga religion. Ghosts may smite their living relatives with disease to the second generation, afflicting grandchildren in either line, and even daughters-in-law, but not the wives of grandchildren, or subsequent descending generations, or even sons-in-law. Brothers' ghosts are the most prone to malevolence; even a child's ghost may harm its own living siblings. It is only grandmothers' ghosts which are at all likely to be helpful. The spirits' malevolence is not punishment for wrongdoing but pure malicious whim. As we have already had occasion to note, the ethical role of supernatural sanctions is almost entirely indirect, operating through human intervention, rather than any concern on the part of the spirit for the character of human behaviour.

The cult of a newly deceased relative is not begun automatically; one waits first to be sure that the ghost will insist upon such a course. Only when illness or other misfortune befalls someone in the family, and the diviner who is consulted ascribes it to the action of the neglected ghost, will a ghost hut be built for it and offerings made. The only offerings definitely prescribed are those made by a woman to her husband's ghost soon after his death, in a temporary tiny hut built for her use. These are the only offerings made directly by a woman; all others must be made for her by a male relative.

The ghost huts (*endaro*) are miniature houses, very roughly and loosely built—just four poles and a clod roof—about a foot high, in which bowls of food and bits of meat can be placed. Only the paternal grandmother of the household head had a more distinctive one. Hers was a fine large hut, separate from the others, and more like a house in structure. It usually faced the gateway, and was large enough for a person to enter it. Inside there was a compartment partitioned off where pails of milk were kept, especially the milk from any cow which had been specially set apart for the grandmother. This milk was not tabu—it was, in fact, later used by the family for churning butter, some of which was in turn offered to the ghost. It would never be stored there, though. Butter was too tempting to thieves. Any stranger might take it, for no one needed to fear the ghosts of anyone else's ancestors!

Obviously, the number of ghost huts to be found in any compound varied with the particular history of ghostly intervention in that family. For example, one of my informants told me that in the compound in which he grew up—that of his father's brother—there were four small ghost huts, grouped near the gateway, in addition to the separate large one for his uncle's own grandmother. There was none for his own father, for no one had been seriously ill since his death. Three were for other uncles—half- and full brothers of the household head—who had had troubles ascribed to them, and the fourth was for his uncle's mother. In normal circumstances, these huts would have been maintained over the years by the current household head, and replaced or added to as needed. Those for ghosts closely enough related to affect him and his family would have been rebuilt by the heir after the death of the household head.

Goat-meat was the offering most commonly used, unless something else, such as beer, was specifically designated by the diviner. When an animal was to be sacrificed, it was shown to the ghost before being killed. 'The ghost is told, "Look what I am going to butcher for you." Then, when the meat is cooked, the bones and some of the meat are placed in the hut, together with some gruel.' Normally, such major offerings were made only when circumstances demanded it, but it was also usual to make minor offerings when materials were available. A little beer might be poured into a pot in the ghost hut when the family brewed, or some gruel given without any special occasion. And when a goat was to be butchered for a feast, it was only sound economy to offer it to the ghosts at the same time for good measure.

When a man makes a sacrifice to some ancestral spirit which has demanded it, he will also call upon the others for whom he has already built huts to share the offering. He usually starts with his father and then proceeds with the rest in order of age, calling on each by name. Sometimes not all of them can be included at the same time, for, just as living brothers may be on bad terms, so may the ghosts. If any ghosts represented by the ghost huts refuse to eat together, a man must kill meat and make offerings for them separately. The ghost of the grandmother whose hut is set apart, as we have seen, is not approached together with the others. She receives offerings of beer and gruel for the most part; occasionally she may be given a bit of beef. But the mutton which forms the staple offering for other ghosts is never given to her: as a woman, she eats only beef.

When making an offering to a spirit, the officiant always speaks to it. He uses a rapid recitative, which is varied *ad lib.* to suit the occasion. This is called to *teretcerera*. Its language is always of the most elaborate and metaphorical sort, though not in any more formal sense esoteric. While this prayer is going on, calling for health and every conceivable blessing and asking the spirit to desist from any injury it is causing, spectators, even members of the family, may gossip and chatter in an unconcerned way. No reverence of any sort is expected of them—not even formal attention. Nor was any awe felt towards the offerings after they had been given to the spirits. A child creeping about the courtyard would with impunity drink from the cup of gruel left at one of the ghost huts, or a dog might disturb the bits of meat without being molested.

Death and Mourning

For all their concern with the ghosts of departed ancestors, Chiga interest in them is strictly limited to their effects upon descendants. I could find no theories elaborated about the nature and powers of the ancestral ghosts. They were simply beings who could influence the affairs of the living. Like the living, they could be mean, selfish, arrogant and demanding—and had fewer checks upon their impulses than a living man must have, who has to live among his fellows. There is no preoccupation with life after death, no beliefs or rituals are directed towards guarantees for an after life for the living or the dead, nor is there any attempt to establish community or continuity between the living and the dead. The newly deceased relative is no longer a co-operating or participating member of the community. There are no recurrent mourning rites, and care of the grave or the remains is inconceivable. Instead, funeral rites are directed essentially towards breaking off any relations of the ghost with his living kin. The corpse is hurried to burial as rapidly as possible. Death is a kind of pollution; the living must be purified, to purge them of the contamination of contact with it. Name and memory of the deceased are erased as rapidly as possible from ordinary living. The belongings of the deceased are purified and some of them are destroyed or permanently discarded. And, as we have seen, offerings to the ghost, except for those of the newly bereaved widow, are postponed until a new relationship is set up—that is, until such time as the ghost's malevolent power actually manifests itself.

Death itself is a calamitous event to be met by the survivors with a great show of mourning and a complete, if brief, cessation of the normal routine of living. As soon as death occurs, the watchers close the eyes of the corpse and the women of the household begin to wail. This special wailing used for mourning (called to *tcura*), like most formal emotional expression, has a fixed pattern and rhythm but free choice of words. There is very loud crying, and expressions like 'Oh, how dreadful! What is now to happen?' are sobbed out.

The outburst of wailing serves notice to the whole village of what has happened. Everyone comes immediately to the house of bereavement. The actual burial and the full burden of all arrangements fall on the close patrilineal kin. Some men set to work digging the grave, others go to notify distant members of the family, all of whom will try to be present for the burial, or at least for the subsequent mourning period.

The burial takes place at once, except that if the head of the household dies at night it will be postponed until the morning. Until the corpse is buried the women and young children wail, the latter adding real crying to the turmoil and excitement. Men, however, are not expected to weep.

In preparation for burial, the corpse is shaved and all the clothes and ornaments are removed. The anklets are cut off with a knife and discarded. The body is not washed or anointed. It is wrapped in a mat, lying on the right side, with knees bent and hands under the head.

The grave is got ready as quickly as possible. For the master of the house, the grave is dug in the courtyard, for the house itself is destined to be moved away in a little while. For other members of the household, graves are dug just outside the fence. The body is never taken through the gateway but through a hole especially made in the fence. The grave is dug by the patrilineal kin, who smear their feet with a mixture of ashes and water applied with a special twig. The first stroke is made ceremonially by the eldest son of the deceased, using a little twig bent into a miniature hoe. Then other men pitch in. One of the tools used is the basket in which the deceased kept his little calabash of butter. Some minor tabus and precautions are associated with the grave-digging: for example, if a rat should get into the grave, it would not be possible to use it and another would have to be dug.

When the grave is ready the corpse is immediately brought out and lowered into it. At this point the wailing reaches its peak. The ropes binding the mat are cut and, if the deceased is a man, the mat itself is removed. (It is left on for a woman.) The earth is shovelled back in and the mats, the basket and twigs used for digging, and the anklets which were cut off the corpse, are thrown on the grave. No clothing or metal must be buried with the deceased; to do so would endanger the lives of the whole clan.

Neither the wives nor any other women with whom the dead man had sexual relations may witness the actual burial. They may see the corpse only before it is wrapped. Similarly, a woman's burial may not be witnessed by her husband. The widow or widower has a special rite to perform in connexion with the funeral, which is called to 'pull out the spear'. The same term is used in connexion with purification after murder. It is not clear what parallel is implied here—whether the spouse is suspect or, more probably, in danger. The rite in this case consists in urinating

on a tree outside the compound gate. This tree may never thereafter be cut down. If a widower should sleep with another woman
before doing this, she would die—and this curse, my informant
told me, would extend up to the number of ten women!

A rite involving urine is also required of the daughter-in-law.
In her case, the urine must be poured over the grave of the deceased father-in-law. (It will be remembered that urine was also
involved in the wedding ritual. It clearly plays a significant—
though unexplained—symbolic role.)

Except for a very young child, whose burial takes place most
unceremoniously, attended only by the closest relatives who live
nearby, all the relatives of the deceased, other than married sisters
and daughters and grandchildren, come to the burial. If they live
too far away to get there in time, they should at least come to
part of the mourning. Anyone who fails to do so is in danger of
being troubled by the ghost and, furthermore, is likely to be
challenged by his fellows for possible complicity in the death.

Married daughters and sisters do not attend the funeral. If
they are present, they must hide when the body is brought out.
Should a married sister come to the funeral, which is neither expected nor customary, she must in any event not stay overnight
and must be given a goat to take with her as a gift when she
returns to her home. This goat 'of the tears' must be killed and
eaten at once by her husband and his kinsmen, and everything
associated with it must immediately be destroyed, for it is con-
taminated by its contact with death. A married sister must
avoid the house where her brother died until a special rite has
been performed, which includes the symbolic eating of marrow
leaves and honey—these are again recurrent symbols of a woman's
assimilation into a family circle (cf. above, p. 54).

Many affinal and maternal relatives of the deceased who have
come for the burial stay on during the formal four-day mourning
period. The women stay at the house and weep and wail, but
men, even very close relatives, may wander about, gossip, and
even transact business. I knew one man who went to collect a
debt from a neighbour the day after his mother's death. During
these 'skipped days' no heavy work of any sort is done by the
lineage-kin of the deceased. On the first day the widows of the
house do not even nurse their babies and the cows are not milked.
All the cows and sheep and goats of the deceased must be brought

in from the fields and kept in the courtyard overnight. If any of them have been farmed out at a distance, round fruits will be used to represent them. Otherwise they could never after be eaten. A great fire is built in the courtyard at the place where the deceased used to sit. Into this fire are put grass from his bed, the fireplace house-post, wood from the gateway, and also various seeds. The fire must burn for the entire mourning period, and then be put out ceremonially by a ritual specialist. If it should rain, the fire must be taken indoors; it must not go out before the four days are ended.

All the food which was in the house at the time of the death must be used up during these days in feeding the mourners. Widows and children have their heads shaved; among some groups it is the custom for them to smear themselves with ashes, though this is not done at Bufuka. Wives of the deceased wear their usual clothes, but no ornaments and they wrap rags about their anklets.

During the mourning days most of the people do not sit on mats or stools. They may stand or sit on the ground, but they do not lie down. They do not sleep in the house, but in the doorway or out of doors. An exception may be made for an old person, who would be allowed to use a mat or stool already there, but none could be fetched for the purpose. Most women who are not members of the immediate family of the deceased do not stay overnight at the house of mourning, but return each day to weep with the next of kin.

Immediately after the burial, the specialist takes the hearth-stones out of the house and places them on the grave. Everything movable is taken out of the house and temporarily purified. The house itself and its ordinary goods are then ready for use again. Things which belonged to the deceased personally are still impure and may not be touched until after the final purification, on pain of leprosy.

On the fourth day the concluding rites take place. If it is the master of the household who has died, the roof-pole of the house is pulled out and thrown on the grave and the bed is torn down. This officially destroys the house; later on it will be torn down altogether. Meanwhile, the widow will cook and sleep on the opposite side of the house from the one usually used, and she will sleep on the floor till a new house is built. (A widower only has to have the house purified and need not move at all; although if there are a series of deaths, even of only secondary persons in the household, he usually will, as the site is clearly ill-omened.)

At this time, also, purificatory herbs are administered to the spouse and the children, and all those who have been sitting at the fire in the courtyard. All the furnishings of the house and the personal belongings of the deceased must also be sprinkled with this 'medicine'. After this, so far as the community is concerned, the funeral is over. Most people will go back to work, except for widows of the deceased.

Especially strong purification is necessary for the grandchildren. They should not be present at all; but those who live there must be very careful, especially to avoid food or cooking things that were ever in contact with the grandparent. This avoidance is for all time. Should a grandchild ever eat food cooked on firewood from the spot where the hearth-stones were thrown away, he would contract leprosy. And this is in a sense retroactive, so they must be given special medicines to purge them of past use of the food of the household.

For some time after a burial the grave is watched lest a witch should try to obtain bits of the corpse for the purpose of black magic. Every now and then someone will go to see the grave to make sure that it is not being tampered with, and it is also magic-ally protected by charms placed upon it. But, apart from this necessary protection for the living, contact with it is avoided as much as possible.

After the death of her husband, a woman gives gruel to his ghost at a special ghost hut (see above, p. 131). After wailing for her deceased husband at a high pitch until the burial, discarding or covering up all her ornaments, shaving her head, and then sobbing and bemoaning her loss through the four-day mourning period, she must go on with a modified mourning over a prolonged period lasting for several months. During this time she lives in a ramshackle hut and must be continent. The grief of a bereaved wife is sometimes very real and very strong, though of short dura-tion. I was told of a number of cases in which attempts at sui-cide were made by widows. One was told me by a nurse at the mission, who witnessed an occasion on which a boat was cap-sized during a storm and all in it were drowned. The island where the hospital stands was the scene of much weeping and wailing, as all the men lived there. One of the women who was

widowed walked right down into the lake carrying her tiny baby
(but was stopped by others who noticed her absence and came
after her). On the whole, however, such intense sorrow was exceptional. The mourning period provides a standardized way of
expressing grief and of readjustment, after which people are
able to resume normal living. They have no further relationship
with the ghost, now completely cut off from the living, until it
makes its presence known in some way.

Usually a ghost establishes contact with its living relatives only
through the medium of a diviner. However, possession or direct
communication, while not very common, is reported to have
occurred. Sometimes, I was told, a person would faint or grow
ill and speak in a strange, 'tiny' voice; this might be a ghost come
to make some demands directly through him. Sometimes what
it wants is a particular girl, who must then be sued for and brought
to the ghost. The family must pay the bride-price and go through
the ceremonies just as if she were the bride of a living man. She
will sleep with one of the living kinsmen of the ghost husband,
but she will cook for the ghost and be considered its wife. Anything which a ghost demands in this fashion is usually granted,
for a ghost has the power to kill. (Some ritual experts, I was
told, claimed to have herbs to counteract these threats, but they
were not considered very reliable antidotes.) One of my neighbours told of having been haunted at one time by the spirit of
his paternal aunt, who came to him in a dream and insisted that
he should marry her daughter. This is, of course, a disapproved
marriage, and the girl's father refused to accede to the demand.
'He married her off elsewhere, and she died within the year,'
my neighbour told me with some satisfaction.

Sometimes a person troubled or possessed by a spirit begins
by talking in a curious, 'tiny' voice, proceeds to make threats,
and ends in what is described as a fit of madness. He may throw
off all his clothes and dash into the woods, babbling nonsense.
I was told of several cases of such seizures within the memory
of my friends in Bufuka. This was the ultimate threat in being
haunted, and cures for it were known to be largely unavailing.

We have noted in the discussion of the vengeance feud that
a man must pursue his brother's murderer and so avenge him
or the ghost will pursue and afflict him. This may be merely

the kind of illness which ghosts ordinarily inflict. But the ghost of a murdered man can also haunt his murderer, if the latter does not protect himself ritually. This is done by means of a four-day purification which is called 'to pull out the spear'. This must be gone through the first time a man kills anyone for whatever reason, and it is also required after killing a leopard.

The murderer undergoing the rite is secluded for four days, during which he must remain constantly awake so that the ghost cannot get at him in his dreams. His relatives may help him stay awake, but must not eat or smoke with him, as that would contaminate them. At first he himself must not eat or smoke either. On the fourth day purification rites are performed. His hair is shaved, his body hair plucked out, and his nails cut. Until these grow again, he may not resume any of his normal relations with his fellows or sleep with his wife. And all the things he uses during this period must be destroyed when it is over—the potsherds he eats from, the stem of his pipe, and so on. He is given medicines and a charm to wear, and a charm is planted at his gateway to keep away evil forces sent by the relatives of his victim. And even after he returns to normal life he must be careful never to come into contact with the spear or other weapons of the man he killed; he may sell them, but not touch them himself.

Most ghosts are of interest only to their own descendants, but there are a few spirits which were described to me as ghosts endowed with somewhat more general powers. Some, for example, can bring and drive away the rain and so affect everyone's well-being. Persons with such valuable ancestors had considerable prestige. Respected elders brought them offerings on behalf of their families. Sometimes many people would come together at one time, to dance while the rain-maker prayed to his ancestors. And after the harvest there might be more offerings and a festival. (There is some question in my mind about the accuracy of this last point. It was reported to me by younger men who had not been active participants; and it is possible that they had confused the dance festivals that took place for the Nyabingi priest with those for the rain-maker; the particular rain-maker to whom the people in and around Bufuka had always taken their offerings became a famous and powerful Nyabingi priest in his middle years.)

Like other religious functionaries, the rain-makers have stopped practising altogether nowadays. I was told that they had stopped in a body many years ago, when they were seized and brought before the British authorities and charged with responsibility for a severe drought. No action was taken against them, but since that time they have refused to take gifts or perform any ceremonies. Officially at least they do not even make charms, such as the herb-stuffed animal horns which people used to get from them to turn away sudden storms. All that is left are homely spells against hail and lightning, which most people know, but which are not particularly powerful.

EMANDWA

In addition to the ghosts of ancestors, there were various spirits of other sorts which played an important role; these were collectively known as *emandwa*, though many of them had individual names also. *Emandwa* were spirits associated in some way with individuals, or groups of individuals, who then made offerings to them and in some cases were able to communicate with them. There was a form of spirit possession involved in many cases, but so far as I could discover it involved little of the painful physical experiences generally associated with spirit possession. The Chiga *emandwa* merely 'sat on the head' of the person they chose and spoke through him. Often the afflicted person himself was not aware that anything had happened until the diviner diagnosed a spirit's presence.

It is not possible to get much information on the nature and attributes of these spirits. Apart from the present non-functioning of all such aspects of religion, the Chiga have little interest in philosophical speculation. They do not discuss the nature and history of the various spirits. Instead, they are content to take practical cognizance of their possible behaviour. The average person will answer questions about the distinctions between various kinds of spirits in terms of behaviour—that of the spirits or of human beings in their approach to them. When speculations do emerge on abstract questions, they tend to be random and very diverse; they are personal thoughts rather than accepted group views.

There were at least two main kinds of *emandwa* that my Chiga informants did distinguish. One was the *emandwa* of the *esiriba*, involving individual magical powers used for socially-approved ends; the other was called *emandwa* of the women. This was an actual cult—or cults—in which initiation ceremonies and secret rites were practised and which had both male and female participants.

The ritual specialist or wise man (*omufumu*) who uses *esiriba* is a sort of consulting sorcerer to the community. He does cures and makes charms—much more powerful ones than can be made by those who just know herbal lore without possessing spirit power. He can also work magic; but he is regarded with respect, not abhorrence, for he sends his spirits out only against evil-doers, not for personal malice. The *esiriba* are the spirit familiars which help him in his work. He keeps them in animal horns when they are not in use. They are said to 'sit upon his head' when he consults them. (I have heard it remarked that 'So-and-so did not need to be much distressed when he had to throw away his paraphernalia, including his horn, for the *esiriba* were in the hair of his head anyway.') From this vantage point the spirits talk to him in little voices which the persons consulting the sorcerer can actually hear. When the spirits agree to help him, they will guide him to the best materials for charms, or will themselves go out on expeditions to carry illness and mysterious afflictions to designated evil-doers (cf. above, p. 123).

The 'horn' in which these spirits live is a large sheep's horn whose wide end is covered by a bit of hide with a hole in the middle. This represents the mouth; gruel and blood are fed to the spirits through it. Inside the horn is something which I was told was like a dried beetle; it can be heard rattling when the horn is moved. The horn must be treated with respect and care. It must be fed even when not in use, kept from the chill in a little fur bag and never be turned upside down. Other paraphernalia of the sorcerer's work include a gourd rattle, bells, and a string head-dress with charms and sacred shells in front. (These shells come from a mountain in Ruanda, and anyone who goes there may collect only as many as the number of children his mother bore, under penalty of death.)

One acquired *esiriba* by being 'given' them by an established practitioner. A payment was always made, even when the transfer was from father to son. The disciple shared the proceeds of his professional practice with his master, who not only gave him the spirit horn, but also taught him the herbal lore and formulae. Usually one or another of the sons of an *omufumu* would serve an apprenticeship to his father, learning first the plants and then their uses, and then, when he was a grown man, probably the father of several children and one who assuredly 'knew wisdom' and was not likely to use his power carelessly, he would be given the *emandwa*.

I acquired an *emandwa* by the purchase of a spirit horn. I was instructed to 'feed it a bit of gruel and a little milk, so it will grow', for having just been made for me it was very young as yet. Feeding with blood would come only later, if it were used for important things. And I was instructed in very delicate terms about the need for giving gifts to the maker. 'When a girl is married, does she not always go back to her family to talk with them, and does she not always bear gifts? The girl is the *emandwa*, and it should give gifts to its father, who gave her gifts before and more to come.' All *emandwa* have names. Mine is called 'Little Luck-bringer'.

Neither of the sons of the man who made my spirit horn is a sorcerer. He would not instruct the elder, for he does not trust him. 'He does not listen well to my words.' And the younger is a Christian. Under similar circumstances in the old days, if there were no son who was apt and interested, some nephew would take up the practice. What is not altogether clear is whether any element of spirit possession is involved in which the spirit takes the initiative. This certainly characterizes all the other sorts of relations with spirit familiars, though sponsorship by one who can teach ritual and charms is also necessary.

The sorcerer who works with the *emandwa* of this type has many powers, among which the most notable is that of sending out his spirits to bewitch an evildoer so that he will make restitution in some way (see above, pp. 123, 141). This socially-approved magic of the *omufumu wesiriba* is called *sisya*. It is performed at a kind of séance, which is usually held in the dead of night at the home of the person who engages the services of the *omufumu*. According to one account I was given, the *omufumu* would himself consult a diviner before agreeing to undertake a particular job. He would accept only if he found that the *esiriba* would be willing for him to do so; otherwise it would be not only useless but actually dangerous for him to try. The séance is not secret and would ordinarily have a considerable audience. However, if directed against a neighbour, it might be done less publicly at the sorcerer's home.

This is the way a séance was described to me:

When the magician arrives for the séance, he sits in the place of honour by the fireside and is feasted with beer and freshly butchered meat. Everyone is in a somewhat solemn mood; there is none of the boisterous merriment that ordinarily accompanies beer-drinking. About midnight the sorcerer sets to work, setting the *emandwa* in its horn upright between his knees in the mortar of the doorway. First he shakes the rattles and then the *emandwa* speaks in a 'tiny chirping voice', asking, 'Why are you beating me?' The sorcerer explains that its help is needed and then makes an offering. A sheep is butchered and the blood is allowed to spurt into the horn. Other titbits are set apart in the back of the house for it. The tongue of the sheep is cut off and eaten raw. After this the sorcerer addresses the spirits again and explains what he wants them to do—to send sickness on some thief whose crime is known although his identity is not, or perhaps to cause green grass to grow on the pubes of a runaway wife whose whereabouts are unknown. An answer is expected in the voice of the person against whom the action of the spirit is directed, who is supposed to have been caught by the horn. He confesses to the crime and tells whether it is possible to kill him or whether he is too well protected. In the latter case they desist and seek out another practitioner with more power. Otherwise, the spirits set out at once on their errand.

Spirits of this type have some special connexion with snakes and often manifest themselves in that form. When the spirits the magician has sent out have done their work and killed a victim, they may infest the grave which is dug for him. Then his relatives will have to summon their master to take them back. No family would risk burying a man in such a grave until the snakes had all been driven forth, lest they too should be killed by the spirits. Or the snakes may return to the home of the man who ordered them to be sent forth, and he will summon the sorcerer to be rid of them.

Not all snakes are *esiriba*, however. Ordinarily one may treat snakes with scant respect and even kill them. But if you see a snake which acts in a peculiar fashion, refusing to go away, or snakes which infest a house or lie across the gateway, it is better to be discreet, for these may be spirit snakes. When snakes appeared about my tent soon after it was put up, many feared to kill them and advised instead that we move the site, as an omen like that portended evil. We had to hold a solemn conference before we could go on building. Most spirit snakes are portents, but the interpretation is not always obvious, and it is well to consult a diviner if you think you have seen one. Sometimes you find that it is necessary to bring sacrifices to the man who is their master, and through him make offerings to them of blood and meat. If you disregard the snakes at a house-building, you and even your cattle may die. It is well to consult a diviner in advance of selecting a site, for should you build where *esiriba* have lived they may still be about but will make their appearance only after you move in and attract them with the smell of cooking.

The sorcerer has other duties and powers which do not involve this kind of magic. He makes charms of various sorts and does cures. Many people have some knowledge of charms and spells, but the *omufumu wesiriba* knows much more and his work is far more effective. For when he gathers medicines or makes charms, his spirits help him. They guide him to powerful materials which could not even be found without such aid. Only he can draw out the more powerful kinds of witchcraft, or plant charm trees to catch evil spirits sent by an enemy (a routine procedure in case of divorce). He can hand on much of his knowledge and skill to a layman, by direct training, but unless such a man acquires spirit familiars of his own, he can only work at a very modest level.

The services of an *omufumu wesiriba* are on the whole very expensive. He is always given an initial gift when he is engaged for a particular task, and another when he arrives at his client's home to make the charm or perform the cure. Another gift of a hoe or a bracelet will have to be given to his assistant 'to open the bag'. The fee paid in addition varies with the services rendered. For important work involving a séance, a sheep would be slaughtered; for magic directed against someone, two more sheep, one as a gift to keep and one to be killed for a feast. However, these are due only after there is some evidence that he has been successful. This evidence may be the return of the stolen goods or the runaway wife and so forth, or some direct effort on the part of the person against whom the magic was directed to get it called off, or it may be the appearance of the snake. A sorcerer gets gifts not only from the person employing him. He may also get gifts from the victim's family, who may try to persuade him to call his spirits off before the victim dies, or even bribe him to direct his magic against the man who originally hired him. People do not, however, seek vengeance on the sorcerer himself. He is too powerful and, in addition, is only acting as an agent. It is because he is so powerful and subject to so many pressures, that such men must be mature and of tested character before they begin to practise.

Some of the performances of the *omufumu wesiriba* have elements of showmanship and sleight of hand. For example, in preparing one sort of charm the sorcerer builds a fire on the roof of the house. This is part of a charm for protection on a journey. He is also supposed to be able to make a stolen sheep's skin, stretched for drying, get up and walk away, or to make fire sweep the courtyard from a torch, or balance a large box on a tiny stick stuck into the ground, or, most remarkable of all, to make trays or mats 'fight' together in the courtyard.

These tricks are not necessarily done only by men who have spirit familiars. Some, it was said, could be just learnt by others. My houseboy's brother was said to be able to do all these things and many others. 'He could cut off and later replace a hand or part of forearm. He could turn one shilling into seven, and pass a string through a leg or through a grindstone.' These were things he had learnt from another tribe of powerful sorcerers among whom he had lived as a child. He had also learnt how to remove black magic by cupping. He does not have a fixed home, but goes about and is well paid for his 'sack' (his magical kit).

There are various other *emandwa* (or kinds of *emandwa*) which resemble the *esiriba* in some respects. Some are used in the more powerful sorts of divination. Some can drive out ghosts which are haunting their master, or go out after a thief for him. Some are not so powerful as the *esiriba*; they can help their master, but cannot be used by him on behalf of other people. Some do not live in his home, but in a little hut he builds for them out in the wilderness, among the rocks. They come to his home only when he whistles for them. All these spirits are dangerous; one must be careful not to abuse the powers they bring, for they may rebound. For example, they may mistakenly kill a man's wife whom he has merely cursed in a burst of anger; or they may themselves infest a place whence they have driven out other spirits, so that their master has to bring offerings to get them to leave.

Emandwa zabakazi, the spirits 'of the women', had a special character, different from that of most of the other spirits. For they had regular group rites, with costumes and other paraphernalia. What is more, these *emandwa*, unlike other spirits, were actually called upon for positive help, especially in helping the women of the family to conceive. Unfortunately, my information on these spirits is even sparser than that on other aspects of Chiga religion, for the *emandwa zabakazi* had been completely overwhelmed by the Nyabingi cult; some of my older women informants had seen the dances last in their own childhood. The designation 'of the women' refers both to the sex of the worshippers—for in this one cult the women played an active part—and apparently also to the sex of at least some of the spirits.

Emandwa cults are described throughout this region, from Ankole, Ruanda, and elsewhere. They all involve the idea of some sort of spirit possession and secret initiation rites. In Ankole the *emandwa* were the spirits of ancient kings, the Chwezi. There were several of these and their worship was part of the organized State religion. In Ruanda, to *bandwa* was to participate in a cult which sounds very like the descriptions I was given, but which was dedicated to a particular spirit, *Ryangombe*. People of all castes participated and all were promised a paradise after death. The king was one among many initiates, and the rites at the palace were described as particularly elaborate.

There does not appear to have been as much centralization in the Chiga cult practices; it is not clear whether there was one *emandwa* cult among the Chiga or a number of parallel ones. Certainly, I never heard any one name assigned to a particular spirit as the centre of the cult. Instead, many separate *emandwa* with different names were mentioned; or the spirits were simply referred to as 'the *emandwa* of so-and-so', mentioning a grandparent or even more remote ancestor. Initiates had different specific spirits to which they were related, but they would join together in the dancing and in the initiation rites.

When a person died, the *emandwa* he or she had worshipped was handed on—by a man to his heir, by a woman to the senior wife of her eldest son. If there was no heir the *emandwa* might choose some other person, whose possession would be announced to him by a diviner when diagnosing his manifest illness.

Before a person could perform the regular rites (*bandwa*) he had to be initiated through the offices of a special sponsor of his or her own sex. Together with other initiates—who were always described as 'old people'—the candidate went secretly to the top of a hill in the dead of night. No one today really knows what went on there, for it was a most carefully guarded secret, but everyone assured me that the initiate was stripped, pinched, and teased into 'doing shameful things'. Thereafter, he was 'like a newly born child who knows nothing of good behaviour'. He violated rules like showing respect for his parents-in-law, and had to be taught such things all over again. People thought that 'he had been butchered and come to life again'.

At least one set of the rites was public and elaborate. The participants wore bells on their legs, capes of pure white sheepskin, pond lilies and other white flowers twisted into a wreath for their heads, and white necklaces. They drank beer 'to make the spirits rejoice', and all spoke in a strange language. (This, too, is characteristic of the Ruanda and Ankole cults.) The dance was peculiar to this ceremony, and was described as jumping up and down with the hands held low. The women faced each other and occasionally clutched each other by the arm. In connexion with the ceremonies, secret offerings were made and then a feast was held. The rites were most often held in the harvest season when plenty of beer was available, often as the fulfilment of a promise made during the year, when the help of the *emandwa* had been sought to avert some calamity.

People also made private offerings to their *emandwa*, both in times of crisis and as a regular matter of honouring them. The *emandwa* of a mother-in-law might have a cow set aside for her, to get her help in conception and child-bearing; the milk would be kept in a special hut, and the animal was never butchered. If a person's own pleas to his *emandwa* were not effective, he would carry special offerings to his sponsor, towards whom he always retained a sort of subordinate relationship, so that his sponsor would help him with his own spirits.

Some of the accounts which I was given, in fragmentary form, of offerings which once were made to particular 'lineage ancestors' appear to have been linked in some way with spirits of this general order rather than with the ancestral ghosts. In some neighbourhoods, there were in the past sacred trees to which offerings of beer were poured, and there were stones which 'made a noise like a drum' at which dances were held, and offerings were given to *emandwa* or other spirits. It did not appear that the right—or duty—of a senior lineage member to make such offerings conferred any special status or authority. And even if it had done so at one time, the position in recent years was completely dwarfed by the far greater prestige and power of the Nyabingi priests.

Nyabingi

And now we come to the pinnacle of Chiga religion, the cult of Nyabingi, to which we have had so frequently to refer all through this account.

There is no doubt that Nyabingi was a powerful spirit cult, whose priests had a direct relationship with the spirit, or with some subordinates of the spirit and, by virtue of this special relationship, were able to exert enormous power over their followers.

The cult was not a cult in the same sense as the *emandwa* of the women, for there were no group rites, no group initiation or dances. The priest who had a Nyabingi spirit—and there were apparently quite a number—built a spirit house for it and there presented offerings to it. Other people could only make offerings through the priests; they had no ritual part of their own to play. Some priests were enormously powerful, demanding gifts—one might almost say tribute—from many people, under pain of striking them with illness (all this of course in the name of the spirit); others had only minor spirits with no demonstrated power to strike down other people, with whom they had a quiet personal relationship, not so very different from that experienced by a minor *omufumu wesiriba*—but differently inspired. These spirits were somehow subordinate to the Nyabingi spirit and their priests were subordinate to the priests who were inspired directly by Nyabingi. Nyabingi herself was female and so were some of the priests she inspired. It is not clear how these subordinate spirits differed from the special *emandwa* category that required initiatory rites. The *emandwa* and Nyabingi concepts at this remove seem very similar; but the practices were clearly different.

The term *mukama*—lord or ruler—is associated with Nyabingi in a somewhat ambiguous way. A priest may be said to *be* a *mukama*, or to *have* a *mukama*. Sometimes the term is used of a person who is suddenly granted great blessings of power and wealth by a spirit. The term Nyabingi itself, as I have heard it used, is ambiguous. Instead of referring specifically to one particular spirit, inspiring different human vehicles[1]—for example, a reincarnation of an early queen of a neighbouring kingdom—the Chiga use the term as though it applied to a category of spirits, and with no historical interest in any earlier state or condition of the spirit. Their concern is with its manifestations and its powers.

These are some of the varying interpretations of the Nyabingi spirits that were given me in an attempt to clarify the picture:

'The various *bakama* (plural form of *mukama*) each have their own names, but they are all Nyabingi, just as all the people are Chiga, though they also have their own names and separateness.'

'Nyabingi is one, something which cannot be seen. The different *bakama* speak for it like the various chiefs speak for the Government. They are sent out by the one who is first representative as the Governor is of the king.'

'The Nyabingi who rules all the others is not a person, but more like the wind. But the minor ones could appear, like real people.'

'Nyabingi is the Mother of all the *bakama*.'

Nyabingi is sometimes represented as a creator: 'All things here below are given by Nyabingi, who with the Rain-maker rules the earth and the heavens, and watches over all the people.'

Different sorts of praise-names are used, like 'The Pitier' or 'The Sun-moulder'.

While the ancestors appear to be more or less independent though definitely inferior spirits, the Nyabingi cult was intertwined with all the other spirits, the *emandwa* of various sorts, which we have been describing. 'All *emandwa* are sent by Nyabingi, who is one.' 'The spirits are merely the servants of the *bakama*.' However, distinctions were also drawn. 'The *mukama* gives power to divine. He is also stronger than the medicine man who cures.

[1] This is the sense in which the term has been defined in such accounts as those of J. E. T. Phillips in *Congo*, 1928, and M. J. Bissell in *Uganda Journal*, 1938.

When such a one goes to where there is a *mukama*, he too must make offerings.'

The first coming of a Nyabingi spirit to a man was heralded by an illness or a dream, which was then interpreted by the diviner to mean a command to build for the spirit; or sometimes a man's priesthood was announced to him through some other, established, priest.

When a man had a spirit familiar he built a house for it with a special inner room which no one but a proper officiant might enter. Here the priest retired to speak to his spirit master, whose voice could occasionally be heard to issue from it. The inner room contained no altar; it was simply a storeroom where pots of beer and other offerings were kept. The priest spent a great deal of time at the special spirit house. By day he would sit there 'to warm himself'. Usually he ate his meals there and sometimes he might even sleep there.

A man might have such a spirit and remain its sole communicant. But if his spirit familiar proved powerful enough to afflict other people, they would have to come to him with offerings for him to present on their behalf. The more powerful priests had very wide circles of such followers and sometimes made great demands upon them. Once the strength of the spirit was established, the demands could be made directly, without intervening illness or other afflictions; these were, rather, merely held over the people as threats should the demands not be met. Gifts were also brought voluntarily, to ask favours of the spirit or of the priest, who as a man of wealth was in a position to give considerable patronage. And often many people would come together bringing their gifts and there would be a great festival, which might last for days. At such a time, if the priest were wealthy, he might even kill a bull and beer and meat would be given to all who came.

People who brought offerings would usually wait while the priest went into his inner sanctum to present them to the spirit. He would talk in the usual rapid recitative used in such prayers, and the old men might pray with him. They would ask for life and strength for themselves and all their families. 'Let us be,' they would say. 'Grant us life and strength. May our children not die; may they grow well and sturdily. For this we will butcher a bull for you.' And, as they pray and make their offerings, they kneel and give thanks for past help. 'Thank you, Rugabo; I praise you for having cured such and such a disease', and so on. Fulsome thanks and praise are part of the accepted pattern of respectful observance to any greatly superior being; it is the pattern throughout this region which is also required of the commoners towards their great kings. This kind of pattern was consistently taken over by the Nyabingi priests.

White sheep, a special kind of spotted cow, and honey beer were offerings particularly suitable for a *mukama*, but other things might be brought—sprouted grain, fermented gruel, tobacco, butter, certain kinds of animal skins. The very poor might even bring green vegetables or firewood. Only goats, peas, and potatoes were unsuitable. Part of the offerings was taken in to the spirits, and some were used by the priest's household; the rest was shared lavishly among the visitors.

Those who had nothing at all to bring came to offer their services. Youths might dance or serve as bodyguards, as they did at the courts of Ruanda; in return, they hoped to receive a wife or a contribution towards a bride-price payment. Girls, too, might be brought to the priests as wives or handmaidens. Such a girl would be taken into the inner room to be presented to the spirit like any other offering, and prayers would be offered for her family's wellbeing. She would then stay there and, if the priest did not marry her, she would be a servant, or she might be given to one of the retainers. Though some parents might bring a girl voluntarily, most of them did so only on demand; parents of pretty girls went so far as to hide them, so that they would not be seen by the priests. Sometimes a married woman might be sent as an offering after the death of her husband. In such a case the spirits might also demand all the cattle her father had received as her bride-price!

The priests—or their spirits—were believed to be very imperious in their demands and very severe on any defaulter who was recalcitrant about paying. People tell many tales of their great power. They tell of a woman who bothered a powerful priest with repeated requests for tobacco until, annoyed, he made everyone in her household ill. Or of a man who sprouted a hump on his back overnight because he was remiss in making an offering. And a pact-brother of one of my neighbours died by drowning because he put off carrying his offering for a day in order to drink beer.

Elaborate ceremonies were associated with the wealthiest and most powerful of the Nyabingi priests. Such a priest modelled his life in considerable part on that of a ruler in Ruanda. According to the many accounts I heard, he did not ordinarily go on raids himself, but he did send out the young men who formed his court. When they came back they would show him the spoils and he would select his share. Servants herded his cows for him. They brought the pails of milk to show him, and he would direct which part was to be churned, which given to people to drink. He had many male and female servants and some of them, together with some of his wives, had the task of staying at home and keeping the house and yard in good condition. Some of his wives worked in the fields like the wives of ordinary men, but he himself did not work. One famous Nyabingi priest had one wife whose sole job it was to spread grass for him to sit on. A priest would also sometimes give a sheep or cow to the old people who brought him offerings.

The house and furniture of a Nyabingi priest were well made and decorated after the more formal and finished style of Ruanda. His stools were well carved and red with continual greasing. The spirit house, which was in a special court behind his own or in an entirely separate compound, was well plastered and often there were designs painted on it. Many had partitions of the elegant woven Ruanda sort. The courtyard was kept well scraped and spread with grass, and visitors were forbidden to urinate there— an unusual refinement, for the Chiga commonly draw the line at defecating. Anyone who urinated in the house of the *mukama*, even when drunk, had to pay a fine of beer.

There were special insignia associated with the cult. Some were like the *emandwa* cult paraphernalia in Ruanda; but others were like the insignia of office of the Ruanda chieftains. There was a special type of spear with two heads, called *keitabagome*— 'Killer of Rebels'. There was also a pot with two spouts, which was usually decorated as ordinary pots seldom were. A priest would have a walking stick made almost entirely of metal, with its point fashioned like a tiny flattened arrowhead, and a special large dagger for cutting meat. The skins of all otters and leopards killed were brought to the priests and purified by a special practitioner. Such skins were dangerous and powerful, and no one else would dare to use them as mats.

Special significance was attached to the drums used in connexion with Nyabingi worship; most of them were imported or
made by the Congo Abahunda, who were invited for the purpose
and paid in cows and beer. They used uncured cowhides for the
skin and brought along the special wood of which the drum was
made. The drum was very powerful, and great dangers were
associated with it, so that rites were necessary to safeguard those
using it. Even the place where it was kept could cause harm:
contact with it might cause leprosy. A person who merely saw it
inadvertently would bear children with their eyes turned in; and
the place where worn-out drums were thrown away was avoided
by everyone.

When a new drum was to be put into service it was taken on
a journey. It was carried by servants, not by the priest himself,
and people would give it gifts. Thereafter it would be used to
summon people to ceremonies or feasts, or to announce the priest's
coming to a village on one of the customary periodic visits which
priests made, travelling in style with youths and maidens and
members of his household. On such an expedition the priest was
fed lavishly, and also given gifts, such as goats, to take home
with him. He covered the whole of his 'diocese' about once in
three years, staying in many places for about a month.

The Nyabingi priesthood is not thought to be hereditary. A son
did not automatically inherit the office from his father, but acquired
it by direct inspiration like anyone else. Theoretically this might
happen to anyone; the spirit may go wherever it pleases and even
leave one man to go to another. In fact, sons did succeed to their
fathers' practices. During his period of service as a priest, a man's
sons served as trusted assistants. One of these sons, not necessarily
the eldest, normally succeeded to his father's position and power.
I was told that in some cases a brother had taken over. But there
were also cases where there was no heir; the spirit had just 'gone
off into the wilderness'.

No clan affiliation was involved in the Nyabingi cult. The
Abayunda had had a powerful priest to whom they usually took
offerings. He lived on an island in the lake in very great style,
and many came to him who were not Abayunda at all. After
his death many of his followers took their offering to an Omusigi
who was a powerful priest.

On the other hand, the Abahesi had no Nyabingi priest at all.

In disgruntled reply to my questioning as to why there was none, which he apparently considered entirely out of order, Mutambuka answered, 'How do we know why? It simply happens that she never came to anyone here.' It is, however, at least suggestive that this very man, Mutambuka, was a very powerful individual, not only in his clan, but also beyond it. A rival would have had great difficulty in establishing himself. I heard one very different report, however, which was so rapidly hushed up as to suggest its truth, that he was himself a kind of assistant or associate of the most powerful of the priests.

Some of the most renowned of the Nyabingi mediums were women, but a woman so possessed could not practise as a priest in her own right. Some man, usually her husband, would build for her and actually speak to the spirit along with her. If a man had the *mukama*, no woman might go into the sacred house, and he had always to ask Nyabingi's permission to sleep with his wives, whom he would refer to as her handmaidens. But if a woman had the spirit, her husband could sleep in the inner room and be as familiar with it as she.

Nyabingi spirits are said to have been able to perform wonders. For example, they could turn themselves into human forms and appear to ordinary mortals. A spirit might so appear in many different guises—as an old man, a young girl, or an old woman. Cases are spoken of where such appearances have occurred to individuals who ignorantly refused favours demanded of them by strangers whose identity they discovered too late, when terrible afflictions befell them in punishment. On the other hand, strange appearances might be the harbingers of power and wealth miraculously appearing.

Some strange natural events were also ascribed to the *bakama*. For example, it is said that a person might see the sun and moon change places in the heavens; this is an ill-omened event; to speak of it was to die. Many such events are believed to have happened as mysterious portents, without any obvious origin; others are supposed to have been sent in order to get the worshipper to make offerings.

There is general agreement that 'Nyabingi has not always been in the country'. Present practitioners are more or less direct descendants of the first priests of Nyabingi, who are cited uniformly as about four generations back. They—or she—are said to have come from Ruanda, from the territory of a Chiga group there, the Abagunze. (However, the cult also flourished, though with less political effect, in Mpororo.) The more elaborate type of sacrifice—great feasts, presents of girls, use of drums and bugles—was said to be even more recent. It is supposed to have begun only during the lifetime of one of the priests who was later captured by the British. This may be an accurate account of the special impetus given to the cult by the political direction of Muhumuza (see below, p. 156).

Whatever the essential connexion between Nyabingi and other types of spirit, there appears to be little doubt that the cult did overwhelm and supersede other cults. It was so antagonistic to the organized rituals for the *emandwa* 'of the women' that to *bandwa* went out of fashion completely. The superior power simply overwhelmed the lesser.

A general movement towards power appears to have characterized this cult; and whatever may have been its original role, its later developments took a strongly political turn. The number of priests whose power reached beyond the limits of clan lines, who modelled their insignia of office and their general style of living on those of the ruling class in Ruanda, who exacted tribute on an increasingly lavish scale, and used patronage as a method of building up a corps of retainers, thus adding the spears of a kind of army to the behind-the-scenes power of the spirits themselves, were all instances of this. It seems quite clear that this force had become a military arm, in rebellion against the constituted authority or the attempted conquest by the court of Ruanda. The sway of Ruanda was never established over the Chiga as a whole, but there were areas where the armies of Ruanda had appeared, won a skirmish, and departed, leaving behind a people whom they chose to regard as vassals, though rebellious ones. Few Chiga admitted that more than the fringes of their territory had been thus subjugated. But the threat was there, the constant warfare both from Ruanda and from a terrible Pygmy army which inflicted untold damage in raids which laid waste whole villages. The protective arm of the Nyabingi priesthood, with its spirit-backed powers, was important not only in resisting any further incursions from Ruanda, or from the north—for attacks came from Mpororo as well—but also in the warfare with the Pygmies. There was probably no organized cohesion among

the priests as a whole. Indeed, there were Chiga clans and lineages who were reputed to have aligned themselves with the Pygmy
raiders. But it is against the background of raids from outside,
and conquest or attempted conquest, that the political aspect of
the growing power of the priests can be most clearly seen.

How much influence Muhumuza had I cannot be sure; but
her name was certainly linked with the Nyabingi cult at its peak
by my neighbours and informants. Muhumuza was a concubine
or subordinate wife of the king of Ruanda; herself a Nyabingi
priestess in the northern part of the territory, she was interested
in increasing the power of her son, who was a provincial chief.
How much unity she succeeded in bringing to the movement is
not clear. The Chiga were no doubt ready to fight with her
against Ruanda, though it seems unlikely that they would have
remained under her son's authority, once it was established, any
more than under any other. What seems unlikely is that there
was anything resembling organized common action among the
various priests. If there was, I certainly could get no inkling of
its machinery—no account of common meetings, of inner initia-
tions, or of any specific pattern of subordination, though certainly
some priests were spoken of as more powerful than others.

The movement was at its height at the time of British intervention in this region, and was stopped by concerted efforts on
the part of Ruanda and the British and Belgian Governments,
after several engagements along various parts of the present boundary. Muhumuza was captured and sent to Kampala where she
was imprisoned. A man identified as her son Ndungusi was exe-
cuted. Reports from time to time arise and flourish that he is
still alive and will come back. A Catholic priest in Ruanda
gravely informed me that this is not unlikely, since there is reason
to believe that the man put to death was not in fact the offender.
After the arrest of Muhumuza there was a general round-up of
all the known priests, who were exiled from the country. Many
spent seven years in prison at Kampala. Some were later allowed
to return, but had to live in districts far away from their original
homes. A number are reported to have committed suicide.

The cult's anti-Ruanda organization was taken to be anti-
British as well. Whatever its beginnings may have been, it certainly became so. Despite the sweeping and vigorous attempts
to prevent any resurgence, priests did return from jail or come

out of hiding and organize large-scale rebellions of a definitely anti-British character.

In the 'twenties there was quite a violent affair in the immediate neighbourhood of Bufuka. A local priest, who had been in prison for about a year and had managed to return to his own home, declared himself a new and particularly powerful *mukama*. Establishing himself in secret, he managed to build up a following, not only of neighbours, but of individuals from the remotest parts of the District and even from parts of Ruanda. They had actually made detailed plans for an attack on the European centre, in which they proposed to kill all the white men. The plot was discovered by some native schoolteachers, whose suspicions were aroused by the organized plundering of their gardens. When the British sent police to the priest's court, they found it filled to overflowing, not only with the usual offerings of honey and beer, but even with heaped-up baskets of shillings! A large number of people were present, feasting and holding a ceremony as a last step before undertaking the attack, for which a day had apparently already been fixed. One of my friends, who was a boy at the time, reports watching the whole thing from behind the fence. Many of the worshippers dashed away, some actually leaping the fence; others tried to get rid of the stools and other paraphernalia. The priest himself managed to escape and committed suicide by drowning. The two sons who were his assistants and apprentices were taken off to Kampala and the movement collapsed. A remaining son is a peaceable, not particularly influential member of the community.

The British, determined to prevent a recurrence of such uprisings, took very sweeping steps to keep the movement from regaining any ground once they had exiled the priests. Anything connected with it in any way was suspect. Honey-beer could not be brewed at all, lest it be designed as an offering to a priest or to the spirits. Every cattle transaction had to be registered, so that no cow could be sacrificed to the spirits without the authorities getting wind of it. It is not surprising that the native interpretation of all this became a general fear of making any sacrifices or offerings, lest someone should ministerpret and haul the worshipper off to jail, even though he was only making a sacrifice to his grandmother's spirit for his child's recovery from illness. This confusion was confounded by the Government's taking the position that witch-doctor's horns—the traditional basis for any powerful charms, the traditional central element in the practice of an *omufumu wesiriba*—were instruments of black magic, to be confiscated when discovered. The confusion led to some very odd views about the regulations. As one man explained to me, 'If a man claims to make a cure, and then fails, we must arrest him as a magician.'

The unexpected result of all this, therefore, was the almost total disappearance of native religious practice in virtually all the aspects which we have already commented upon. No religious education could be effectively carried on in such an atmosphere, as fathers were afraid their children would tell on them. Whereas the Chiga had been the people who wore most amulets in this region—the people known to their neighbours all about as the most powerful sorcerers outside the Congo forest regions—they became conspicuous for wearing no charms of any sort. Not only public festivals of a religious character, but also private ones, were stopped or took place on a small scale in someone's back room; even ghost huts disappeared. In all the parts of the country which I visited, I heard of only one man who still had one standing, and that I never actually saw.

While confusion and fear of punishment are essential elements in this total lapse of religious practice, they do not account for the whole picture. The Chiga were never inclined to accept authority quietly. There is another factor which they themselves point to, and which certainly played an important part in what happened. This is the fact that, as they see it, the old spirit forces, which worked by terror, have more than met their match. They have been successfully conquered and driven from the land, and no one need any longer be afraid of them. It is not a matter of not believing in them. Everyone agrees that Nyabingi and the ancestor spirits were powerful in the old days. In fact, even the Catholic Church phrases part of its achievement in terms of having driven Nyabingi from the land. The point is that all agree that it is gone, at least for the time being. It has been driven from the land by the 'govamenti' (cf. above, Ch. 6). Therefore, no one, not even the pagans, need be concerned about practising the old forms of placating the spirits.

The reaction of scepticism to the older beliefs, which is sometimes expressed, may be a superficial or spurious one. When

Kaborama said to me, 'We used to believe in Nyabingi, but it was only the wind,' he was perhaps only whistling in the dark, though he may also have been trying to skirt a dangerous area when talking to someone who was a friend, but also, after all, a 'European'. But there is no question that the absence of fear does cut very deep. The law-suit for recovery of a cow from a priest's son (cited above, p. 121) is a case in point. The men who demanded the cow had no pretensions to Christianity. They simply claimed that it had been given in vain, for their father had died of the disease which the offering was intended to cure. The case was taken to court just before I got there, and was won by the claimant who carried off the cow with no apparent fear of evil consequences.

All of this has, of course, deeply affected the growth of Christianity. Most children are receiving some Christian education as a matter of course; and hardly any are receiving any instruction in the older way. Many women attend the village churches, though not all of them are baptized. Not so many of the men attend, but few make any effort to prevent their children and their wives from doing so. And when they do attempt it, they sometimes meet with very successful defiance. Kaborama's resignation when confronted with a real dilemma, is probably quite usual. As he presented it: 'What can I do? Both my wives are Christians, so there is no one to brew me beer for offerings. I couldn't very well do it myself, even if I wanted to.'

It is, however, important to remember the comment of Mukombe, to which we referred earlier (see p. 126). Mukombe insists that 'many of the old practices still go on, though in secret, and the old faiths are what the bulk of the people trust, despite their protestations to the contrary. It is only fear which restrains them, and they would quickly return to their old ways if the British suppression was modified.'

The High God

While the ancestral ghosts and the *emandwa* and Nyabingi spirits represented the functioning aspects of Chiga religion, there was also a high god who was often referred to but had no cult. He was generally conceived of as entirely good and as in some sense a creator; this view apparently antedates the introduction of Christianity. This god had many names. *Sebahanga*, the most popular, is derived from *hanga*, to fashion or shape, as is *Ruhanga*, the name the Christians now use for God. Many other names were also used; these are praise-names, referring more or less explicitly to noble attributes of the god: *Kazoba*, 'the one who makes the sun set'; *Rugaba*, 'the one who gave everything on this earth and can also take it away'; *Kazoba talenga*, referring to the fact that what he wants he takes that very day, without having to wait even one more; *Biheko*, 'he who carried everyone on his back', and so forth. (The last name is most interesting, as it is identical with that of an important Ruanda cult spirit.)

There is no contradiction in the overlapping of some of these terms with terms also applied to Nyabingi. They are not so much names as descriptions based on attributes and possibly, like human praise-nicknames, they are not even intended to be taken too literally.

The high god was held responsible for many events, good and bad alike, for which no other specific cause could be discovered. When all attempts at placating the forces originally diagnosed as responsible failed in a particular case, *Sebahanga*, who could not be influenced like other spirits, was assumed to have been at work.

A few of the characteristics of the high god may be influenced somewhat by Christian concepts. When, for example, a woman explains that the Chiga high god lives in heaven she may merely be seeking an identification with her new Christian teaching rather than accurately describing an older belief. But two of the most militantly pagan of my acquaintance have called upon *Ruhanga* in my hearing, in what seemed an automatic response and could hardly have been an attempt to impress me. 'He hath given and taken away' and 'So hath he created' were expressions used in connexion with the death of an infant, while 'May *Sebahanga* guard me, he is the ruler' is another common expression with a decidedly Christian flavour which I have heard used by some who would never go near the church or its school.

For all his power, the high god received no sacrifices or other formal rites, but this is entirely in keeping with the general pattern of Chiga religious attitudes. Offerings are designed to placate malevolent spirits. The high god is benevolent, so these are unnecessary. There was a custom, not observed with any regularity or intensity, for the monthly recognition of the rising of the new moon; this too falls outside the regular Chiga pattern of fear and placation. There is, however, no indication of any association between the moon and the creator, except perhaps as both may be related to some older or at least distinct religious stratum. The moon worship, if such it may be called, is exceedingly simple. At the new moon and at the time of the first eating of the crops of a new season, the master of a household customarily addresses the moon. He speaks informally, as in all Chiga religious appeals, saying something like 'Oh, appear well for me and my children and my wife, that they may receive life and strength. May your passing not find me dead.'

The absence of cosmological interest leaves this gesture very much of a puzzle; I could discover neither legends surrounding it nor hypotheses of explanation. Not even the most philosophically minded of my Chiga friends could so much as guess at its significance, either as to what might be expected from it or as to the relation of the moon to other spirit forces. It was regarded as a habit rather than an act of great religious significance. The only references to the moon that I could discover in tales or conversation were trivial and shed no further light on the problem. The moon, I heard, is 'coming from its father's' when it is new, but as it approaches the full it is said to be 'coming from its mother's', where it is better fed. There was no indication of any attributes or names assigned to these mysterious parents— too elusive and too characterless to be termed mythical. There is also occasional reference to the moon in proverbs and riddles.

The absence of any concern with dramatizing the moon is seen in the fact that the dullest-witted of Bufuka girls knew that the apparent rapid flight of the moon is merely an appearance due to clouds. And the full moon is welcomed principally as an opportunity to be out of doors at night, for by its light young people may visit and dance.

I could find no evidence of any interest in the stars. There may have been esoteric lore, but there was no popular interest. There were no names for the various stars or constellations, except for the evening star. It is held to presage bad times when it appears without the moon.

The only myth-like tale which I came across was one dealing with the origin of death: The first person in the world gave birth to a son. When he grew up his father arranged a marriage for him. After he was married, his mother fell ill and died. The son started to bury her and she said to him, 'Watch for me. In a short time I will call to you. Then you must take me out of here.'

The boy went to herd the cattle, and left his wife with instructions to stay at the grave and fetch him when she heard his mother calling. As soon as he had gone, the mother started to call. Her daughter-in-law, hearing her, began to pound the earth with the handle of a hoe, saying, 'The dead do not come to life.' The mother said, 'Take me out of here, my child, and when your father dies, he will come to life again, and when your mother dies, she will come to life again, and your children will all come to life again after they die.'

But the girl refused, saying, 'No. The dead do not come to life.'

Then the mother-in-law died again. When the son came back from herding, he asked his wife if his mother had called, since she had not come to fetch him. She said, 'No.' So he remained sitting there. And from that time on all the people have died and remained dead.

DIVINATION

We have already seen the important role that divination plays in Chiga religion. It is the diviner who discovers the cause of any trouble and prescribes the remedy. He may suggest an offering to an ancestral ghost or some other spirit, or diagnose magic at work and suggest some method for its cure. Sometimes a diviner is consulted to get advice on important steps before they are taken. Is a house-site safe or infested with dangerous spirits? Has one need of any special charms for a proposed journey? And so on.

There are several different divining techniques. Not all are considered equally effective. The most powerful and accurate— such as killing a chicken, and observing the course of the blood and the condition of the entrails—are always used for such critical problems as accusations of witchcraft. A diviner who uses such techniques gets larger fees—from a wealthy client, perhaps as much as a sheep—and will probably be summoned to the client's home instead of just working casually in his own compound.

In other techniques leaves may be pounded and beaten to froth in water; or a little stick is thrust into the nose, so that the diviner can whistle through it and then interpret its sayings. Calabash seeds or bits of bone may be cast on a board, or a bit of potsherd thrown against an ash-smeared stick. There are numerous others.

'When you go to consult the diviner', I was told, 'he will ask what you intend to give him for his services. When you have given him food or bracelets, he instructs you to spit, saying, "*obuhoro* of my house" ' (that is, greetings and peace; very much the same as the Semitic '*Shalom*'). With each specific question that you ask, you repeat the spitting and the blessing or greeting. 'You can ask him, "Will I still be here when the next harvest has ripened?" and if someone has died, you may ask whether the "things that killed so-and-so will also kill me." ' If the diviner finds a bad indication in his omens he will also tell you what to do about it. 'He may say, "I catch the ghost of your mother. It is good, but someone in your house will die." You ask him, "Shall I kill meat for the ghost of so-and-so, then? Shall I ask it to come out of my child?" and he tells you to do so. Perhaps he may say, "But there is also the ghost of your father, which wants you to find a goat to butcher for it." Or he may tell you that you must also give a bull or beer to Nyabingi, or put beer in the pot of your grandmother's spirit, before your child will get well.'

The diviner, in most cases, has every opportunity to manipulate the materials he is dealing with, as well as to vary his interpretations. I had the opportunity once to question a diviner, who was showing me 'how we used to do it', and incidentally predicting safety and good luck for me on my impending journey home. He was using a blob of green froth in a bowl, which he twirled and tilted in his hands. When he allowed it to come to rest, he would point to the contours of the blob as indications of the good results he was getting in answer to all the questions. 'How would it look if the prediction was a bad one?' I finally asked him. 'Oh', he said, 'then it would look like this,' immediately showing me a resulting blob which was jagged and streaked, as it had not been before. His audience did not seem to consider this peculiar, or implying any unreliability, and there is no reason to think that he did either. However, divining 'in the head', without the use of any external materials, is considered a rather unreliable method. Not all diviners are thought to be equally skilful and trustworthy, nor are their predictions expected to be uniformly accurate. If a diviner makes a mistake, it may be the fault of the spirits who have misled him, or it may even be that he is lying. A diviner may try his readings a number of times until he gets results he considers satisfactory. If the client is dissatisfied, he may have him try again or he may go to someone else in the hope of getting better results.

Some diviners are just people who have learnt one or two of the special techniques; others, however, combine various divining skills with making charms and doing cures. For any type of divining it is necessary to serve an apprenticeship to learn the technique, and then to have a sponsor initiate one into the actual practice of the art, which he does with such ritual as setting a torch on the head of the novice. The more powerful diviners usually claim to have special power or wisdom as well as an acquired skill, wisdom which usually passes from father to son and announces itself in a special dream. Every diviner I knew claimed to have learnt through a dream; and every one was the son of a diviner of exactly the same sort as himself.

The diviners were obviously a basic support to the whole structure of Chiga religion, since most offerings were made only on their advice. However, diviners were regarded not so much as major functionaries, but rather as everyday consultants and advisers. They were not invested with the awe and fear which tended to surround the sorcerers, priests, rain-makers, and other such important practitioners. Although the diviner appears to have had it in his power to make or break the reputation of any priest, the Chiga apparently saw him as subordinate to the latter. Some in fact today insist that it was from the *mukama* that the diviner got his power, and that he had to pay him an initiation fee and make continual offerings thereafter. There is no reason to believe that the dependence on Nyabingi is basic to divination, for divining is certainly much older than the Nyabingi cult, but some interrelationship may have developed. However, the actual relations of power and dependence, and even connivance, which may have existed, cannot be disentangled in the present non-functioning of the institutions involved.

MAGIC

There are magical practices for good as well as for evil, but it is not clear that the Chiga see them as related categories. The sorcerer who practises with the help of the *esiriba* does both kinds, and in a context of social acceptance. The term *omurogi* (witch), one who practises black magic (*okuroga*), is sometimes applied to him when he is sending out his spirits to harm someone. More correctly, however, that term applies to a person who secretly and illicitly practises evil magic on his own behalf.

The Chiga believe that witchcraft is the cause of a great deal of disease and death, as well as of various other misfortunes. A great many types of magic are known and feared, and there is little doubt that much of it is not merely feared but actively practised. On the whole, the Chiga consider themselves rather prone to practise witchcraft—much more, they say, than the Nyaruanda, though not nearly so much as the dangerous sorcerers who live in the forest country to the north-east!

Two of the women who lived in Bufuka when I was there were believed to have been witches at one time in their careers. However, neither was punished as a witch, as they were not accused of causing any specific local trouble. One of them had had her witchcraft 'beaten out of her' by her husband soon after her marriage and was no longer considered dangerous. She was a fully accepted member of the community. The other woman, morose and solitary, was suspect still. Witchcraft materials were said to have been taken away from her once when she was very ill. Now people are afraid to eat her food lest it be poisoned. I have heard since coming away that lively accusations have sprung up against her again, as she is reported to have been found wandering about at night naked, behaviour which could have no possible legitimate explanation. There were also two accusations of witchcraft made against other women while I was in Bufuka, but both of these were considered to be pure spite and jealousy. They had no community support and were quickly dropped.

On the whole, women are more commonly accused of witchcraft than are men because they have fewer alternative resources; a man would be able, and would prefer, to take more direct action. This is so much the case that socially-disapproved witchcraft is often referred to as 'women's witchcraft' to distinguish it from the work of the regular practitioner. However, one man in Bufuka was considered something of a witch. He was a successful thief, and was thought to practise a good deal of magic in his calling. As a result, he was shunned, particularly by some of the women and girls, who avoided his compound except when formal obligations took them there.

Except for the special type of witchcraft practised by the professional sorcerer with community approval, Chiga witchcraft contains little supernaturalism or dealing with mystical forces or spirits. It involves no bodily substance or emanation. It is accomplished rather through charms, spells, and the use of evil materials, and much of it is available to anyone who really desires to make this serious break with acceptable human behaviour.

There are several reputedly effective ways of killing by magic. The saliva, urine, nail-clippings or other such parts of the victim's body may be treated magically with herbal charms; or powerful herbs may be administered directly to the victim. These may drive him mad, so that he wanders about before he dies. Or one may use contact with some object associated with the violent death of a relative of the victim's—a bit of the boat in which he was drowned, or a spear that pierced him. The liver of a dead person or dog is extremely dangerous, especially when mixed with tobacco so that the victim will smoke it. This will cause him to die of a terrible liver affliction and is so contagious that it will afflict his relatives too, unless they take special preventive medicines and for ever after avoid eating liver of any kind. It is also possible to kill a person by bewitching the site on which he is building a house. That is why people do not usually sleep in a new house the first night. Instead they put stones in the roof which will attract the magic designed for the house-owner. These different forms of magic have many different names, but they are all equivalent in evil, and may be called *roga*.

In addition to causing victims to die or to sicken lingeringly, magic may bring other ills. It may be used to get people to spear each other in a drunken quarrel; if a man is stingy and refuses to give others beer, magic may be used to make him vomit or defecate on the spot. There is also magic to keep a child from growing, or a girl's breasts from developing, or to cause a victim to be struck by lightning, and so forth. You can also kill a man's flocks and herds by witchcraft. All cases of such afflictions are ascribed to probable witchcraft, though no one in particular is necessarily accused.

There is another way, besides the use of black magic, to injure another person. This is not called to *roga*, but to *kungura*; on the whole, it is considered almost as evil. To *kungura* is to perform some act which is tabu in order to bring about the threatened evil consequence. Some of these may be done in sheer ignorance or by accident; but evil intention is always suspected. There are a great many such acts limiting a wife's conduct; she must not sprinkle water on her husband to wash him, or put his food on the baby's sling. She may use the threat of such acts sometimes as a means of getting her way in a difficult situation, but on the whole this is playing with fire, as her reputation will suffer. Some such threats may be used in an extreme form to prevent an undesired marriage or to bring about a divorce; for such tabus are often contingent. Like much of Chiga magic, they have a kind of delayed action and will take effect not immediately, but only after the injured or threatened party takes some further action—usually sleeping with his wife, for example. There is, therefore, little a man can do, if his wife takes such a desperate step, but send her away. In the same way, a married woman when visiting her family may tie up her brother's sheep, or handle other possessions of his in a familiar way. This ruins them for him and he can do nothing but give them to her to take home to her husband. Altogether, a shrewd, but disgraceful, manœuvre.

The term *kungura* is not limited to such malicious human acts. It may also be used of evil omens, some of which are ascribed to the intervention of spirits. In that case, the spirit must be appeased by an offering, but in other cases counter-spells may work. The evil consequences of some portents may be averted by a kind of simple denial of their occurrence. For example, it is a dangerous thing for a sheep to bear four offspring at one birth. If it does happen, the herder can quietly kill two of them on the spot, and all will be well provided he remembers never to speak of it. If he does tell anyone, all the sheep in his flock will die and perhaps he and his family also. For some evil omens it is possible to employ a professional who can administer purificatory medicines to counteract them. But there are also cases where you are powerless to do anything. For example, a hawk is a particularly fearful harbinger of evil. If one comes into your compound, you may escape any dangerous consequences by having the proper charms and medicines applied to your home and its members. But if you come upon a hawk's nest there is nothing at all you can do, for a hawk is reputed to build its nest of human bones and magical herbs. It is immediately fatal to the finder.

In general, the antidote to witchcraft is intimately related to its various causes. If it is sent with the help of spirits, then it can only be removed by spirit help. An official sorcerer will have to be consulted. If it is caused by witchcraft materials, these must be removed—from the body by vomiting or cupping; or dug up from places of concealment in the house or compound, and so forth.

Charms

In addition to black magic, there are many forms of magical protection. Such practices are never called to *roga*. Charms of various sorts used to be extremely prevalent. The most powerful were made by the regular sorcerers, some according to very complicated recipes, with many ingredients contributing to their effectiveness. There were great trees planted in the dead of night, which were designed to catch and stop spirits sent out by enemies. There were baskets with numerous separate charms, which were buried in the courtyard at the spot where the master of the house was wont to sit and which protected the sheep and cows. These included a bit of the horn and a hair from the tail of the oldest cow in the herd. The flocks were believed to be bound to this, so that if a thief did come, he would be unable to get them to follow him—unless his own magic was so great that he could find and dig up the whole basket, in which case the animals would themselves follow it. There were animal horns which could function in various ways. One could drive away lightning, another would be used in cupping or smelling out witchcraft.

Many others were simpler and some of them could be made by anyone who knew how. A bit of carved wood stored in the rafters of the house would be gnawed before a journey or after dreaming of spirits or at any other time of peculiar danger, to protect one from enemy attacks. The iron bracelet from a dead parent's arm served to prevent haunting by spirits. And a bit of wood prepared properly and fastened in the right way to a baby's wrist kept it from colic. (This is the only charm I actually saw in use, and that quite commonly. It may be that it had in fact a more formidable purpose, but no one would admit to anything other than this mild medicinal aim.)

Words contain great power, and most charms include them. The sorcerer gathering dangerous herbs will spit on them, saying, 'May you kill maidens and women, youths and men.' Some charms are mostly verbal. Often free variation is possible, playing on the meaning of words. Names themselves have potency; so a man who is hiding must not have an awl on him, for an awl is *omuhinda*, and might make his enemies turn aside (*hinduzayo*) and find him. And he must avoid the creeper *emirondorondo*, for it would make his enemies search him out (*rondo*). Often little mimetic acts are carried out. Grain stalks which are bending over are touched with a monkey-skin so they will 'jump up like a monkey' and ripen straight and tall. The general idea of averting evil from oneself by diverting it elsewhere is popular, both in dramatic scapegoat rites, like the important one for peace-making already described, and in more everyday forms. For example, if rats are eating your peas, you get rid of them by pulling up a stalk and putting it at a place where paths cross. The rats will leave your field and go to that of anyone who steps over it. Another common notion is the idea of beginning again (*shubuza*) to get rid of a jinx. You go home and start out on a journey afresh if you have met a bad omen; or you repeat a ceremony because a mistake was made that is causing difficulties later. Herbs, properly gathered and sometimes recited over, are also used for purification in many kinds of charms and especially for curing sickness. There is no clear dividing line between these uses of herbs; all are *ebiti*. One is likely to have to eat one kind to help in a case at court, and to have another thrust into the rafters of the house to cure an illness.

This whole pattern of disease-curing is, from our point of view, essentially magical. Whether it is so from the Chiga point of view is a more difficult question. A native sorcerer apparently put the use of *ebiti* in quite a different category from the invocation of spirits, when he told me of his interpretation of the European edict banning native forms of worship. As he explained it to me, he would of course not practise any forms of curing which required taking his *esiriba* with him, for that would clearly be a violation of the ban. 'I have explained to my *esiriba* why I cannot treat my horn as I used to', he told me, 'so that they will not be angry at not receiving the sacrifices to which they were accustomed.' But he would undertake to do work merely involving *ebiti* (though, and this is unfortunately the critical point, I do not know how widely he would interpret the legitimate scope of their application).

In any case, the Chiga confronted by illness goes through a series of steps which have an apparent theoretical progression from a naturalistic to a supernatural approach. There are many home-made remedies which people will try for simple ills—poultices, blood-letting by making a few cuts in the forehead or by cupping, or taking well-known herbs. Home-made cures include less obviously practical measures, like wearing a bag with hyaena vomit in it, or having a person lick your ulcer and then lick a frog. In any case, the next step, when such procedures are of no avail, is to get a neighbourhood specialist to try his hand at similar cures. It is only when all these fail that you take the more complicated and expensive step of consulting a diviner to determine the cause and so prescribe the cure—purification or some other form of counter-magic, or an offering to a designated spirit.

This problem has, of course, more general implications. It involves the whole question of the way in which the Chiga conceive of the supernatural, and the extent to which they distinguish it from the course of ordinary events. It appears that, instead of any sharp differentiation, there is for the Chiga more or less of a continuum. Their adoption of the British Government as a category of supernatural power, their lack of any word for this concept, their extension of the term *omufumu* (wise man) or *obufumu* (wisdom) to any type of knowledge, without any separate term for the specifically magical or supernatural, all point in the same direction. It might, of course, be maintained that, so far as the Chiga are concerned, the whole problem is an academic one. They are interested only in results and in procedures for achieving them, not in theoretical explanations; attempting to find the point at which a line should be drawn is not merely hair-splitting; it is an attempt to split a non-existent hair.

DREAMS

There is probably a considerable body of belief and lore regarding the interpretation of dreams, of which I got only faint echoes. Dreams contain some element of description or prediction of the immediate future, but not always in recognizable form. For example, one of my friends dreamed once that a girl in our village was pregnant. She said that she had probably had the dream because one of the other young girls had been carrying her little son, and people had laughed and asked her when she bore it. Just seeing the girl the next day she took as a kind of fulfilment of the dream.

To dream of a bad thing or a dead person is bad and will bring bad luck. To avoid this, after a bad dream you must get up early and put some ashes on the back of each hand. Then you blow on them, saying, 'I blow ash on them.' Then clap your hands once and remain quietly seated for a little while with your hands clasped. This will prevent the dream from having any bad effects.

Dreams are also connected with the regular supernatural agencies. Most of what I have described as haunting takes the form of bad dreams. Ghosts may haunt you; you will die if the ghost of your murdered victim should pursue you in your dream. The ghost of a leopard also has this power. That is why it is necessary to take the special precautions described above and to avoid going to sleep at all for four days after killing a man or a leopard. The *emandwa* may also haunt you. This kind of dream is the source of power for some types of divination.

TABUS

To *kungura* is to perform a forbidden act which will bring harm on someone else. There are also some forbidden acts whose threat lies not against another person, but against the performer. The penalty of these acts is usually leprosy. It is for example forbidden (*zira*), under threat of leprosy, to eat of the food tabu to your clan; to step over the grave, or eat from the bowl, or use the hearth-stones, or in any of a number of other ways come into contact with the remains of a deceased grandfather; to marry a widow of a household when you have pulled up the house-pole after a death; to eat of an animal killed by a spear which killed one of your relatives; to sleep with your wife after killing a leopard or a person before the purificatory rites have been performed; and so on.

Some tabus are tied to very specific situations, such as pregnancy and menstruation. A menstruating woman is not so dangerous that she has to be secluded, but she must be careful, for should she drink milk, the cow might dry up, and young plants of beans or tobacco would be injured by her passing among them. Pregnancy tabus affect not only the expectant mother but members of her husband's family. Any carelessness about them would injure the baby. And there are hosts of others.

Thus we find the Chiga individual surrounded by a universe full of sudden evils and vague threats. His own ancestors, instead of siding with him, themselves menace his health and that of his children. Greater and more powerful spirits may threaten him and demand great sacrifices to 'let him be'. The *emandwa* appear to have been a little more helpful, but they too are more or less powerless before the superior powers of the Nyabingi spirits. The malevolent wishes of other people readily take active form, if not in immediate recourse to the spear, then in witchcraft of diverse kinds. And a man may be irrevocably trapped by his own actions, or by purely chance happenings.

But the typical Chiga response to this forbidding universe was not one of anxious fear and trembling. One armed oneself so far as possible with protective charms; then when specific misfortune struck, one sought advice from a diviner and took the best steps possible to right things again, aware always that these steps might be of no avail. A man accepts the blows of fate as they fall with some degree of resignation; but this resignation is tentative and temporary, ready to be discarded at any sign that the threat is weakening. It is a capitulation to force, but it is not abject. For all their resemblance to the touchstones of safety, familiar to us as devices of the neurotic to allay anxiety, the protective charms as well as all the tabus and omens which surrounded the Chiga must have been very different in their emotional implications. For the Chiga they were matters of ordinary daily routine, important enough to attend to, but not worth brooding about. The speed and completeness with which the use of charms was dropped when the Government banned them indicates this very clearly. The outward contrast is most striking when one crosses the border into Mpororo and sees the quantities of charms everywhere, on everyone's neck and arms and about the houses. The Chiga, despite the belief in the prevalence of black magic and the uses to which various kinds of body dirt can be put, do not burn or bury hair and nail clippings, but merely throw them into the bush. Spirits are worshipped and placated only after they have given specific indication that offerings are in order, and not in a constant routine of conciliation. And even burial rites, for all their emphasis on contamination and ritual purification, reflect a business-like acceptance of the fact of death.

8

EDUCATION

EDUCATION among the Chiga contains none of the formal features which we so often find in East Africa. There is no development of the age-grade idea, no formal schooling, and very little compulsion of any sort. Chiga children, like Topsy, just grow. They learn the ways of their culture by observation and participation, and only occasionally by precept. And they grow up differing from each other in skills, interests, character and habits, but all within a limited range of cultural standardization.

For many months the care of the baby is exclusively in its mother's hands. It lies strapped against her bare back during her waking hours, and sleeps with her at night. Not until it is a toddler will it ever be left in the care of other people for any length of time. The mother carries it with her to the fields, setting it down beside her while she works, and interrupting whatever she is doing to suckle it whenever it cries. When she takes it from the leather sling, she massages it firmly but gently, bending and stretching its arms and legs, and running her hands over its skin 'to make it supple'.

On the whole the baby's body is treated as rather tough. It may be quite uncovered in the chill of the early morning, when the mother sits in front of her house and nurses it; it is sometimes sheltered from the full glare of the sun when it is lying out in the fields, but often its head is quite exposed. The way the sling is tied to the mother's back allows the head to bob and jounce with her every movement, yet she will not hesitate to jump up and down a few times in high good spirits if she passes some girls who are dancing. The baby learns very early to assume the spread-eagle position with its legs which fits it comfortably against its mother's supporting back, and before long it can be transferred to a safe sitting-place on her hip. When a mother holds a baby out, or hands it over for someone else to hold, she may swing it casually by one arm, as though it were snugly and strongly of one compact piece.

Chiga babies receive rather rough handling, but they seem actively to enjoy this. The atmosphere of human contacts in which they live is certainly a warm and affectionate one. Not only the baby's own mother, but many other women and children, will pick it up, fondle it, kiss it on the lips, coo at it, dangle it rhythmically while singing to it, and so forth. Most babies enjoy the contacts with many people which occur at any casual gathering; some, however, tend to retreat into mother's arms. This the Chiga deem an unfortunate sulkiness, a sign of an unpleasant bad-tempered disposition.

Although babies are nursed for a long time, supplementary feeding is begun quite early. Liquids like thin gruel are smeared into the baby's mouth from the mother's hands. Solids are carefully chewed by the mother and then fed to the baby directly from her lips. However, cow's milk is not used, and these other foods are not considered a substitute for breast-feeding. A mother whose milk fails, or a father left a widower, must make arrangements for a foster mother for the baby; otherwise it is extremely unlikely that the child will live (cf. p. 72).

Unlike many other East African peoples, the Chiga have no ban on intercourse during lactation. A child is given the breast until another child is on the way. Only then is a determined effort made to wean it. Bitter substances are spread on the breast to discourage the child from sucking, but difficult feeding problems do arise. One youngster of my acquaintance, a boy of about three, was sent to stay at his grandmother's 'till he forgets', for his mother, newly pregnant, complained that he hurt her breasts. But when there is no other child on the way, there seems to be no more anxiety on the mother's part than on the child's to break the bond, and no social pressures operate to discourage it until the child is four or five, when people may begin to tease it a bit. A child of three or four may still return to the breast at bedtime, lying beside his mother in the bed, or held in her lap until he falls asleep.

As soon as the baby is able to sit by itself it is left alone on the ground. No special point is ever made about not eating things picked up from the ground, with the exception of human or dog excrement. Nor is any special effort exerted in training the child itself in excretory habits. It is not forced in any way until it is old enough to understand. A baby may be lifted up and held off when it urinates or defecates, but there is no accompanying tension or emotional excitement; younger children's lapses—defecating in the path or the house, for example—are simply considered embarrassing as an evidence of bad manners. In general, there is little discipline of any sort to make young children conform to uncongenial patterns. Babies are fed when they are hungry, soil whatever they happen to without reproach, stuff anything tempting into their mouths, joggle happily on their mother's back, are kissed and fondled, seldom frowned upon or scolded and, so far as I observed, never punished.

No special interest is manifested in the baby's crawling, but its first efforts to stand and to walk are encouraged and assisted. A devoted mother will spend as much time as she can spare with her child at this time. She will sit on the ground with her arms open for the baby to tumble into after a few steps. It is also joggled up and down on its mother's knees, and stimulated through play to make independent efforts at rhythmic activity. Since it also gets early training in Chiga rhythms through being tied to its mother's back while she dances, many a baby begins to dance as soon as it is able to get about alone, and while its walking is still a little uncertain. Young children early become agile and surefooted, able to undertake the long daily walks over precipitous paths which work in the fields will soon make necessary. Young children even go considerable distances from home alone, sure of a lift on friendly adult shoulders should they grow tired.

Many of the children learn to talk rather late, or at least do not use speech much. The babies seemed to me rather silent and not given to making many random speech sounds. When they do start to talk, there is eager interpretation of their efforts, and they very quickly graduate to sentences. Children often handle most categories except those of tense rather well by the age of three. No baby talk is ever used to them, and the only baby pronunciation which is allowed to persist is in proper names. Humming starts early. By the age of three both boys and girls are fond of casting all sorts of phrases into the musical pattern of the men's joy songs, a rhythmic and rapid recitative.

As the child passes from the status of baby to that of toddler, it continues to live in an indulgent and protective atmosphere. It may go along with its mother to the fields, where it can play and tumble about, or stay at home in the charge of a grandparent or loafing father. It is only when the child reaches the age of five or six that it is likely to be left in the care of older children and to be exposed to their petty tyrannies. As a 'follower of the herd-boys' the child—at least the little boy—gets much less attention and indulgence. The older boys avoid the younger ones as much as possible and subject them to a considerable amount of ragging into the bargain. They may complain about this, but adults seldom intervene. The lot of the little girl is somewhat different for her time is more likely to be spent closer to her mother. But she too may be bossed about by senior siblings or children of her own age but senior in status.

I saw at least one example of clearly marked jealousy arising out of this situation; this was a boy of about six years old and next to the last in a large family. He was an unprepossessing child, given to sniffling, and bearing the marks of rather bad burn scars on his face; he had reached the awkward age when adult pampering had ceased and the independence of the herd-boy not been achieved. His younger brother, already nearly four years old, was still nursed by the mother and generally pampered by the family. The parents frequently commented on the older boy's difficult behaviour. They saw him as sneaky and rather malicious, but paid little attention to him except when his 'constant mischief' happened to end in behaviour that was annoying to someone, as, for example, when he lost or destroyed his little skin cloak. Then he was cuffed. But I never heard anyone comment on the obvious jealousy underlying his conduct, even when it took the extreme form of beating, and really attempting seriously to injure, his little brother. It is not possible for me to say whether such situations are typical; if they are, they may be very important as supporting factors in the typical break-up of fraternal households.

When the children are free they are not ordinarily underfoot. The play groups I saw were small and of very miscellaneous ages. Large groups come together mostly at some adult function, where they usually either sit about watching, or dance and otherwise imitate the adults. If they do try to take a few dance steps in the group, they will be admired for their showing-off, or told in an amused and tolerant way to 'stop spoiling the rhythm'.

A great deal of the children's play is imitative. Little girls strap bundles of leaves on their backs as babies, boys build little houses. Their imitativeness is sometimes very ingenious. One bright lad was a great hit when he made spectacles like my sunglasses of papyrus pith and reed. There are some semi-formal competitive games, such as racing and dart throwing. Formal games are lacking. I noticed that on many occasions a group of children playing together were really each engaged in quite separate activities. A few toys are made for the children by their parents —little bows, and various objects made of reeds. The children do a great deal of rhythmic marching about and sing improvised songs, while older children sing the standard songs. A girl of not more than ten was very good indeed at these. They also try, or pretend, to help the adults and slowly acquire proficiency in the basic techniques. A little girl accompanying her mother to the fields practises swinging a hoe and learns to pull weeds or pick greens while playing about. She learns the work rhythms, the cycle of the seasons, which crops must be planted in 'hard' fields, and how to tell whether a field is 'soft' and useful for certain crops, or ready to lie fallow. A boy tagging after his father watches him milk the cows or thatch the house, whittle a hoe handle or roast a bit of meat on a stick. Playing with a small gourd, a child learns to balance it on his head, and is applauded when he goes to the watering-place with the other children and brings it back with a little water in it. As he learns, he carries an increasing load, and gradually the play activity turns into a general contribution to the household water supply.

By the time children are six or so they are helping with many chores, and at eight or ten can do a number of tasks without supervision. A girl of that age may spend a long day working in the fields and come home to tend the fire and even to cook a simple meal, such as boiled corn or potatoes. She can carry her baby sister securely on her hip, and fetch firewood from a considerable distance without adult direction. A boy her age would be able to wind a carrying pad, tie sticks more or less securely in the various ways in which they are used for building, make bird-traps, and take care of a few sheep or goats. On the whole, the boys spend more time in groups and playing about than the girls do. The boys' most important task—herding—is a group activity, and allows plenty of time to whistle and play pranks, to sit and whittle, or even to take a nap. The herd-boy is learning the man's approach to work, relaxed and leisurely and broken by jokes or a song. His sister, approaching puberty, is more likely to have a single bosom friend. They share secrets and giggle together, spending as much time together as possible, much of it at work. But their work is neither relaxed nor joint work; the best they can do is plant neighbouring corners of their respective families' lands.

This assumption of work and responsibility comes about gradually, and largely on the child's own initiative. A child of six or seven who is reluctant to work will be prodded and teased, but not forced, to work. However, a boy of seven can scarcely find satisfaction very long in playing about with the children who are at home; as he joins the older boys, he will naturally undertake more and more of what they are doing. Any assumption of adult ways and attempts at adult skills or responsibilities is praised and applauded. As a result, most steps—like a girl's deciding to don clothes instead of going about with just a little cloak, or giving up goat-meat, or trying to cultivate a small plot by herself—take place long before the time when anyone would insist upon them or take them for granted. This respect for the individual and his right to make work choices underlies Chiga treatment of young children throughout. Even at adolescence, when obedience in other respects may be rigidly demanded, youngsters are allowed a good deal of initiative and responsibility about how they will use their time.

The same assumption that responsibility rests with the child underlies most of their educational practice, whether of habits, character or skills. The child wants to learn and sets about doing so. And he must manage to learn by example, not explanation. There is little supervised training and less lecturing. There is amazingly little verbalization in the whole learning process. Children seem never to ask the 'why' questions which are so much a feature of learning in our culture. They will pick up and examine an object new to them, and are always anxious to know its name and functions. But they are completely uninterested in the question of how it came to be. This is rather a striking feature of the adult psychology as well. As we have noted, there do not seem to be any myths or origin legends, and Chiga are not at all given to speculative elaboration of their own beliefs and practices. The very term 'why', in so far as it can be found at all in the language, refers really to end rather than origin, and means literally 'for the sake of what'. And adults, teaching a child, simply correct specific errors as they occur—by demonstration—instead of talking about the process, or trying to analyse in any way what they are doing or what the error was.

A girl will, for example, take up the art of weaving baskets when and as it pleases her to do so. Her mother or sister will take her early efforts in hand to correct her mistakes, but not to analyse them. They never say, 'Make it tighter' or 'Set the awl in higher.' At the most, they will show her the correct way once more when she asks. They will not slow down the process or guide her hand. Should the beginner find the process discouraging and the trials unsatisfactory, she may abandon the whole effort, to renew it again at some later date, or perhaps to forget it altogether. As a result, many women cannot make pots—or cut skirts, and so on. Even for such everyday household essentials they will have to depend on what they can get by 'begging' or trading.

The resulting range of interest and ability is great even within single families. For example, one girl made some of the best mats and baskets in the village. She even tried to find out what she could about old-style methods of decorating them, and tried to copy the high peaked covers for personal baskets which she saw when she went on a short trip to Ruanda with me. On the other hand, her next younger sister, an energetic and hardworking girl, was clumsy, and totally uninterested in handicrafts. She had tried her hand at a basket once or twice but had laughed along with the rest at her efforts and had long since given them up. She will grow up as a woman of energy and good character, but with no specialized skills. Meanwhile, another, younger sister, about nine years old, had begun a basket which hung prominently on the wall. Her efforts were praised, but she was not especially urged to work at it. It was she, rather than her older sisters, who was most interested in learning to make pots, a skill of which their mother was mistress. She and one of her half-sisters used to help at it, especially at kneading the mixture of clay and water with their feet in a great trough, and tending the grass fire. They would grow up potters; their sisters would not.

There is a similar range in men's activities. All boys must eventually learn to prepare building materials and to carry out the basic steps. It is not unusual to see a ramshackle play-hut

put up behind the family compound by a ten-year-old, for practice. But when it comes to more specialized techniques, boys too
vary in their interest, attention and skill, and so in their ultimate mastery. Weaving the crown of a house, or very highly
skilled crafts like iron-working, are all handled the same way, by
apprenticeship, and the boy's own interested attention. A boy
interested in learning to be a smith will start working the bellows,
learning which woods are good for charcoal and so on, when he
is about ten. Such a boy need not be the smith's own son; if he
is not interested, his shirking, while deplored, would be tolerated,
and the help of some other lad would be accepted; he would
move into the smith's house, and remain there, sometimes for
years, slowly 'learning by doing', with a minimum of verbal
training.

Religion was absorbed in the same way, by observation and
practical apprenticeship. In older days, all children saw the offerings made at the ghost huts, and they were present at various
ceremonies to the spirits. If a child did not get in the way, he
was often allowed to be present even at very important ceremonies. The various experiences of his family while he was
growing up taught him the essential practical points. He readily
learned that spirits might safely be neglected in normal times, or
until something went wrong. He knew when diviners had to be
consulted and what sort of formula one uses in any converse
with the spirits. Even young men today had as children been
witnesses of all these activities and of the great festivals for the
priests, for very young children could be underfoot almost anywhere and older ones, if not allowed in sacred places, were not
above peeking. Tabus and similar regulations were learned only
through such observation and some early correction if the child's
own behaviour was involved.

There were no really complicated rituals or theological formu-
laries to learn. All special techniques in religion, like divining
and healing, which required some special knowledge, were learnt
by apprenticeship; young boys in training might go along to
'hold the sack' while herbs were gathered, and so on. For some
of these religious specialties a form of initiation was required,
but this was ceremonial not instruction. The actual knowledge
had to be acquired through experience and observation.

It is easy to see how this educational pattern has furthered the religious disintegration. Children are subjected to direct Christian training, but can learn little of the older ways. Their fathers, even those who want to, have little experience in describing or explaining their practices, and they dare not let the children take part in any ceremonies they may risk performing in secret, for children may be informers.

Basic aspects of social organization and the way it functions are acquired readily enough by everyone through ordinary daily experience. A child learns who his relatives are, and which among them one may greet, or which one must wait to be greeted by, and so forth. But the extent of the knowledge of kinship principles and genealogies varies greatly among different adolescents and even young men. One youth may be able to present relationship terms, genealogies, and obligations quite systematically, while another will know very little of all this. It will depend upon the keenness with which adult discussions as to relationship, relative age, and so forth have been followed. None of this is taught by way of formal instruction.

The same basic attitude underlies Chiga treatment of all problems of character training. Personality differences are recognized as definitely established very early in the child's life. By the time he is a few months old a child is regarded as an individual with his own disposition, likes, dislikes, and temperamental quirks. The preferences of a three-year-old will be carefully consulted whenever possible, and his behaviour habits accepted as more or less fixed and just about as unmodifiable as those of an adult. There is no essential difference between child and adult, except that a child does not 'know sense' in most matters, so that it cannot be held responsible until it grows to fuller knowledge. Character is assumed to be fixed early. One child is 'probably taking after her bad-tempered father' (from whom her mother is divorced) because she turns away from people who approach her, runs to her mother, and scowls. She is just a little over a year old. Another little boy is 'sneaky. He'll be a thief' because he does not eagerly share his food with other children.

Since variations in behaviour are accepted as expressions of more or less inherent personality differences, there is no serious effort at correction. Children are scolded, but without much hope of effecting a real change. There is not much point in holding up a good child as a model; he is simply more fortunate in his traits. Lectures about behaviour are rare; they deal mostly with specific points of conduct, such as bringing a light for a visitor, and very few tales with morals could be recalled by my best young informants. And punishment is not used systematically as a disciplinary technique. When it occurs it is vindictive rather than aimed at correction. I have seen a father throw a handful of stones at a two-year-old child who was ordinarily a great favourite of his. On this particular occasion, however, he had a headache, and her singing, which he usually fatuously admired, annoyed him. On another occasion I saw three grown men pursuing an eight-year-old girl determined to beat her; they were furious at her for breaking the pot in which they had been making beer.

While general reform is not very seriously expected, attempts are sometimes made through threats or scolding to deter a child from the performance of some particular act of mischief. A mother may promise to tell father to administer a beating; and I have heard a co-wife used as a kind of bogey-man. It was particularly interesting in the case in question, since the woman whom the mother threatened to call was certainly a much gentler person and had had only the friendliest of relations with the youngster in question. None the less, the threat reduced a two-year-old to tears. Other bogeys are invented, too, such as enemy clans coming to harm the child.

The difference in children's reactions to adult scolding or annoyance is very marked—some sulk, some weep, and some retort in kind. The first response is considered 'very bad' even in children—since, like sulky adults, they may be brooding on some serious act of vengeance. The child's expected response is often weighed by the adult. One seven- or eight-year-old was a real problem, given to 'stealing' and to throwing stones at other children and even at adults. His mother claims (with some possible exaggeration) to have tied him up and beaten him with thorny twigs (punishments usually reserved for adolescents or young wives), but to no avail. Now, she says, she 'can't very well beat him severely, for he would run off and sleep in the woods, and that would be dangerous'. Others too have mentioned fear of losing a child's love as a reason for not using punishment. On the other hand, if a child is recognized as 'bad' his own parents may warn people not to have him in their homes.

In line with this acceptance of a child's behaviour as an indication of a general habit which has to be put up with, there is considerable indulgence of the child's whims. Sometimes they really have the upper hand. One child is left at his grandmother's for a protracted visit 'because he won't come home', even though his mother must make frequent trips to see him because he is not completely weaned (it is a journey of about an hour). A mother will go to fetch the water for cooking because her daughter, aged seven, says she is weary. Refusing flatly is one of the first patterns any child learns for handling a situation, *nayanga*, 'I refuse', being a part of his very earliest vocabulary. Gross insolence will often be accepted from very young children. I have heard a father chuckle with delighted amusement when his young daughter, annoyed because he was in the way of her play in the courtyard, called him 'Snot'. And a mother, mildly shamefaced at the grossness of the insult, when her six-year-old son said to her, 'Aha, yes! You always want to go into other people's houses to steal,' apologetically remarked, 'He's always showing off.'

However, not all children take advantage of this indulgence, or go on demanding the centre of the stage for very long. If they do, they are 'spoiled' (precisely our idiom is used); and as they get a little older, it ceases to be amusing. By the time they approach adolescence, the whole picture has changed. Just as they assume responsibilities, so they must assume appropriate social behaviour. Adolescents must be respectful; and they must accept parental control. Girls must clothe themselves, boys must take care of the herds. At this point they will be reminded, nagged at, and if necessary more severely dealt with. However, since habits of obedience have not been especially nurtured, parental control is not always automatically effective. It was sometimes necessary to resort to drastic measures to enforce it. Boys and girls might be beaten, tied to a post in the compound for a whole day, or threatened with curses of a very potent sort, if they rebelled against parental decisions. The threat of such punishment was enough in most cases, and one heard from the more docile adolescent girls such expressions as 'My mother'll kill me if I'm not home soon,' said with precisely the same exaggeration that such an expression would ordinarily imply among us. On the other hand, as we have seen, girls have been disowned by their fathers or put to death for sexual offences before marriage.

This method of character training, corresponding as it does to the general 'just let them absorb it as they go' educational methods, is not, of course, absolutely negative or neutral. The child, with a minimum of lecturing and specific instructions, learns the rights and wrongs, virtues and vices considered appropriate in Chiga life just as he learns what to plant and how to plant it, how to build a house or dance in the proper rhythm. If there is little direct moral adjuration to the young, there is plenty of name-calling, good and bad, and plenty of gossip for them to hear, with very clear implications of praise and blame. Besides, as in other phases of the learning process, specific errors will be commented on, derided, or corrected. And in addition, impressive in their total weight are the ethical or characterological implications of the social institutions themselves, in which the children as they grow older increasingly participate.

Every girl, for example, has before her the example of the good woman: quiet and modest, yet self-reliant; fulfilling her social role with dignity, though always in formal subordination to her husband. Woman's subordinate role is sharply institutionalized; any young girl knows that a woman may not own property or be a diviner or take part in marriage negotiations. She has seen how her mother defers to her father's wishes, and has heard the neighbours tease a young bride who forgot to call her husband 'master' and used his name instead. But she has also seen enough to understand that this subordination has a formal character; it does not make a woman a drudge or a chattel.

She has learnt a good deal more about her own future role. She knows that women who are respectful to their husbands may none the less have considerable influence over them and enjoy a measure of real independence, while those who are rude or inconsiderate are threatened with divorce or beatings and are generally spoken ill of. She has seen the tact with which good women handle their relations with their co-wives, and knows how quickly accusations of sorcery fly if they do not. She has heard women who shout and scold called 'bringers of shame' and she has been embarrassed by such shocking gossip as the story of so-and-so's wife, who is suspected of having smeared faeces in her co-wife's house in order to discredit her with their husband

—possibly an object-lesson in wickedness, as well as a warning against it.

Another thing she has learnt early and well is that women work hard and have a kind of puritan attitude toward work. This is realistically grounded in Chiga economy, which assigns to women the essential productive tasks and leaves them largely masters of their working time. That this attitude is inculcated early in life was brought home to me very strongly at the first wedding I attended, when several of the girls, after dancing most of the night, went off in the early morning, while everyone else was sleeping, to put in a few extra hours' work in the fields before the afternoon festivities began.

The term *omufu*—lazy—is an opprobrious epithet which applies only to women. It implies laziness but it also means shiftlessness and general lack of intelligence. A woman who is *omufu*, who shirks work to the extreme point of neglecting to provide adequate food, is likely to resort to thievery into the bargain. Such complete failure to live up to minimal obligations would be adequate grounds for divorce or the payment of a fine or bribe by her family; and such litigations are the subject of wide discussion by those concerned and unconcerned, so they provide an excellent object-lesson on the dangers of slackness. Of course, if all this is not enough to develop good working habits by adolescence, there will be beatings and penalties, if necessary, as we have seen, for a girl's reputation for industry is an important talking point in marriage negotiations.

There is another term for laziness which is wider in its implications: while *omufu* implies low intelligence, *omurofwa*, also applicable to a lazy person, means filthy as well. Perhaps the connexion lies in the energy required to be clean. Neglect of the hair is laziness rather than dirtiness when the approved hair style permits it to go unwashed for weeks at a time, and hair-dressing requires hours of patient work. Since washing is closely associated with oiling the body with butter, the lazy person may well be the one who finds herself without the butter, or does not trouble to apply it. Certainly laziness and filth went together in one woman whose husband tried to divorce her for being an *omurofwa*. Not only did she neglect work for gossip and was frequently to be seen with mud-caked feet, but she was accused of being so lazy that she would not leave the house to defecate—which is,

even by Chiga standards, an inexcusable extreme. However, some
of the emphasis on washing may be a reflection of modern mission
teaching. A distinction was drawn in the case of another woman
who was conspicuously unwashed but not otherwise lazy. She
would clear the house or court of dung with her hands—everyone did that, though usually youngsters had the task as an assigned
chore—but would then proceed directly to the rest of her work.
Her house, too, was certainly swept less often than it might have
been, and I have seen sheep's dung there in the afternoon.
However, she was known as an energetic and hard-working
woman; and it was only members of the younger mission-
influenced generation who referred to her as *omurofwa*.

Related to this is the conspicuous playing-down of any interest
in personal appearance. A dance does not produce a gala dressed-
up throng. Apart from fringe and metal adornment on skirts,
which some girls wear all the time and which is partly a function
of wealth, there is really no holiday costume, no special woven
or feathered or beaded or ornamented dress to wear for special
occasions. Head-dresses of flowers were used in certain religious
rites in the old days, but since the rites have died out the head-
dresses have disappeared too.

This lack of interest is reinforced by the critical comments of
contemporaries. When one girl put on her 'over-the-ropes skirt'
(that is, one ordinarily kept hanging up, not worn every day)
and all her necklaces for a wedding, it provoked the malicious
comment of other girls that she was seeking to attract undue
masculine attention. This was coupled with comments that the
skirt was clumsily cut, and the necklaces not very effective since
she had not washed and oiled herself! The critical girls had
similar finery but had not donned it. Distant visits were the
only regular dress-up occasions I observed. Even an extremely
clean and tidy girl, who washed more than most and was rather
proud of her arms, which she oiled and even set off with braided
grass bracelets, seldom bothered to wear her necklaces or her
decorated cape, as this would have provoked comment.

Modesty is one point about which women are very self-
conscious and in which little girls are actually drilled. They will
be reminded, rather sharply, to tuck their legs under when they
sit down—long before they wear any skirts to pull down over
them. Maidenly modesty is important, and I have heard it

particularly pointed out that a mother of growing girls must be circumspect in her own sexual behaviour, for does she not need to set them a good example? A mother will also scold her daughter for other kinds of unmaidenly or unwomanly behaviour. Tomboy pranks, for example, which girls may indulge in when alone, are derided by adults who observe them; such behaviour is unseemly and incongruous in a woman, for it is men's behaviour; indeed, it is a usurping of male position that is actually very dangerous (see p. 166 above). A Chiga girl must not whistle, or eat goat's meat; she must dance like a girl, beating the rhythm on her skirt, while her brother leaps with the men; and while he is learning to show off and boast, she may practise the ceremonial ululation appropriate to women and girls, the piercing, long-drawn out *ayi* . . . that celebrates any triumph, their own, or their families'.

Shame, modesty, the strict disapproval of any association with strange boys, all combine to produce real shyness in many adolescent girls. They hang back, refrain from talking in company, and may even cover their faces or mouths with their hands, look down and giggle with embarrassment, if any attention is paid to them. Even a girl in Bufuka who had eloped twice, so that her own father had given up any hope of decent, respectable marital behaviour from her, was 'eaten with shame' at the idea of coming with me to a dance in another village. More acutely shameful situations—being caught with menstrual blood on one's leg or accused of being alone with a boy—would provoke a flood of tears in a sensitive girl.

On the other hand, it is worth noting that excretory functions ordinarily provoke no embarrassment. A most proper young lady would not hesitate to tell everyone that she was going off to the bushes because she had taken a laxative medicine, and the most lady-like of my women friends would step casually off the path to urinate.

Boys are less given to shame over such matters than girls. Men will even urinate in the house when they have been drinking. This is unseemly but not particularly shameful. People are likely to laugh about it and comment on his drunkenness. It only becomes shameful in some respect-demanding situation, as when there is a mother-in-law present or when it is the house of a respected priest. The Chiga do show a strong disgust for the actual products of excretion—dog as well as human, though not for those of sheep or cattle—but for the process itself there is no shame.

A boy gets a very different picture from the girl's of the role he is to play and of the ideal ways of playing it. Men, of course, are the masters, the brave hunters and fighters. A boy easily learns his right to be boss and whom he may boss. And he learns early, too, that a man is admired for being brave. He has heard of the brave stand of the Chiga against Ruanda, and the way they have been pressing the people of Mpororo back from the fertile pasture-lands to the north. And he has heard the proud boasts of all the killings in inter-clan vengeance fighting. He may even have come along on a raid, when he was old enough not to get in the way, and seen the fighting at first-hand. In any case, he knows what bravery means. He knows it may include a surprise attack by a whole group upon a lone traveller, an ambuscade, and even such trickery as the sudden stabbing of a man come as guest to a feast, so long as it is cast in the pattern of the vengeance feud. He knows that running away to safety is conceded to be the better part of valour in any tight pinch, and no occasion for shame. In fact, 'he who runs fast' may even be a name to be proud of. Making a valiant stand against odds has point only in so far as it is successful, and not at all as a last fine honourable gesture. Was not a major stratagem in fighting against the fierce raids of the Pygmies a mass running-away, moving on to islands or hiding dwelling-places securely in the swamps, and then just letting the raiders pass on?

And he learns early, too, that he need have no false modesty about his achievements. The formal *evuga*, the recitative patter which accompanies the challenge of the spear dance, is ejaculated at every sneeze, and expresses any general feeling of well-being, is an account of a man's own achievements and those of his ancestors, mostly in battle, and grossly exaggerated. 'We went to a village of the Abakongwe, and we killed four thousand, two hundred and seventy-three people; and we drove away five thousand a hundred and ten cows.'

The nicknames, too, which men give themselves and each other, are praise-names of a glorious sort: 'He wounds people' and 'He puts the enemy to flight'; 'He who burns enemy houses' or 'The one known and feared'. Nor do they only celebrate bravery: 'He who jumps over fences', for example, commemorates a proud occasion when a young man narrowly escaped the spears of the irate brothers of a maiden he was trying to seduce.

These names need not relate too closely to actual happenings or traits. One man was nicknamed 'the tall one', and I remarked that he was not, as a matter of fact, particularly tall. 'Oh, that's nothing,' I was told, with evident surprise at my *naiveté*. 'Surely it's all right for his friends to flatter him.'

Something very closely akin to boasting is seen in the less standardized but fairly common 'showing off'. While this is considered a trifle undignified and unbecoming in a mature person, it is not seriously frowned upon. The term *moga*, which means to show off, implies playfulness and amusement rather than derogation. In one field of activity, dancing, it is considered entirely acceptable to try to take the centre of the stage and call attention to the excellence of one's own performance.

Another form in which the typical male assurance is expressed is in betting. Anything may be seized upon as the excuse for a wager; the stake never seems as important as the glory of winning. How many steps had been cut in my path to the lake, when should we arrive at a particular place, and innumerable equally inconsequential points were heatedly argued. The betting came as a climax to such debate; the wager, when at all considerable, was placed in neutral hands to ensure payment. The essential point was not so much competitive achievement as personal satisfaction and vindication. While the defeated person might be taunted for his misplaced assurance, I never noticed anyone seriously shaken in his own self-confidence. I have heard girls join in such betting and boasting, but it would be highly unsuitable for a grown woman. Small boys are an eager audience, and often make their own small bets alongside the grown-ups.

Chiga boys see this example of masculine pride and bravery about them. They know that it is good to be quick to take affront and to revenge an injury; that it is good to rush bravely to the defence of your honour or lands or possessions, and those of your relatives. But they also learn that it is not good to be merely quarrelsome, or to fight with your own kinsmen. It is not good —but it is also very usual and very hard to avoid.

For example, men all drink whenever they can. It is good to drink, as it is to feast and fill one's belly. But drinking often leads to serious fights. For when a man drinks and feels good he starts to boast; and very soon his boasting changes from a formal rhythmic chant, which can be admired by his hearers as an artistic endeavour, to an argumentative kind of ranting which may lead to entanglements and serious quarrels. If possible, drunks are put out alone to sleep it off at this point, but the noisy and bumptious cannot always be stilled, and stabbings occur, even between brothers. Boys are underfoot and in and out at drinking parties. They know that such fights happen, that drunkenness is common, and that the effects are usually over-looked if no one is actually killed. Sometimes a father may seize the occasion to warn his sons of the effects of excessive drunken-ness, but it is not likely that such warnings will be very effective. For the boys know also that such behaviour is accepted as all too common. Indeed, it is the exception that is worthy of com-ment. One man, for example, is proud of the fact that he has always come home from beer-parties the same night and slept off the effects without getting into any fights or other trouble. *Mutayomba* they call him—'He who never shouts'. But no one would consider his good behaviour typical.

The Chiga are truly concerned with this problem of fighting. There is a whole range of terms dealing with the various shades of anger and their consequences. Ordinary anger (*echiniga*) is a reaction to which anyone can give way—indeed should, under due provocation. But the good man's anger will be moderate; he will try to settle things by arbitration or leave the way open for reconciliation. Violent bad temper (*omujinya*) is different. It is likely to be generalized and to lead to unprovoked acts of vio-lence. One of my neighbours was known as 'a man of bad temper' and of 'bad ways'. His glowering looks and sour humour, which were fairly constantly apparent, were accompanied by a history of numerous acts of disapproved behaviour which went unchallenged because his neighbours and kinsmen were afraid of his violent retaliation.

Outbursts of violence that are postponed are even more dan-gerous, whether they be postponed through guile—as a way of achieving a difficult vengeance point more effectively—or as part of a habit of brooding. Many Chiga are prone to sulk (*chungura*) when they will retreat, behave unco-operatively, even stop talk-ing. Such a mood is considered potentially far more dangerous than a forthright and immediate expression of anger. In the latter case, they will say, you get it all out of you; but when you brood there is likely to remain 'a little thunder brewing in the heart (*akahinda*)'. This may burst forth with greater vehemence or, what is worse, finally express itself in some act of devious malice like arson or witchcraft.

We have noted elsewhere some of the other traits that boys and girls alike learn to label good and bad. To be generous, for example, is important and meanness is 'to steal'. But even a child of the most respectable and indeed warm-hearted household knows that sharing beer can be avoided by keeping the pot in the back room, and that when supplies are short this may be necessary. To tell lies or gossip, or inform on anyone (*beiha*) is a bad trait. But almost everyone does it—or at least is constantly accused of it. And in any case, are not ties of kinship and friendship stronger than any abstract obligation to be a 'man of good customs'?

All through such learning, then, runs a kind of thread of balanced opposition, of goodness as an ideal that is surely not required and really hardly expected, of most kinds of wrong as all too common. Anyone may succumb to them. And there is not much point in ascribing any particular moral blame to one who does. For while bad traits and bad behaviour are unfortunate, even deplorable, they are in a way afflictions rather than wilful evil. There is no sharp distinction between character and ability; poor intelligence, misfortune, and bad temper may be the results of bad luck or witchcraft or just the way you happen to be. And what can anyone do about it—except, of course, be on guard?

This thread of wariness and suspicion underlies interpersonal relations and is quite explicit. It is a matter not of personality—though it would no doubt be profitable to explore the deeper levels on which this operates—but of a specific, overt concept of human nature, which includes the expectation of selfish, treacherous, and spiteful behaviour from almost anyone. Children do not need to develop suspicion as a character reaction. They are taught by all they see and hear that mistrust is the wisest course —not only towards strangers, all of whom must be regarded as potential enemies under the vengeance-feud pattern, but towards relatives as well. 'A person one can trust' is primarily someone

from whom you can expect a kindly interpretation of your own
behaviour, no malice, and some generosity. It is true that most
brothers are friends in these terms. But not all are, so that, as
we have seen, the pact-brotherhood, with its well-nigh inviolable
oaths, is a safer basis for trust than is close kinship. And apparent
friendliness is no basis at all. For, as the Chiga see it, one never
really knows other people. Your own brother may be plotting
against you even while he greets you amicably. As one man put
it to me, 'One may outwardly be on very good terms with a
person whom one really hates and wishes to kill.' Indeed, such
behaviour was a more or less regular feature of vengeance-killing
strategy. One of my friends expressed it, 'A man may come and
drink beer with you. Then as soon as you are thoroughly drunk,
he may stab you.' And apart from calculated duplicity, there are
sudden anger and changes in mood. 'A man will look at you
favourably one day and come to stab you the next'; and 'A person
may be suddenly angered by some slight and kill another, but
be very penitent about it the next day.' Their attitude of uncer-
tainty about other people's true reactions is perhaps best summed
up in a characteristic expression, often heard: 'How can I tell
what he will do? Do I sit at my brother's heart?'

In some individuals the realization that trust should be extended only with caution and rarely expected in return is accompanied by a general hypersensitivity and cautiousness which is
almost anxiety. My closest Chiga friend would counsel secrecy for
all sorts of Machiavellian reasons. She suspected practically everyone of lying, cheating, and stealing; people who visited me were
motivated by greed; and presents had best be hoarded, lest they
be stolen or begged away. And her attitude, while possibly a
little extreme, was quite consonant with general Chiga attitudes.
Anyone unfamiliar with currency always assumed that an offer
to pay him in half-shilling rather than shilling pieces was an
attempt to cheat him of his just wages. Trading was conducted
in an atmosphere of mutual distrust. To *zimba*, cheat in trade,
asking excessive prices and so forth, is particularly characteristic
of the Ganda, according to Chiga allegations, and the word
itself comes from that language; but many of the Chiga are
known to be capable of it. Blacksmiths, of course, are cheats,
who traditionally fail to live up to their agreements. And stick-
ing to the shrewdly constructed letter of a contract is at once

legitimate and sharp practice. 'He who summons himself can pay himself', they say, by way of warning.

Curiously enough, in some individuals this mistrust breaks down at precisely the point where realistic evaluation would seem most to justify and demand it. They are readily taken in by strangers, particularly the more trading-wise Nyaruanda and Ganda. One of my porters, for example, once gave a total stranger his sheep to take to market for him, and was amazed when he never showed up with the proceeds. This man is a little simple and this is an extreme case, but making loans that are difficult to collect to people whom one has no reason to trust, going with partners on a trip and being cheated by them, are incidents that commonly occur.

This attitude of suspicious mistrust, as we have already noted, pervades not only human relations, but attitudes towards the supernatural as well. The outer cosmos and the spirits themselves fit into the same framework of hostility and hypocrisy. All spirits, including those of recently deceased relatives, are chiefly important to man as potential sources of disease and destruction. Most religious rites are directed not towards securing the positive help of the spirits but towards getting them to cease inflicting some evil or to call off one which is threatened. Even when the sacrifices called for are made, one cannot count absolutely on their having the desired effect. One cannot build up certainty towards the future any more than one can towards people. Even charms are a gesture in the direction of protection rather than a completely reliable defence.

As we have already noted, luck plays an important role in this world-view. Spirits sit on anyone's head, and a man becomes great or remains unimportant exactly as his spirit familiars, interpreted through diviners, will. The man whose flocks and herds and wives bear plentifully and with a good balance of females, has a 'lucky court' (cf. Ch. 5, p. 108). Others are just unfortunate. Whatever they turn to somehow comes out wrong. It is their canoe which overturns; it is their sheep which wander away and are eaten by a leopard; and when Kagaga, who rates as an unfortunate by the above type of occurrence, despite his wealth and position as a sub-chief, married his young brother to a satisfactory wife, it surprised nobody when, in keeping with his luck, the marriage broke up within a few months. This too was what would naturally happen to an unlucky person. And there is no telling whence good or bad luck comes, nor how long it will last. The source of such mishaps is not something specific which can be discovered or prevented. While some evils do come as a result of breaking tabus, they also come from witchcraft— the work of an enemy or merely a randomly malicious person— or from the unprovoked evil exertions of spirits. And good luck, too, is causeless and is not a reward for good behaviour or the fulfilment of obligations.

This is the world-view the young man grows up with. He learns to accept afflictions as they come, to prevent them when possible, and to take what satisfaction he can in the immediate goods of daily living—lying in the sun, drinking beer, and the occasional excitement of a fight or a sex adventure.

This world-view and the attitudes it involves are explicit Chiga ones. The analysis given here is a cultural not a psychological study. It would be interesting to explore Chiga attitudes and feelings further, from a more psychological perspective. What is the meaning of their moodiness, their sudden swings from laughter to anger? How sensitive are their sorrow and their sympathy? How are the likenesses and differences among them related to their child-rearing practices—overt and covert—and to later variations in individual experience? What, in particular, sustains the individual Chiga, living in a world so full of expressed dangers and hostile forces? Is his apparent strength related to the warmth and permissiveness in early childhood, which are often declared to set the scene for a secure ego? How are the nonconformity, the low level of guilt feelings, and the independence of his fellow's opinion of him, which appear such striking characteristics of the Chiga, as well as the suspicion, mistrust, and individual self-reliance, tied together psychologically? And how are they related to the erratic imposition of disciplines in early childhood? These are fascinating questions suggested by this material. But this study was carried out before techniques for the depth study of personality had become familiar research tools. The exploration of such aspects of education, of personality and culture and their interrelations, must, therefore, be left to later field research.

9

FOOD AND ITS ACQUISITION

CERTAIN general characteristics of Chiga material culture have been introduced in preceding pages. The Chiga live in bee-hive shaped grass-thatched huts, grouped in small fenced compounds which form independent and sometimes geographically isolated units. Their villages are rambling affairs with fields stretching out and up the surrounding hillsides for a considerable distance. They keep cattle, but depend for food mostly on their crops. They make and use metal tools and weapons. Baskets and mats, almost entirely unornamented, plain soot-blackened pots, and a few wooden stools and bowls make up their entire household furnishings. For clothing they wear the hides of animals, scarcely treated, and with the fur retained—the garment of the south, not the bark cloth of their northeastern neighbors.

One is immediately impressed with the great inferiority of Chiga craftsmanship compared to that of their neighbors. Actually, the Chiga understand and use the techniques essential to virtually all the crafts that are common in this region, but their finished products are rougher, cruder, and much less decorated. This is as true of houses and furniture as it is of baskets and ornaments. Today art, even in the form of ornamental scars and elaborate coiffures, is going out of fashion.

Economically the Chiga are entirely self-sufficient. They make virtually all the things that they use, depending upon trade with their neighbors for only a few items, which are luxuries rather than necessities, and for all of which there are native substitutes. Chief among these imported luxuries are pipes made by the pygmies. They also prefer pygmy braided belts and bamboo carrying trays. Today they also use salt, tobacco, cloth, and soap bought in the Indian shops.

Chiga economy makes careful use of the available resources. Both firewood and building wood are scarce, and obtaining them takes time and trouble. Therefore, only canoes, large troughs used for watering cows or brewing, and the one or two small stools that most households boast are made of large solid wood. Most Chiga building is wattle and daub, using the much more readily available pliable vines for the horizontal, and slender poles for all the uprights in the walls, so that only the few upright posts inside the house that help support the roof need to be made of heavy wood. Grasses and reeds, together with tree bark and to a leaser extent animal sinews, are very extensively utilized for weaving baskets and mats, tying the structure of houses, carrying pads, and innumerable other purposes. These are cut and prepared as needed. Iron ores and clay deposits are other raw materials whose uses are known and exploited by Chiga craftsmen.

This is a country of little wild vegetation; in most regions forests have long since been denuded, and even the "bush" country runs to small growth, with only an occasional tree. There are neither fruits, berries, nor nuts to be had. Mushrooms and various edible greens are gathered for food; game animals and birds are hunted and trapped; and locusts are toasted when they chance to rain upon the earth. But cultivated plants and domesticated animals are more typical of this region, even though it is too high and too cold for bark cloth, bananas, or sugarcane, nor are peanuts known. The horticultural techniques, based on slash and burn gardening with little rotation, will be discussed in detail below. Animal products are pretty thoroughly used, except for the milk of sheep or goats and the readily available chickens, which are despised. Hides are used for clothing; flesh, blood, organs, and even intestines are eaten. Cow's milk is drunk or churned for butter which is important as an unguent for both skin and clothing. But here, as with the wildlife, the extensive exploitation is not a correlative of ample supplies thus made available, but is rather a function of scarcity. Chiga economy is a meager one, even where there is careful husbanding of resources.

For their food supply Chiga depend principally upon the products of their fields. They grow large and small millet, beans and peas, yams and some corn, as well as increasing quantities of the newly introduced white potatoes. There are also various gourds, whose flesh and seeds are eaten, and peppers. The country is for the most part too cold for plantains, and these are not grown except as an occasional experiment or curiosity. Neither sugarcane, favorite dainty of the Chiga, nor the groundnut, basic staple in

Ruanda, are grown here. Of the various vegetables locally grown by Europeans for their own use, the only ones which have thus far provoked any interest are tomatoes and strawberries, but no general attempt is made to grow these. This may be in part because the only available source for the plants is theft from European gardens. The crops also include tobacco, and gourds to be dried and used for utensils.

From these crops come the main meals of the Chiga. These are simple and not very varied. Plain boiled yams and beans, or perhaps a mixture of corn and beans, or greens and peas, are most usual; thick millet porridge may be eaten with what ethnographers of this region call a "relish"—meat or a little wild vegetable food such as mushrooms or succulent grasses. The leaves of gourds, peas, and beans are also eaten as greens. The only additional course in most meals is a thin gruel of eleusine, or occasionally beer, but beer is usually taken as a meal in itself.

Another important source of food is the cattle and the herds of sheep and goats. In most households, meat is an occasional luxury rather than a staple, but those who can afford it eat meat often. Sheep and goats are butchered on many occasions, much as sacrifices and feasts; they may be killed for meat or for their skins for clothing. Cows are rarely killed, but their meat is used when they die. In addition to meat, the herds supply butter (more often used as an unguent than as a food) and buttermilk. Fresh milk is rarely drunk. Blood, both from slaughtered animals and drawn from living cattle, is also used as food.

Meat is also obtained by hunting. Wild ducks are eaten, though chickens, which are kept for divination, are not. Chickens are considered unfit for food, except for tiny children to whom the chicks killed for divination may be given to be cooked and eaten. Various antelopes are the choicest game. These, like beef, are allowed to be eaten by women, who are forbidden to eat sheep or goat meat.

Eggs are not eaten at all. They are looked upon as a kind of excrement. Some of the young people do eat them today, under European and the Europeanized Baganda influence, but such persons are mocked at for their unclean ways. The Chiga are on the whole very uninterested in and antagonistic to strange foods. They see no prestige point and no advantage in eating white man's food, and have not the Baganda interest in food variety as much. The only strange prepared food that I observed was enjoyed by my villagers was plain sugar, which they found to be a wonderful delicacy. Hard candy they liked, too, considering it much the same as sugar, but chocolate was vigorously spurned even by a child of three. There is a tentative willingness to try bread, since its ingredients are all vegetable and intelligible, and tea is the one gesture chiefs make toward European customs in food, but neither of these is enjoyed. As a matter of fact, so fixed are the food habits that for many who have never had an abundance of cattle, butter was not a luxury to be striven for, but was something which, since it was not eaten habitually, was therefor undesirable—even somewhat nauseating to think of as food.

Salt is much desired. It is used very sparingly in cooking, and not at all in the various dishes made of flour. Plain rock salt is treated as a delicacy to be used rather like a lollipop. Honey is relished when it can be gotten, and is used either by itself or mixed with beer or gruel. Another special treat comes from the lake. Tiny frogs and fishes can be caught, and these are eaten broiled, or more commonly merely smoke dried.

Smoking is general though not universal. Many who do smoke are thorough addicts, even waking up during the night for a draw at their pipes. Pipes are passed around freely; to refuse anyone's demand for a drag at yours would be a serious offense. I never saw it happen even with my houseboy, who was very finicky. Today, even tiny children sometimes smoke.

HORTICULTURE

Chiga territory is very hilly, and the houses lie clumped in the hollows or along the gentler slopes of the hills. The fields lie about these, stretching from close proximity to the houses to a considerable distance at the top of the hills, or in the gullies running down the sides. They may be a half hour's walk or climb from the house or even farther away. From a distance, the fields look like a crazy quilt of irregular rectangular patches. Each cultivatable area is divided up into tiny individual plots marked off from each other by little ditches and by the steps of the slight terracing which their hillside location makes necessary. The country is very extensively under cultivation in many parts, but even where this is so, some of the land usually lies fallow at any given time, and can be used for grazing.

Chiga horticulture follows a well-marked seasonal round. As is usual for East Africa, there is a period of hard work when food tends to be scarce, followed by a harvest period of partial holiday, with food fairly plentiful. This is the time for weddings and beer parties; the weather is dry and hot, and no major work can be done in the fields. In so far as time is counted, it is reckoned by these harvest or dry periods. But it is the coming of the rains in August or early September that marks the beginning of the year. It also marks the beginning of the year's work.

All Chiga crops are seasonal except for potatoes. The provident housewife sees to it that enough of these are planted at odd times to assure adequate food for her family when the regular crops are scarce. Millet, which is the chief crop, is planted in January or February, and the work of preparing the fields for sowing begins much earlier. It will be ready for harvest in July or August. Corn and beans are planted at the beginning of the short rainy season in mid-September; for the most part, fields which have already been farmed over are used. As the beans ripen, corn may be sown among the rows, and an extra crop of peas, which are very quickly ready for harvest, may also be sown. At the same time ground is broken for *buro,* the small millet or eleusine, which is preferred for porridge though not for beer. By the time this is sown, it is November or December, and time to begin the heavy work of millet preparation. A little millet may be sown in fields where early peas have been grown, but most of it is planted in freshly broken ground, which must be dug up and burned over before it is hoed and sown. This is the heaviest part of the gardening, and the one gardening task which is regularly men's work.

The short fall rains are followed by a short dry spell, which gives way to a steady downpour in February or March. This is a low point in the food cycle, though not the lowest. Corn and beans in some quantity, and the chief harvest of peas should be ready in March. The fresh peas as they ripen are likely to be the only food available in many homes at this time. As the heavy rains get under way, the *buro* ripens for harvesting. Second crops of beans are usually planted at this time, and sometimes peas and corn. These should be ready to help in the low ebb before the millet harvest, if all goes well, though weather fluctuations may spoil them.

Below is a chart of the cycle, accurate only as a general pattern:

September–
November:
Light rains. Corn, peas, beans planted. Eleusine ground prepared and sown. Some corn and beans may be available from very early plantings. Otherwise food is remains of previous harvest, and potatoes. Toward end, preparation of millet fields begins.

December–
February:
Should be fairly dry. Crops ripening, but there may be some shortages before they are ready for harvesting. By mid-January, millet is sown. By the end of February, corn is ready, and fresh peas and beans.

March–May:
By early March, peas and beans are dry and ready for harvest and storing. Rains start in March or April. More peas, sometimes more corn or beans, may be planted. Buro should be ready in April.

June–August:
Dry season. Regular millet harvest. Any second crops of corn, beans, etc. also ready. July can be very lean if the crops are late, as earlier stocks are likely to be exhausted. Potatoes may be the only food available, and not everyone has those left.

The weather conditions are actually subject to considerable variation, and this is likely to cause serious trouble. The year I was in Bufuka, the rains were too early and heavy, and then the dry season came on too soon. Sprouted beans died from lack of rain; later other crops were hit by hail, which is very damaging. There was also a short locust swarm which did considerable damage, so that the harvest of grain was a particularly meager one. The planting arrangements are not flexible enough to be shifted to suit variations in actual weather conditions, nor are they even exactly synchronized to the expected seasons. The Chiga calendar is lunar, but it is very vague. Most people would name the month by observing what the season occupation or the state of the crops actually was at the time, and there might be individual differences of a whole month in the reckoning.

The determination of planting times appears to be rather a hit or miss affair, except that the village as a whole is a unit as to schedule. There may be great variation from one village to the next. I noted a difference of a month and a half at one time between the beginning of planting a particular crop in two neighboring hills. When the next village began to plant corn, a number of people in Bufuka remarked that conditions seemed good for it, but nonetheless, they waited for their own neighbors to begin. The explanation they gave of this reluctance to rely on their own judgment was that the risk to any one field from bird marauders would be too great. I think, however, that there is no doubt that the root of the matter lies in the defunct institution of the rainmaker. Proper rites were performed in the old days to bring the right weather at the right time; clearly there was no point in individuals starting separately, nor in being much concerned with the behavior of people on a neighboring hillside, who had their own rainmaker. And these habits have persisted. In any case, when Kamara decided to go against tradition, and start his millet independently, the village laughed at him for a fool, and nodded with great satisfaction when his fields dried up, despite the fact that at the same time other people lost corn, beans, and peas. This was blamed not on the fact that they had started them too late, which by comparison with other villages seems to have been the case, but rather on the excessive dryness of the season.

Chiga horticulture is of a slash and burn pattern, in which fields are cleared and burnt over, used for a few years, and then allowed to grow back. The major tool is the hoe, somewhat like that of the Baganda in shape, but with a long handle, so that work can be done without stooping. This is used for digging up the fields as well as for cultivating and weeding. The large curved men's knife is used for cutting down bush and for harvesting standing grain. Some weeding is done by hand, and the *buro* is gathered by cutting with the small knife. The only other tools and implements needed in gardening are baskets for seed, and large open-work baskets for carrying home the harvest. Materials for threshing and winnowing will be described below.

Work in the fields differs with the various crops. Millet is sometimes planted where peas have been pulled, but the bulk of the millet crop goes into "bush," land which has not been recently used, so that it is heavily overgrown. It is the task of the men to clear this of its overgrowth, cutting and chopping down the brush, and stacking it in long horizontal rolls about three feet apart, which are then burned. Kleusine is also sometimes planted in "new" fields, but more commonly in fields used for a previous crop. Some crops are planted by preference in "soft" fields, that is, fields from which crops have recently been harvested. Others are planted in "hard" land, which has been unused for a season or so but is not yet bush. There are various rotations practiced; a number of crops are planted together, or one is sown in the fields of the other when the latter is being weeded. None of this is a vary accurate or scientific procedure of rotation. The preferred procedure is to allow a field to lie fallow every other year; after millet has been grown in a field for two successive seasons it is considered to be exhausted.

Work is always started at the top of the field—literally, for the country is almost vertical—and the work proceeds slowly downwards to the lower edge. Fields are almost always wider than they are deep. If a field is very large, they sometimes start at the middle, working down, and leaving the top half as a separate field. This is the only customary variation. So standard is the pattern that great surprise was occasioned when on our journeyings my porters came upon some people working their field in vertical rather than horizontal strips. There is no careful marking or measuring. Vertical boundary lines are dug when two people are working adjoining plots at the same time, so that there can be no dispute about the actual produce. The slight terracing which is necessary for most of the fields, because of the steep hillside slopes, marks off horizontal boundaries, which are usually little steps nine inches or so deep. The sizes of individual plots vary, both with available space and the energy of the housewife, and with the types of produce to be grown. Corn is most often grown on a single large field, while other crops are grown on several plots, in the various different fields about the village. Any one hillside will be given over to one or more types of produce, and almost all the villagers will have one or more plots there. For example, on a hilltop just beyond Mutobi there were millet, pea, and bean fields. There were thirteen plots belonging to Kaborama's wives and children, four to Makubiri and his sons, six to their cousins (Basasa and Kanyugunygu), four to Rwebitara and his sister, eleven to other people from Bufuka, four to Toizikoga and her father, eight to Kalira of Mutobi, and five to other from Mutobi.

The actual plots vary greatly in size. Maliamu, for example, had, under cultivation at one time, in plots in these fields and others, roughly an acre and a half of millet. One was a very large field of more than half an acre. The others were small fields about one-third that size. One of the smallest was ordinarily a potato patch. Only one of these millet fields was in Bufuka proper and this was quite a small one. She had also planted a little millet in her corn field, which was a single tract of about three-quarters of an acre. In addition to these gardens, she had several acres of peas, in three large gardens up the hill, and one small one near her home. She had about half as much beans. These measurements were taken after the *buro* harvest, so that there were no fields of that grain under cultivation at the time. There were some gourds and a few experimental peppers, together with a bit of tobacco, growing right off the compound. These measurements are all very roughly approximate; they were taken by pacing the boundaries of the various plots, and the obvious inadequacy of such a technique was further exaggerated by the irregularity of the ground in most places. Maliamu's fields were larger and more numerous than most, as she and her two daughters were all vigorous workers, and her husband sometimes helped.

For millet and *buro,* the ground is turned and broken rather deeply by Chiga standards—that is, to the depth of about a foot. So far, the British agricultural adviser has made no progress in persuading them that the expenditure of some additional energy in digging a foot or so deeper would yield manifold returns. Initial preparation of the usual millet field represents about a month's work, so that one or two new fields a year is all that most families can arrange for. When the ground has been dug over deeply once, it is reworked lightly, the loose top soil being spread out evenly. The grain is then sown broadcast.

For beans and potatoes the ground is first worked over lightly, only the surface being turned. Then, when grass begins to sprout, it is worked into little hillocks, about a foot high, and several feet apart, arranged neatly in rows. Beans are dropped into little holes in these hillocks, and then covered over. Potatoes are planted by their creepers. These are pulled up root and all from the field were they are growing, and carefully stripped. A tiny rootlet, with only two leaves, is stuck into the top of each hillock.

Maise is planted in separate fields, like millet, or scattered in among the beans at the time of the planting or the weeding of the field. Peas are sown broadcast on ground which has not been previously worked at all, and are then lightly worked into the soil with the hoe. Peppers are planted merely by breaking one over new ground, and leaving the split seeds to take root. Gourds and squashes are usually grown among the beans, but sometimes a tiny separate plot is given over to them.

All the crops but peas require some weeding. For the large millet and most of the others, the hoe is used, to cultivate the soil about the stalks. Weeds are uprooted in the process, and any large clumps are picked up and thrown away. Small millet is delicate, and must be weeded by hand. This is a very tedious task and must be done twice, especially as the weed called empunika is advancing through the country. Ironically, this weed is on of the very few growing things that produces a real blossom.

The process of harvesting and preparing the various foods for storage takes considerable time. Millet is cut down with large curved knives, arranged in rows, and left to dry in the field. It is flailed before storing, and the grain dried on mats. It is then put away in large bins that stand on stilts in the courtyards. Small millet is cut head by head with a small knife, and is sometimes dried and stored in the head, since there is no waste stalk with it. If it is to be stored in the grain, it is thrashed by treading, after preliminary drying, and is then dried again. Corn is cut down with large knives, and dried in the sun, stripped of its husk. It is usually stored in the ear, but sometimes for greater compactness the kernels are separated before storing. This has to be done by hand, the kernels being rubbed off with the fingers, or the friction of another ear. When peas or beans are used green either the pod is plucked or the whole stalk cut. But the bulk of the crop which is to be stored is allowed to ripen much further. Pears are gathered only after the stalk and leaves are yellow-brown and are beginning to dry. They are then pulled up by the roots or out at the base of the stalk, and left on the field in heaps to dry still more. Later these heaps are flailed and then lifted and shaken, so the peas drop down. They are winnowed and dried, and then stored. Husks are sometimes burnt, but most husks, straw, stalks, and any stubble left in the fields are used as fodder for the cows.

Tobacco is known to need particularly rich soil. The Chiga practice no manuring of their fields, though cow dung is plentiful, but they do recognize the extra richness of a deserted house site where such manure has accumulated. This is therefore a preferred place for planting tobacco. They know that tobacco must be carefully weeded, stripped of its top or flowers and some of the leaves. All this represents a good bit of unusual care, as does the gathering. It should be cut, stripped, soaked, and put into a basket covered over with a certain grass (*akabindizi,* which grown over the houses and fences) so that it will "redden." Then it must be "pealed," pounded, and dried in the sun. Rapid hearth drying is said to prevent its being properly "sweet" (a bit of unconscious irony appreciable to anyone who has even so much as smelled native tobacco). Because there is so much painstaking and uncongenial work involved, many people do not bother to grow tobacco, thought they are addicted to its use.

PREPARATION OF FOOD

Obtaining the food supply is only one part of the picture of food getting. There is also the important task of preparing the food for consumption. This entails a great deal of work, all of which falls upon the women.

Cooking is done in pots balanced on an open hearth of three stones. A woman also needs a wooden ladle, a straw whisk, and large calabashes for fetching water and for churning. Every household needs a grindstone, which is one of its most prized possessions. Pots are made in a number of shapes and sizes, but only a few are in regular use for the daily cooking; others are kept stored on a shelf in the roof. There are also baskets and shallow basketry trays, for serving and eating, together with baskets, calabashes and straws for drinking. Meat cookery is a special department, much of it done by broiling. For meat cooking and eating, knives are required.

The simple Chiga main meal is eaten in the evening, sometime between four and eight o'clock, depending upon when the mother gets home from work in the fields. She usually brings a load of firewood with her, and gets to work as soon as she returns, sometimes sending one of the children after the water she will need. This meal will consist of one main course, boiled potatoes, perhaps, or dried corn and beans. If there is meat or a green vegetable, this will be cooked and a large quantity of a kind of doughy porridge will be prepared to go with it. The main course may be washed down or followed by gruel, warm, or preferably cold, and old enough to have begun a mild fermentation.

Any eating at other times during the day is haphazard; there is usually no other cooking. A mother going out to work in the fields will usually see to it that there is a pot of cooked food placed where the children will be able to dip into it. She may even take some food along with her for her noonday rest. The only times a heavy meal is eaten in the fields during the day is when there are hired hoers; their food is part of the expected payment. There may also be extra cooking if an unexpected guest arrives who ought to be honored. If there is no gruel in the house to offer him, some will be prepared at once.

Preparing flour is a particularly time-consuming task. It involves not only the actual grinding of the grain, which is a long, slow task, but also a series of preliminary steps. First the grain must be threshed and winnowed, then separated more thoroughly from the husks by pounding it in a tall wooden mortar with a long wooden pestle. It must then be winnowed again, and thoroughly dried in the sun. Someone must be in attendance to turn it over form time to time, and to keep the birds off.

If the flour is to be used for beer or gruel, the grain is soaked before it is dried for grinding. The soaking causes it to sprout, and thus provides the malt necessary for effective fermentation. The soaking is a complex process. The grain is winnowed carefully, and spread out on a mat. Then ashes are blown over it, and it is tied up in grass or bark, and soaked for a whole day, either in the lake, or in special pits dug to catch rainwater. After that it is kept tied up for four days before it is spread out to dry. Then it must be pounded and winnowed again. Soaked grain may take several days to dry. It must always be taken in at night, and spread out again the next day. Grain drying may be hastened by toasting it at the fire, but this is said to spoil it, and would certainly never be done with sprouted grain.

Ground flour made from eleusine, unsoaked, is one of the chief staples of the Chiga diet. It is used, as bread is with us, chiefly to go with something else. It is used to "cause to eat" not only meat, but also greens, or even just gravies, though the latter are not so varied as among the Baganda.

Kleusine porridge is made by tossing the flour into a large quantity of boiling water. For convenience, a special pot is used which has an open mouth and no neck, and this is set on the fire at such an angle that the lower edge of the large opening is halfway to the ground. The water is tested by sprinkling in a tiny bit of the flour; when this boils up the whole is poured in. It is allowed to boil for a few minutes; most of the water is poured off, and the sticky mass is stirred with a large ladle until it is all brown and pasty. It may then be covered and allowed to soak for a few minutes longer. Finally, it is put into baskets for eating. Sometimes it is used luke-warm, and sometimes kept until the next day. Occasionally, a bit of salt is used in the cooking.

Another important diet item that is made from flour is a kind of watery gruel, which is used as a drink between meals or after a meal. Flour and cold water are put into a pot and cooked, with some stirring, until thoroughly heated. This can be drunk hot, but is preferred after it has stood for a day or two and fermented slightly (it always cools uncovered so as not to become watery). For this drink, malted grain is preferred. Sometimes, as a great treat, it is set to cool in a pot in which there is a little honey.

The most important use for the malted flour is in beer making. Beer making involves a great deal of work. Flour must be ground, and weed and water fetched. Usually large quantities are brewed. The beer cannot be kept in any way, but must be used as soon as it is ready, which is not less than ten days after the first step has been completed.

To make beer, a small quantity of drinkable "gruel" must be prepared first. Water is boiled and poured into a pot; to this the flour is added. Then these are thoroughly mixed, and the color of all the flour darkened, cold water is added to fill the pot and this is set aside. After about a day, this froths up and can be drunk. It is left to ferment for about a week, or even longer. Then it is boiled down to about one-quarter its volume and stored again. It is not drinkable at this stage. After this a small quantity of flour is sprinkled on it, but not stirred. The next day a great deal of flour can be added, being carefully mixed with the whole arm. By night of the next day it froths up, a thick and very intoxicating mess. Now it is ready for the last process. A paste of flour and hot water is made, to which cold water is added. This is just like the very first process, except that a much greater amount of flour is used, so that it is necessary to work the flour well with the hands to break up all the lumps. When this is cool, the strong preparation previously made is added to it and stirred with a ladle. This has-tens the fermentation so that it is ready to drink by the next day. The beer is very thick, and contains quantities of gruel which is fermented but not so intoxicating as the liquid part. Some take only the nearly clear liquid, but the gruel "dregs" are eaten by many. The beer is drunk out of large calabashes, which are passed around, and with straws directly from the pot. The "dregs" are scooped up by hand after the rest has been drained off, either out of the whole pot, or a particular calabash.

Beer made with honey is much stronger and much sweeter than ordinary beer. Making it is now against the law, but occasionally it is drunk surreptitiously. The country is too high and cold for plantains to grow properly, so the "banana beer" of the Baganda, while known, is rarely to be met with. The occasional experimental plantain grower makes his beer using the Baganda recipe, which is a very simple one. The cooked plantains are crushed, and a little flour is added to their juice. This is allowed to stand, and quickly ferments. The beer is ready in about two days, and cannot be kept at all without spoiling.

In preparing vegetable food for eating, there are a number of standard simple cooking procedures. Most common is boiling, and, except when dried foods are being boiled, as little water as possible is used. Foods are sometimes roasted in the coals of the fire, but this is considered more suitable for a snack than for a meal. Some things lend themselves to a kind of dry toasting done on potsherds over the fire. In boiling, the mouth of the pot is covered over with the bark of the wild plantain, or with leaves.

Potatoes and yams are usually not peeled. They are boiled, whole or sometimes cut into pieces, with very little water; or a few may be roasted in the coals. The person eating them pulls the skin off each one as he eats it. Though they may be eaten cold, they are preferred very hot—freshly pulled out of the boiling water. Potatoes and beans are the staples of many families. Sometimes grain is boiled whole instead of being made into porridge.

Fresh peas are usually shelled, though sometimes they are cooked pods and all. Salt should be used—added when they are about done, allowing them to boil up again. The water is then drained off and they are cooled a few moments longer. Greens— pea leaves and pods, and wild greens—may be put in when they are nearly done. Dried peas are boiled for several hours, in a great deal of water. They are troublesome to prepare, because there are usually stones mixed with them, which winnowing cannot get rid of, and these must be sorted out by hand. Sometimes peas are roasted on a potsherd held over the fire. They are stirred with the hand to keep them from burning. They "pop" and may fly off when they are done. For this toasting, the peas must be dry but not too dry. When stored ones are used rather than freshly threshed peas, they must be soaked for a few hours, and then briefly dried in the sun, before they can be toasted. Beans, like peas, are cooked both green and dried, in the former case often in the pods, merely stripped of strings. They are particularly liked boiled with corn kernels. Beans or peas may be cooked with potatoes. More than one pot is used only when porridge and a relish are being prepared.

Corn is not as important a staple as millet and eleusine. Select ears may be boiled or roasted whole. Dry corn is usually shucked by rubbing with the hands or rubbing two ears together. The whole kernel is cooked, but occasionally corn is ground into meal which is mixed into gruel.

Gourds are cooked whole or cut in half. They are not peeled or seeded. They need to be cooked for a long time in very little water. Young ones are eaten skin and all; the older ones with tough skins are peeled as they are eaten. The seeds of very ripe ones— too ripe for eating—are themselves good eating. They are dried in the sun and then roasted on a potsherd, sprinkled with salt water, and dried again. They are a delicacy, not a substantial food. Another delicacy is millet stalks. These are chewed for their sap. Those which because of some blight will not ripen, and so can be out before they are dry, are the best, but stalks are also sometimes "gnawed" after the heads are cut off.

Mushrooms of various sorts are used. Clumps of soil are removed as much as possible, but the mushrooms are not washed, as this is believed to spoil the flavor. Small ones are cooked whole, large ones cut up; pepper as well as salt is added when they are nearly done. Pepper may be used in greens, peas, and beans as well, but not so imperatively.

Water lily roots are famine food. They may be eaten roasted or boiled. As a casual tidbit they are even eaten raw, plucked going by in a boat, or children as they play about at the shore of the lake.

It will be noticed that salt is an occasional item in the Chiga diet. Nowadays, the salt is obtained in the form of a pink rock salt which is bought from Indian traders. The huge lumps are broken up by pounding on a tray, and salt is so much of a luxury that the tray is sought after for licking afterwards. Before this commercial salt was obtainable, there were two sources of salt. It was made either from the salt-earth, which is now used for cowlicks, or from lily roots. In the former case, the soil is stirred into water to be used for cooking, the sediment being thrown out. The other method involved drying the water lily, stem, leaves, and all, cooking it and then pounding and mixing it with a bit of water to form a solid ball to be used as required. It too was sometimes sucked, but not so much as is the modern salt. Things cooked with this turn very black.

Meat preparation is the only task associated with cooking that is done by men. They do all the butchering, and some of the cooking, particularly broiling. Most men can butcher, though not all are very good at it. The animal's throat is cut, while the legs are held. The skin is slit up the belly and up the backs of the legs. Then it is hung up by a rope tied around the hind legs. The insides are removed, and the skin is taken off all in one piece. For this a small knife is used, but the meat is cut up with a large curved knife. The head is skinned, but not the ears, nor the part underneath the tail. All the meat is utilized, and all the organs. The intestines are cleaned by squeezing out their contents, with knots made as the work progresses, to keep it going in only one direction. They are then washed, and broiled for eating. Often the stomach sack is used as a container, sometime for the blood. The liver and other internal parts are considered great delicacies. They, and all the curious small bits into which the meat is cut up, have definite names.

Meat is prepared by broiling over a fire on a stick, and by boiling. The broiled meat may be hung away and dried for future use. Sometimes boiled meat is dried over a fire for storing. When meat which was previously boiled is to be eaten, it may be reheated, sometimes with salt and butter. The water in which meat has been boiled is drunk.

Sometimes the blood of the slaughtered animal is poured into the soup in which the meat is cooking. It is stirred with a stick which should have a bit of meat at the end. The meat is taken out till the blood thickens, and is then reheated in it. Blood may also be cooked separately—it may be stirred in a cold pot, which is then set over the fire. This blood can be allowed to dry and is stored, to be cooked as desired. It is considered very good cooked with peas or greens. It is added to them when they are boiled, after draining off any cooking water that has not been absorbed.

FIRE

A great deal of time goes into gathering firewood and feeding the fire. The Chiga know how to make fire by means of fire sticks, but this is a cumbersome process, avoided when possible. While hunters and herders sometimes carry sticks about with them, anyone will, if possible, resort to borrowing a flame, even from a total stranger. Women going to the fields, if they expect to need a fire either for roasting a few ears of corn, lighting a pipe, or warming themselves, carry a light out to the fields with them, in coals on a potsherd, or smoldering in a foot-long bundle of slow-burning grass or in a kind of fried cat-of-nine-tails. In the house, the fire is carefully banked at night, so that the coals can be readily fanned into a blaze in the morning, if indeed it is not so cold that something of a fire must be kept going all night, tended by the little boys sleeping beside it on the floor. Anyone stirring it up during the night must remember to bank it carefully. If, despite this care, the fire should go out, a new one would be started, preferably by fetching a brand from a neighbor's house, rather than by using the sticks.

The fire sticks are called respectively "the woman" and "the penis." The former has a slit cut in it, in which earth is put. The other stick is inserted and twirled between the palms. It makes its own tinder, for a great deal of sawdust accumulates before the sparks appear. When it starts to smoke, you must not comment on it, or it will go out. When the tinder is alight, tiny bits of grass are added, until a real blaze is started. The lower stick is always set on a knife blade, or the corner of a skin cloak—not on the ground.

There are a number of precautions that must be exercised int he use of fire. Two people must not take fire from the house at the same time. If both need it, one must give it to the other in the courtyard. Nor should you ever bring fire into a house in which a fire is already burning. If you find a fire burning when you come into a house with some, you should throw it outside, not on the hearth. When you take a torch of burning grass into the courtyard, always extinguish it after it has served its purpose—do not bring it back into the house.

Gathering firewood is in itself a most onerous task. This is because there are no trees and large bushes available which can be cut down for the purpose. All the fires are made with whatever small dry sticks can be picked up. Every one coming home from the fields brings what bits of twig and brush he has found, and sometimes special trips of quite a distance must be made for the purpose. The men do not consider this their task, though they may help if convenient. The people of Bufuka were doubly lucky in their nearness to the lake, which provided papyrus for fuel as well as a readily available water supply. A provident household will have a few extra bundles of firewood stacked up by the side of the house, but this is hardly likely to be more than a day's supply. The actual process of cooking is lengthy, too, because of the quality of the wood. It must be fed into the fire twig by twig, to the accompaniment of much blowing, to keep it glowing hotly. It is necessary for someone to be constantly in attendance for even the simplest meal of boiled yams.

The Chiga have no lamps. The only artificial lighting besides that supplied by the fireplace itself comes from dried rushes, which burn with some glow for a few moments when lighted. These are used as emergency candles—to see something stirring in the courtyard at night, or to look for a pot of beer stored in the dark back part of the house.

WATER

Water is seldom used for drinking, though if someone is quite ill he may drink a little hot water. Even those on the shore of the lake seldom wash, unless they are under the influence of the missions. The water is needed for cooking, yet nearness to its supply is not considered at all important in choosing a house site. Many villages are built way up on a slope, with water available only in a muddy trickle at its foot. As a result, fetching water is often a serious chore, and even the mite which the tiny child fetches half in play in a small cup is a real contribution to the water supply. When even this is not to be had, pools to catch the rain may be dug in the courtyard—about a yard in diameter and several feet deep. These are especially useful for soaking grain.

Provision of adequate watering facilities for the cows is more important. These do not need to be near the houses. Artificial improvements may be necessary because of the danger from leeches (see below). Sometimes pools are dug near the edge of the water. In that case, there is danger of a cow's slipping and falling into the ditch. An old boat may be used as a drinking trough, into which the water is ladled. With the curious lack of concern about comfort, which is a Chiga characteristic, cows may be habitually taken to drink at a spot where their trampling makes an important path muddy and dangerous.

CATTLE-KEEPING

Herding does not set the tempo of Chiga life. There are no seasonal migrations. There are not even designated grazing grounds. The cattle feed on whatever lands happen to be unused for gardening, eating the grass, or the stalks of the previous season's corn or millet. The pasturage is thin, and neither cattle, sheep, nor goats are a plump and comely lot. Most of the herds are small. Even the wealthiest of the Chiga seldom have herds so large that they need to be divided after the fashion of their pastoral neighbors. More commonly, in fact, herds are pooled for convenience in tending them.

The work of tending cattle properly belongs to the men, but most of the daily routine except the milking is actually done by children. The children take them to water and pasture, while the men milk and do such special tasks as bleeding, butchering, and doctoring.

In most families, all the animals—cows, sheep, and goats alike—are taken out to pasture together. In the morning, though not before the sun rises, as among the Bahime, the cows are milked. Shortly after sunrise and sometimes even later, they are taken out under the care of small boys, who keep them from straying onto the planted fields, and who are ready to give the alarm should any danger threaten. This is simplified by the fact that there are no lions, and the leopards seldom approach the herds in the daytime. Perhaps there was more supervision of the children in the days when enemy raids might have been expected, but now there is little. In the early afternoon the cows are taken to water. Care has to be exercised lest the cow swallow a leech, which would cause trouble and might prove fatal. Many of the watering places are artificially constructed to avoid this. Occasionally, the herds must be taken to the natural salt licks. This is the only way in which I knew salt to be supplied to the herds, but perhaps where these licks are not available, the Bahima method of feeding them prepared salt is used. They are brought back at about five or six o'clock and milked again. Then the gate is barred for the night.

Baby animals are not taken out with the others. They are kept sheltered inside the house. At night, all the goats and sheep are tethered with them, while the cows are penned outside in the cen-

ter of the compound. The size of the herd is usually reflected int
he size of a man's compound, just as the size of his various families affects that of each of his houses. A poor man may even have
a house without a compound, and keep the one or two cows that
he does own with the herds of some more fortunate man.

The typical pattern of this region is followed with respect to
milking. The cow is broken to it by allowing her to lick the skin of
a calf. This is prepared by placing the skin of a calf's head upon a
stick and spitting salt and special herbs on it. The herder "intoxi-
cates" the cow with this, so that she believes the calf is about, and
allows the harder to approach. If the cow does not give milk, irri-
tating materials such as a very sharp-edged grass, are thrust into
its womb.

When milking, the man squats at the left side of the cow, the
pail held between his knees, so that both his hands are free. The
milk is collected in a pot and then, in a family wealthy enough to
boast one, it is poured for keeping into a wooden milk pail. It is
rarely drunk fresh. One of the common regional beliefs that the
Chiga share is that if a cow's milk is struck by the sun, the cow
will become weak and sickly. But this does not cause them to rise
before daylight, as their neighbors do, and milk their cows by
firelight. They are merely careful to keep their milk pots covered.
The milk is put aside for three or four days, and then churned. The
buttermilk is drunk, and the butter stored for use as needed.

Blood is obtained not only by catching all the blood of any
slaughtered animal in a bowl, but also by bleeding the cows periodically. This is done by shooting a short arrow into a vein on the
right side of the neck. A rope is tied just below, which is loosened
to stop the spurt when enough has been taken. The blood is caught
in a bowl. This bleeding is said to be very good for the animals.
The process takes some skill and a number of participants. They
must catch and hold the animals, hold the bowl, and in other ways
assist the man who does the actual shooting. The people of Bufuka
never did this while I was there, for there was no one who was
sufficiently skilled. There was much talk of getting someone from
the next hamlet to bleed the animals for them, but they never got
around to arranging it. In this next village the process took place
at least once every few months. Many people took part, and the
cows of several households were attended to in one operation,
taking the better part of a morning.

The Chiga do not share the exaggerated reverence for the cow, which is so important a part of the culture of their Bahima and Batuttai neighbors. They do not draw a sharp distinction between cattle on the one hand and sheep and goats on the other; in fact, they may even herd them together. What is more, little girls are allowed to her cattle.

This does not mean that no distinction at all is drawn between the cows and other animals. Cows are, of course, very much more valuable. The procedures surrounding the sale of a cow are quite special, and even the meat is treated differently in exchange. There is also some distinction in the uses to which they are put. Only cow's milk is drunk regularly. Goat's milk is never used regularly; little boys sometimes milk the goats for practice and then drink the milk. Goat's milk is seldom churned even by the poor, and the butter made from it is never eaten. A further distinction is seen in the rule that women must not eat mutton or goat meat, though they may eat beef. Nor may goat or sheep meat be cooked in the same pot as beef.

Tabus govern the care of the cattle, but they are not so elaborate as those of their neighbors, nor so centered upon the sacredness of the cattle. Most of them are just ceremonial and magical elaborations of fundamental cattle care.

The first milk that a cow gives is not used by adults. The little boys who take care of the cattle churn it and smear themselves with it. The second milking is also not used. It is put into the ghost hut for the grandmother of the owner of the cow. A special ceremony must then be performed to make it possible to drink the milk without danger to the cow. Various special foods—different kinds of mushrooms, toasted peas, chicken meat, smoked frogs, sweet potatoes—are prepared. Two children, a boy and a girl who are the successive children of one mother, are the main participants. The little girl is placed on the cow. The boy drinks of the cow's milk and then the girl has a sip, and so on in rotation until they have emptied the vessel. After that they must take each of the foods in turn. This makes it safe to drink the milk. It also lifts the tabu that has been in effect on all these foods ever since the birth of the calf. If anyone in the household had eaten any of these before this rite, the cow might have had a hemorrhage.

When a cow with an unweaned calf is mounted by a bull, they take the calf away and herd it with the other cattle, so that it will stop trying to suckle. The milk which the cow still gives is not treated as ordinary milk. It is tabu to adults, though children may drink it, and it is not made into butter. After four days the cow is bled, and a little of the blood is used to construct a charm that will help prevent the cow from aborting. It is mixed with husks of old grain and a twig much used in charms and these are set up in the peaked part of the roof over the doorway, with words to the effect of: "We have set you up in the roof. Do not come down again." It is believed that the cow cannot have the calf until this is taken down. It must be taken down when the cow goes into labor. The remainder of the blood from this ceremonial bleeding must not be eaten by the young men, but only mature ones, for it will act on the young ones as *enziburano*—that is, it will prevent them from being fertile.

When a calf is seen to kick in its mother's womb, it becomes dangerous to beat the cow, or it will abort. If the kicking is on the left side they believe that the calf will be female; if on the right, male. When the calf is about to be born, the herder is careful to be on hand, though it may entail sitting up all night. He must be ready to give any necessary assistance. For example, if the calf is being born legs first—a very dangerous thing and an evil omen—he will have to push and pull to assist the birth. Also he must cut the hooves of the calf, and put bits of the trimmings in the mouth, nose, and ears. This is done to prevent the cow from eating the afterbirth, for if it should do so the calf would die and the cow would be unable to give milk. The calf's own dung is smeared on it, for the mother likes to lick its excretory parts. The herder carries the calf, if it has been born elsewhere, back to the house, where it will be sheltered for some time before it goes out with the other animals.

A cow that has borne twins does not thrive if its milk is used outside the home, and by people not of the clan of its master. This applies likewise to the butter. And neither the mother nor her twin calves may be sold. Their meat must all be consumed at the compound of the owner, and the bones collected in a basket and buried in the center of the courtyard.

Multiple sheep births are not so important. One of the twins can be taken away and killed. The tip of the tail of the remaining one must be cut after six days, so that it will not fatten. A goat sometimes has four kids at one birth. Two would be butchered and two kept. But if a sheep has four, this is a very dangerous omen which bodes death to the owner. If the herder who is present at the ill-omened birth is wise, he can avoid the consequences by killing two on the spot, and bringing home only two, and then never speaking of the matter to anyone.

HUNTING

Hunting was once a way of getting extra meat and was also a favorite sport. Today hunting is prohibited by the British authorities, in a policy of game preservation. The ban is much resented but seldom broken. Everyone speaks with longing of the days when any man who liked hunting, and had dogs of his own, went hunting almost every other day. Hunting was likely to be particularly good after a rain. People hunted alone or in groups, with and without dogs, by means of nets, traps, drives, and pitfalls. The spear rather than the bow was the favored weapon. The latter was known but more as a pygmy weapon than their own. There was no use of animal disguises.

When a group of people went hunting together they started out very early in the morning. The expedition was arranged the night before by a dog owner. At the sound of a bugle, the participants gathered with their dogs, weapons, and any other paraphernalia planned to be used. Anyone who wished might join in, providing they were prepared for the hunt; it was important that they had neither slept with a woman nor been in a house with a menstruating woman the night before. Usually, as many dogs as possible were brought along. These wore bells, stuffed with grass to keep them quiet until the animals were sighted. Care was taken not to alarm the animals too soon—so whistles were used rather than calls. Lookouts were stationed at several places. When they sighted the animals, the dogs' bells were loosened. The dogs were used to start the animals while the hunters closed in. Sometimes the animals were driven into nets by the hue and cry. In that case, men were posted at the nets, ready to spear the animals when they became entangled. Sometimes they were hidden in little shelters put up at either end. Sometimes stones were thrown, aimed at a point a little beyond the animal so that it would be startled and run toward the hunter rather than away from him. In any case, the actual kill was usually made with a spear.

When a group hunted, a bugle call announced the close of the day's activities. Then they gathered to divide the spoils, according to careful rules. Should the party be having no luck, the bugle might summon them while it was still early. They would all lie down as though they were sleeping out for the night, and then start out afresh, hoping by this device to rid themselves of the effects of whatever it was that was causing that day's bad luck.

The hunting net was made of double-twisted rope. It was attached to two stakes, on which it was rolled up for storage and carrying. These were thrust into the ground when the net was in use. It stood quite high, taller than a person, "lest the animals be able to jump over it." The cooperation of several persons was needed for this type of hunting, to start and drive the game, to hold the net, and to spear the animals when they became entangled in the net. The large traps and pitfalls sometimes used were also necessarily joint ventures, for it took more than one person to dig and maintain them. The person who initiated the project would have to share the meat of any catch with those who helped him. Sometimes a group could build several traps, one for each of those engaged in the work.

Pitfalls were sometimes quite simple, trusting entirely to their depth for their effectiveness, or they were filled with pointed stakes, or even had a trapping rope at the bottom to secure the prey once it had fallen in. The hole that was dug was covered over with grass.

A favorite kind of trap worked by bringing a heavy weight down upon the animal. The weights ranged all the way from winnowing trays, used to catch small birds, to posts covered with heavy stones, which have been known to capture leopards. The principle was the same in both cases, except that in trapping birds the operator could remain on the scene to pull away the supporting sticks when the bird was under the trap, while the leopard trap was designed so that the animal sprang it himself. The bait was set in such a position that in order to get it the animal would have to disturb the supporting posts, thus upsetting the whole precariously balanced structure. The roofing poles were lightly balanced on the post, and heavily weighted. The whole thing was usually built in a circle, with the bait inside.

Several types of noose traps were also made, arranged to strangle larger animals or hang smaller ones. An approach was usually set up so that the animal was led to place its head into the noose from the proper direction. The noose was either hung from a supple pole, which would spring back when the restraining twig was disturbed, or it was set into a cleft stick. Many variants of these general patterns were in use. One was set into the ground at the entrance to the animal's hole. Another, designed to catch rats, was set into a small hollow bamboo stick.

BEE-KEEPING

Keeping bees is a very special pursuit, followed by relatively few people. When a man dies, his power over the bees has to be handed to his eldest son in an inheritance ceremony, or the latter will not be able to keep bees. At the ceremony a small model of a beehive is given to the son, at the same time as the cows' lead rope and other such symbols are given him. Bee-keeping is surrounded by many ritual precautions.

There are tabus associated with the honey itself, special carrying pads and charms for moving the hive, and tabus on the keeper's behavior. He must avoid building fires with certain types of wood; his wife must avoid adultery, or there will be holes in the hive. There are many secret tricks for keeping the bees from leaving the hive, such as planting a child's walking stick in the ground nearby. Removing honey from the hive also calls for a careful procedure. The hive owner must remove all his clothing. He removes the lid of the hive and then smokes the bees out by placing a potsherd with fire on it in the hive, and blowing upon it. The bees are driven into the back part of the hive; he can then cut the comb away and give it to the child assistant who has come to help him. The child wipes it and puts it into a collecting basket. Then the fire is removed and the hive covered.

There are several types of beehive in use. One is woven, rather like a small storehouse. Another is made of small planks, sewn and bound with papyrus. Still another is built of a split log about a yard long, hollowed out and then fastened together with tough vines. The bark is usually removed and the surface roughly finished. In any case, the hive is hung high up in a tree, and well thatched to keep out the rain.

FISHING

Fishing is not very important for most of the Chiga, but some is done at Bufuka and other places along the shore of the lake. Frogs are caught and smoked, otters are speared for their skins and their magically potent genital bone, and the tiny fish that seem to have been recently introduced into the lake are caught, mostly for sale to the Baganda.

Fishing is done by means of crude weirs which the men weave of green papyrus. These are long double cones, made by inserting a short basket with a hole at the tip into a longer one with a closed bottom, and then binding the rims together. The tops are plastered over with anthill clay, which serves as bait, and the traps are tied among the papyrus at the edge of the lake. The tip is stopped up with grass to prevent the escape of fish that have swum into the trap. Usually the traps are baited, stopped up, and hung in the lake at night. In the morning the fish are removed and dropped into a basket. Sometimes, because otters are likely to eat the traps, people fish at night instead, setting the traps in the late afternoon, and removing them about ten o'clock. Both fish and frogs are caught this way. Both are very tiny—just a few inches long, and quite thin. The fish are killed and set in rows on stakes to dry. Frogs are usually cooked in water first, and then dried by spreading them on mats. Both are then smoked, spread out on a large surface such as a house door. The Chiga claim that the process of drying fish was taught them by the Baganda recently, but I had no opportunity to check the accuracy of this.

Otters are speared in the water with a special triple-headed spear. Few people are adept at it, and like the successful leopard hunter, the man who has killed many otters is entitled, or perhaps really required, to wear the charm which is also the insignia of the man who has killed men in battle.

10

COPING WITH THE
ENVIRONMENT

HOUSEBUILDING, and keeping the houses in repair, is one of the most onerous tasks of the men. The roof should be looked to quite often, and a new house, or at least a complete new thatching, may be necessary about once in five years. In addition, whenever people move because an important member of the family has died, or because of desire for adventure, or dearth of land, or a quarrel, they must go through all the major parts of the house building. If the new site is near enough, the old posts and some of the thatch may be used again.

The old-style Chiga house is grass-thatched over a wattle and daub framework. It is a "beehive" shape, with the walls and roof in one. It has an arched covered doorway, and no windows. It is always built as small as possible for the size of the family to be accommodated, and since goats and calves are kept inside at night, it is very crowded indeed.

A recently introduced modification of this house has become rather popular, modelled after the Baganda house. This has plain vertical walls that are plastered over, the separate roof having eaves that overhang the walls and do not touch the ground. It is larger than the old house, and is much more difficult and laborious to build.

Here and there an individual has experimented with a third kind, which has nowhere met with much approval. It is rectangular instead of circular, with windows in the walls, and a general attempt at imitating the government camps and similar public buildings built of native materials. One of those attempted in Bufuka was very unsuccessful, with its roof sagging sadly.

In the old type of housing, all the houses of one family are built around a center court, with all their doorways facing inward. The outer walls of the houses are connected by a fence of living bush, and there is a wide gateway opposite the entrance of the oldest wife's hut. The cows are kept in the courtyard at night, and milked there morning and evening. There is usually a large tree in the center of the court, or at least a stake, which is related to the protective charms of the household. The master of the household usually has a favorite spot in the courtyard where he sits and suns himself.

Most of the grain drying and other such outdoor work is done not in the courtyard itself, but in a little flat clearing prepared outside the gate to one side of it. This is out of the path of the cows, and so it can be kept clean, hard, and dry. No attempt is made to keep the courtyard itself dry and clean. Cow dung is allowed to lie until it is partly dry and is then removed by hand, usually by one of the children, to a large heap at one end of the courtyard, which is ordinarily unfenced. Here broken things are thrown when they have no further use, and any garbage is also thrown there. But the mud churned up by the cows is allowed to lie, and it is thought better not to smooth it out, as otherwise the rains would drain right into the houses. Sometimes an attempt at drainage is made by digging a channel through the fence at a low point. Ordinarily, however, during the rains, the courtyards are covered with ankle-deep mud.

Nowadays everyone has a fenced privy outside his fence. This is one of the government edicts which has come to be generally respected. For the most part, these privies are actually used. Occasionally, someone is guilty of soiling the inside of a house, but this is considered very filthy, and is quite a disgrace. I have even heard of a jealous wife secretly littering the floor of a favored co-wife's hut in order to get her looked down upon by their joint husband. In the days before privies were built, each family had a place in the woods where a little mound was convenient for squatting. Here a stick was kept with which to shove away the accumulation and keep it from becoming excessive in one sport.

No special provision is made for urinating. It is not quite *comme il faut* to use the floor of the house, though during drinking parties this is common. It was a great disgrace to soil in this fashion the house or the courtyard that was the dwelling place of a priest with a great spirit. Aside from this, both men and women urinate quite casually in public, though most of the younger people today are "ashamed."

A courtyard also contains a number of smaller buildings. Grains are stored in large bins, set up on stilts, and in most households there will be more than one of these for each wife. There also used to be tiny huts about a foot high and sometimes one considerably larger, built for the convenience of the ancestral ghosts. These have almost entirely disappeared.

The gateway of the compound is closed up at night simply by piling branching logs on top of one another. The house has a door that is set in the doorway at night. This may be made either of wicker or of twining. Men generally exercise some care to make them neatly. They weave the doors out in the courtyard. The two end posts are thrust into the ground, and the whole thing, as it grows, is supported from behind. Doors are always made with peepholes, so that the master of the house can rise during the night and make sure that there is no thief among his cattle.

Partitions within the house are made of papyrus, woven in regular twining; sometimes they are strengthened by binding on a bundle of withes running horizontally. None of the care lavished upon the doors is exercised in making the partition, although the basic technique is the same. While most of the doors that I saw were regular and even in workmanship, the partitions were almost all very crude and rough in finish. They may be plastered over with a kind of white earth or cow dung or a mixture of the two. Sometimes they are decorated, but even the decoration is crude and rough in contrast, for example, with the smooth elegance of Ruanda styles. Here it consists merely of large geometric figures scrawled haphazardly in black and red outline on the whitish clayey surface of the plaster.

The hearth is an important part of the household. It is always in the front part of the house, on the right side, just off center. The fireplace itself consists of three stones, as evenly matched as possible, so that the pots will balance readily. A good deal of significance is attached to these stones. They are set into place the morning after the house is finished, and must never thereafter be moved. Should they be moved to another house, the married sister coming for the traditional ceremony of eating marrow leaves cooked at the hearth would be in danger of leprosy.

The chief cooking of the household takes place at this fireplace. It is also lighted for warmth when necessary, and the family sits about it. Behind to the right, next to the wall of the house, is a low bedstead which serves as a couch. It is reserved for the master of the household to sit or lie upon at his pleasure. Sometimes a stool will be drawn up at the other side of the fire. In addition to the chief fireplace, a house often has another fireplace in the back part of the house behind a partition. Here a young son may cook a bit of sheep or goat meat while his mother prepares the doughy porridge to go with it out in front. Here girls may cluster during a ceremony, when men are sitting about the front fire. And here one can cook a bit of beer when making just a small quantity and when one does not wish to advertise it to the neighbors.

Fires may also be built out in the center of the courtyard, where the master of the household likes to lounge. This is just for warmth, not cooking, and there are no hearthstones. It may also be used to burn up refuse. In a very large household, fires would be built in the courtyard for brewing large quantities of beer.

There are few furnishings in the house. The beds are built in— a low couch to the right of the fire, and one or two more behind partitions. They are woven of twigs, supported by poles resting in forked sticks thrust into the ground at the four corners. This is a modern innovation. Old-style beds were built directly on the floor, being made merely of piled wood. Both the old and the modern styles are covered with grass, frequently renewed. There are no other bedclothes—the hides worn as clothes by day are used as covers by night.

The built-in beds and various partitions, together with the center pole that is part of the structure of the house and the fireplace set near the door, fill most of the available space in an average-size house, leaving only enough room for the family to sit about in the front part of the house; the back, some distance in from the doorway, is dark even on a bright day. There may be a shelf up above the couch on the right hand wall, on which large pots may be stored. Others are kept in the back of the house behind the partition. Baskets hang from the veiling, and various small belongings hang upon the wall from pegs. Tools may be stowed in the roof, or piled against the posts or walls of the house. Sometimes there are one or two stools or wooden bowls. Pots of beer or of cooked food are kept in the back part of the house.

Food supplies in bulk are not kept in the house. There may be little baskets and bamboo tubes containing seed, or chunks of dried meat on sticks stuck into the rafters above the door, but most of the food is kept stored in the special storage bins that are in the courtyard. These are of two main types. One is of the same wattle and daub construction as the house, and the other is of woven wickerwork like the doors, the strands being split withes. They are from one foot in diameter to five or six, and are usually a few feet high. Some are so tall and large that in order to get the grain out a child has to be lowered in. They are frequently set up on a sort of tripod arrangement or on banked earth, straw, dung, or stones to keep them dry and to keep the animals out. The floor of the compound is very slippery; little pools stand amid the mud during the rains, and the bins must at least be raised out of this. They are covered with lids which are rather like the house roofs, except that they are removable; but some of the larger ones have an opening in the side below the roof, instead, from which the food is removed. This has a stick protruding from it and is thatched like the house roof. The bins themselves are commonly plastered over with a mixture of earth and cow dung.

BUILDING THE HOUSE

Houses are built on cleared sites which are carefully prepared by hoeing. In making the old-style house, a circle is measured out and a trench dug, into which neatly pointed stakes are set at fairly regular intervals, and firmly packed in until they stand by themselves. These posts are then bound together at wide intervals with bundles of withes which are tied on with papyrus rope. The roof is built from the top down. First the top of the roof is made, sometimes rather elaborately. It is fundamentally a spiral structure on a basis of radiating spokes. When the spiral has gone around about three times, it is taken inside the standing circle of the walls. The heavy bundle of withes is carried spirally counterclockwise downward. When the roof is raised high enough, making one continuous structure, the spokes for the roof are joined with posts of the houses.

The house is then thatched with grass from peak to ground. When finished this looks rather formless, but it is applied after a regular pattern. The thatching grass, after being carefully dried, is bound into bundles which are tied all about the house, their butt ends to the ground and the thinning tops twisted in among the poles. The second row is tied on about a foot higher. Then the top is covered. The bundles are thrown up to someone standing on the roof, who arranges them in position, with a sort of peak toward the top. A thick coil of the type used for the roof spiral may be laid on top to keep the grass from blowing. The finished house always has the stick that was the center of the roof structure protruding at the top. This is symbolically important. Its removal is the way in which a house is "destroyed" at the death of its owner. The actual tearing down of the house may then by postponed for months. Sometimes there is a bit of potsherd set on the stake.

The doorway to a Chiga house forms a little entrance way. An opening is left for it when the framework is constructed. A stick is set between two poles about four feet up from the ground, and below this the withes are bound in an incomplete circle. Before this opening, a double row of stakes is set for some little distance. These are connected into a sort of archway by sticks bent over their tops. When the house is thatched, this is covered over along with the rest. Inside, the neat alignment of slender posts is often plastered over, and sometimes decorated with crude painted designs.

CLOTHING

Chiga clothing is made of hides, with the fur left on and worn next to the body. Men wear a skin with the legs knotted together slung over the right shoulder, and sometimes another over the other shoulder. Ordinarily, the garment hangs free, reaching the knee. There is no belt or joining of the sides, and there are no modest scruples about keeping covered. When working energetically, this garment is often discarded, and one skin wrapped skirt-wise about the hips. A man may even occasionally discard his clothing altogether when working in the fields. Sitting indoors, the garment will be dropped a bit, perhaps drawn forward between the legs to cover the genitals. Nowadays, a cloth tied skirt-wise about the hips is the modish imported fashion. With this a square of cloth or, if possible, two knotted together, forms a cloak for use against the cold. Little blue trunks run up by the Indians are seen occasionally, and the *kanzu* is still the special badge of European service, whether domestic or in office. This is a long white or orange nightshirt-like garment popular throughout East Africa.

Men's clothing requires no manufacture beyond the preparation of the skins. Women's clothing, however, is more complex. No woman may ever be seen without a skirt. Girls begin to wear skirts as they approach adolescence, and a first crudely draped skin soon gives way to a girl's skirt properly cut and sewn to-gether after the traditional pattern. Women wear skirts which are differently cut and draped, which hang longer, and for which two skins are required. A woman's skirt is first wrapped, overlapping to the left, and tied with a belt, usually of plaited rope. The top flap is then folded over. The clothing may be decorated by cutting fringe, or attaching little metal bangles at the edges, and some-times even here and there on the surface. Women, too, wear skin cloaks, hung over the right shoulder. Sometimes the knotted leges are twisted once about the upper arm.

Skirts and other hide garments are worn with the fur sides in-side. The leather side must be smeared with butter before first use, and from time to time thereafter. The fat, made into a little ball, may be daubed with powdered iron ore or mixed with red earth. This colors the skin slightly and improves its appearance. The skin is put on the ground and the fat worked in with both hands. Married women and girls about to be married may perfume their skirts by smoking them over a fire of various leaves and roots. These are cut into scraps and burned in a potsherd, and the skirt is spread on top over an old wicker basket. Young girls do not per-fume their skirts, but may smoke a new skin which is to be used only as a covering.

Cutting is a specialist's task which only some women can per-form. The skins are laid out on the ground, and the cutting is done with a knife. The pieces are sewn together with twine, which may be either of sinew or of soft shredded bark, both of which are kept stored, and spun as needed. The work always proceeds forward away from the worker, although this may mean continually turn-ing the heavy skirt around.

In the initial sewing a sort of raised seam is made, the awl pass-ing at once through two thicknesses, so that a sort of overcasting stitch is employed. In mending, a different stitch may be used, but the same stitch may be used for mending very different things. I have seen cracked calabashes sewn together; the holes in oppo-site pairs are made by the awl, the stitches run parallel to the crack, on the outside.

Women wear metal ornaments made by the blacksmiths. There are coiled wire anklets, worn by the dozen, which are part of the standard costume of the married woman. There are also heavy metal bracelets, and little clips to be sewn on skirts an capes. Girls

used to wear beaded headdresses, but these are seldom seen nowadays. All babies, and many girls, wear braided grass bracelets,
made by splitting the cylindrical grass in six parts, leaving a bit of
the base to connect the strands, but removing the core, and then
weaving all the strands together in a regular six-part circular braid.
The initial core is inserted into the end and the circle completed.
In the same way a long belt is made which all girls wear under
their clothing.

HYGIENE

Techniques of personal hygiene are very easily—and very
briefly—described. Washing of both person and clothing have
but newly come into fashion, under mission influence and under
the impetus of the newly introduced cotton clothing and store
soap. Body washing as performed by the most particular today
requires just one small calabash of water. Most are content with
occasional hand washing done by pouring a little water into one
palm, cupping and rubbing the hands together, possible rinsing
with another handful. Water is treated as a scarce and not very
desirable commodity even by those living directly on the shore
of the lake.

Washing as such is not new; it is a long-established preliminary
to oiling the body, which should be done as often as circumstances
permit, and at least before all festive occasions. A great many of
my friends, however, partly because of poverty, greased themselves only rarely, so that their skins habitually had a greyish cast
because of dirt and dryness. When the body is to be greased, butter is used (long-stored butter, very often!) and is rubbed sparingly over arms, torso, and face. If there is enough butter, the
anklets, which married women wear in great numbers, are also
greased; and when work in muddy fields is under way, a careful
woman protects her anklets by wrapping them in bits of plantain
bark. Mud-caked feet and filthy hands by wrapping them in bits
of plantain bark. Mud-caked feet and filth hands that have worked
in mud or even in cow dung are not an acute source of discomfort,
and I have often seen people make no effort to remove the debris
even after the work was done. While there is a great deal of personal variation, there is no question that the Chiga present a strik-
ingly filthy appearance in contrast to the washed and laundered
Baganda. This is not a function of skin clothing exclusively, for I

have seen individuals among them dressed in skins, but with the body washed and shining.

Abhorrence of water is quite strong. No one considers it a fit drink except when brewed into gruel or beer. And though I was told that some of the Abakendje on the far side of the lake could swim, none of the people around Bufuka ever went near the water, although this is one of the few central African lakes that contains neither hippos nor crocodiles nor even the dangerous little snails that burrow under the skin. To some extent, perhaps this may be tied up with the notion of the lake as an enemy because it has killed one's relatives. Or it may be a carryover from the prevalent actual scarcity of good water.

As for other aspects of body care, the most careful attention is paid to body hair. All of this should be removed, by plucking. Pubes especially must be kept carefully denuded, particularly by young people; their elders may begin to slacken with middle age. There is a special proverbial expression for disgrace which is phrased in terms of a bride being found to have hair on her pubes. In addition to removing hair, brides, ritually, and other young women who are concerned about sexual relations, smoke their private parts with scented herbs, as they do their skirts. This probably has some cleansing as well as perfuming effect, thought the herbs used have an odor that is musky and rather unpleasant to our taste. They are probably supposed to be aphrodisiac.

Despite the absence of body hair, body lice are plentiful. They lodge happily in the furry side of the hide clothing, which is worn next to the body, and in the well-greased goat's hair anklets. I was told that if one used a separate skin for a cover at night, hanging one's daily garment up to air, the pests could easily be kept at bay. Not everyone has a separate cover; a great many do, but do not use them at night, keeping them only for dress-up wear. Most people seem to be so inured to the parasites that they pay little attention to them beyond an occasional half-hearted and almost unnoticed scratch. Others, however, make every effort to get rid of them. I have seen even a busy woman sitting in the sun for several hours, sunning her cape, and chasing and killing lice in her clothes and anklets. Apart from this, the only treatment accorded the clothing is a massage with butter applied to the outside from time to time to keep it soft. This is necessary because the tanning process is not really effective; but this hardly serves to discourage the guests. They are killed when caught, never eaten. There is apparently no way of effectively fumigating the clothing, and many of the younger people, who have quickly responded to mission influence on this score, dislike wearing the native clothing for this reason, preferring the washable, though certainly not warm enough, cotton clothing. The mission and government are waging a strong war against the women's anklets, but these have a firm traditional hold; the practice of hospital removal is deeply resented. That it is necessary is clear from the serious typhus epidemics that rage up in different river valleys periodically.

Treatment of head hair is very simple these days. The practice of shaving the entire scalp has come into vogue for both men and women. Some of the people who do it are under the impression that this is part of the requirements for a true Christian; if so, it is an invention of the local "teachers" exclusively, for the missions have not themselves insisted upon it. In any case, it is now popular and by far the most usual fashion. Some wear a modification of the Ruanda style of elaborate patterns in tufts, similar to clipped poodles or fanciful box hedges, but usually the tufts are much shorter—just a few weeks hair growth with a spiral path shaved through it. The effect of this latter style, which is popular particularly with adolescent girls, is very pretty. The old-style hairdo here was much more elaborate. It called for a coiffure of tiny twists of hair twined with cord to supplement its length, caked with grease and sometimes even with clay to make it more substantial and secure. These curls hung in several layers all about the head in a circlet, and when properly done reached the shoulders. Sometimes beads or other ornaments were added to some of the curls. The headdress was left undisturbed for a month or more at a time, and when it was to be renewed the knotted ends would have to be cut away and each strand untwisted patiently. This style has gone out pretty completely. A few of the young girls sometimes let their hair grow in to try it for fun; I saw only one middle-aged woman with these curls and one man. I did see a number of wigs made of clayed and greased twists of cord, arranged on a bandeau in imitation of the old effect. The "curls" were decorated with beads and metal clips, and the whole thing worn as an adornment by a young girl. The wigs are not a new invention. Belles wore them in the old days over their own curls as a supplement and to carry extra ornamentation. Now it fits conveniently over the shaven poll; but only a few girls wear them.

While the Chiga tend to treat lice as a necessary evil, they approve of careful treatment and removal of chiggers. These are fleas that burrow into the skin, usually under the toenail, where they lay their eggs if unmolested, leaving larvae which feed upon the flesh. Even shoe-wearing Europeans get them. They present an incessant but manageable problem. Most people are quite skillful at removing them with an awl or better still with the point of a European safety-pin. If they are removed as soon as they enter, no damage is done an no scar caused. But the sign of their first entering is a very slight persistent itch which is easily disregarded and does not last long. It requires experience to notice and identify it. If this sign is neglected through insensitivity or laziness, there is usually no further itching until it reappears suddenly in very acute form about a week later. At this point the insect has grown a huge egg sac, which must be removed intact. Otherwise, larvae remain and cause the real wounds which deform the feet of numbers of the Chiga. The Chiga consider well-cared-for feet, with pared toenails and no chigger scars, one of the prime marks of beauty. The major symbol for description of an orphan's state of neglect is "he has no one to remove his chiggers." The deformed feet that come from prolonged chigger neglect may be bad enough to cause a hobbling gait, which many of my friends thought very funny.

Care of the teeth is not so elaborately stressed. I have never heard it discussed; but from time to time one picks up a twig with a fibrous pulp, chews the end into a rough mass, and then uses it to massage the gums and rub the teeth. This is done as one happens to feel the need, not as a routine habit.

TOOLS AND UTENSILS

Basketry

The Chiga make both coiled (sewn) and woven (both checker and wickerwork) baskets. On the whole, the former is women's and the latter men's work. Men make the openwork carrying baskets, fish-weirs and winnowing trays, and also the house doors and storage bins, which are sometimes woven rather than built. Women make baskets and trays, and they also make twined mats. Men use their ordinary knives for preparation of materials, and much of their work is quick and temporary. Women have a specialized basketry tool, an awl with a lanceolate blade at the end of the handle.

The winnowing tray is made of bamboo. Because the material is not locally obtainable, the trays are usually bought from the people of the mountains to the south. I did see one being woven; the weaver was a man from the south who had come to visit relatives and brought the materials with him. The tray is of checker weave, which proceeds from the center outward, extra cross-strips being inserted as needed. It is encircled by a hoop of flexible wood, and every row of the weaving ends with a loop over the hoop. The hoop is tied on at a few places ad the work proceeds, and is afterwards bound with split bamboo. The bottom of the finished tray is coated with white salt earth and dung.

The carrying basket (*orutete*) is of very open wickerwork. It is crudely woven of irregular supple twigs on a basis of stiffer split ones. The basket is a deep cylinder in shape, squarish at the bottom, and holding considerably more than a bushel. Usually a carrying rod is fastened to the bottom, for support in balancing it. Its principal use is in carrying crops home from harvest.

The basket called *omuhinda* is also made of checker weave. These are always very crude. They are used mostly to carry fish and the anthill stuff used in fishing, and I have also seen them used for storage. Usually they are squarish at the bottom and round at the top. There may be a handle. I saw one that was almost cradle-shaped and was used for keeping tanning pegs. Widish strips of dry papyrus are used, and it is not necessary that the checks be absolutely close. The bottom is a plain square checker weave, and the corners are turned up abruptly. The top is round because the top rim is bound on. It takes very little time to make one of these, and it is also a simple task for a man to make the more complicated fish weirs.

The *etcihembo* or fish weir is made of fresh cut, not dry papyrus. The weaving is wider, and the spaces large. It is wickerwork. More than one strand may go round at a time, but if so these will be parallel, one above the other, not twined together. The inner surface of the papyrus is used outside on the warp strands. The work goes counterclockwise, starting from the bottom. The top is finished off by wrapping the warp strands each around the other; these are folded down and wrapped in. The cover is made in the same shape but smaller, and it is then placed inside the other, and the rims securely bound together.

Women's baskets are of two basic types. The one called *etcibo* is a deep basket, and the *entemere* is a shallow disk, used as a plate or as a lid. They have a great many uses. The flat disks are used as trays and as dishes for serving food; the baskets for serving porridge, for storage of valuables, sometimes even as drinking vessels. Most of the time they are undecorated, for the Chiga say "you can drink beer just as well out of a plain basket." But occasionally they are decorated with designs in black, especially when they are to serve for storage of valuables.

The coiling is done upon a foundation of finely split papyrus. Large papyrus is selected and the usable bark stripped off in strips about 3/8 of an inch wide. These are dried in the sun for about two days. When they are ready for use, the entire length is shredded into wisps as fine as straw, concept for a solid bit left at the base.

For the outside, various materials may be used. The favorite is a heavy three-cornered reed. The most beautiful one is a shiny short grass which needs no preparation other than drying, but it is hard to find in sufficient quantities. The reed is cut when young, and dried only for a day. When the side pieces of the skin are cut off from the core, some of the core comes away with it. These pieces, each about 3/8 to 1/2 of an inch wide are rolled up. Starting at the tip end (which is the good end) each piece is wrapped about the hand clockwise over and away from the operator, and fastened with a loose knot. If left unlooped it will spoil. These loops are strung on a waste bit of reed or papyrus, dried in the sun, and then hung away. Most huts are fastened with strings of these, hung on pegs thrust into the wall, waiting for the mistress of the house or one of her daughters to get to work. When the basket is being made, these need further preparation. Several of the bits of looped material are soaked in water. Some part of the attached base, and any irregularity at the sides, must be removed. Then this material is cut into strips about 3/16 of an inch wide.

In beginning a basket, a bundle of split papyrus is wrapped tightly from the left to right with the sheathing material, the free end being caught underneath. When this is about a half-inch long, it is made into a circle and the second row started, wrapped along with the first, but worked now toward the right, the material being brought over from the back. When the circle has been secured by one wrapping, the stitching starts. This proceeds spirally, the bundle and the work going round to the right.

The stitching material is pointed slightly with the awl blade. It is inserted from the side near the operator, pulled with a little jerk after it goes through, to make it tight, and is then brought forward again from the back for the next stitch. For the bottom, the plate-like object is stood on end and worked on its top. If the object is to be make an *entemere,* the work proceeds on the far edge of the circumference, so that the awl and the stitching go from the inside to the outside, while with a basket, when the bottom is finished it is turned so that it is worked with the outside as the work surface, the stitch going from the outside as the work surface, the stitch going from the outside into the basket. Thus, the *entemere* is bet-ter finished on its inner surface, while a basket is more regular in texture on its outer surface. Each stitch is made into the upper part of the coil below, except when a design is being made. Then it is inserted at the right-hand base of the row below, so that the stitch is double in length. This self-decoration, without variation in color or material, and often without any regular pattern, is usually the only decoration, if there is any.

When new base material is added, it is merely thrust in with the other just as that begins to thin. Sometimes a few unattached wisps may be added here and there to keep it even. The shaping is done simply by adjusting the position of the spiraling coil upon the next one. When a new stitching strip is needed, it is put in from the front and pulled through to the back till only a tiny stump remains. The long end is brought forward, taking care to keep it well over to the left so that the end of the previous strand is caught. The free end in front is caught in the next stitch, but leaves a tiny fold or bump that can be seen on the right side of the finished basket.

If a black design is to be introduced, it may be made with *embatabata,* which is naturally dark. This is the standard Chiga way. Few knew the Ruanda trick of soaking strips of papyrus in cow's blood that has been set aside for a few days. This, Maliamu reports, used to be done much more in her youth—now people are just lazy. Soot may be rubbed on, too. The material is then smeared with fat, dried, steamed, and smoked.

Making Mats

Mats are made of grass twined with widely spaced rope, and are used mostly for bedding. These too are usually undecorated to-day, although techniques are known, and occasionally employed, for decorating them in black.

In making a mat, several kinds of swamp grass may be used, although the favorite one for baskets is not quite as good for mats. The grass is cut and then pounded, a small bundle at a time. It is slightly twisted, in order to crush the fibers. Then it is spread thin and dried in the sun.

In the actual weaving, the bundles of grass are arranged with base ends of the grass alternately in opposite directions, so that the two ends of the bundle are about equal. Two pieces of bark rope are knotted together, and wrapped twice about the middle of the first bundle of grass. The next bundle is laid next to it, and the rope twined about it. This rope must be twisted as it is worked, about two twists overhand to the right each time. The work proceeds directly away from the worker, who kneels on the ground and to the right of the mat. As each bundle is wrapped, the left hand holds the ropes in place, while the right twists the upper rope and carries it forward. The right hand seizes the rope and grass so as to hold it fast, leaving the left to pick up the grass, which must be placed over the rope. The piece coming out from underneath is always to the left. This is the one that must be yanked back toward the operator to tighten it. At the last bundle, the row is fastened by a triple encircling and a slip noose knot. The last bundle is twisted twice toward the worker before it is fastened.

The next row is started at the same end as before, about two inches to the left of the previous row. The spacing will vary with the worker, and the neatness desired for the finished mat. When half the mat is finished, the end is bound off by twining two rows right next to each other, and the last time pulling the rope tight not merely by pulling back, but also over toward the right. The work is then begun on the other half, starting next to the first finished row, and still working with each row to the left of the last finished one, but starting with the initial knots at the other end. The ends of the rope beyond the binding strip are all hacked off. During the weaving, the grass is kept from overdrying by being kept out of the sun, and by constant sprinkling with water. The bark is soaked as it is to be used, to soften it, but must not be kept in the water too long lest it get slippery.

Sometimes a half-mat (*omutcweka*) is made. This time, too, the work is begun at the middle of the bundle, but each bundle is folded over, and the other half included with the next one. The work then proceeds in the same way.

Most Chiga mats are undecorated and rather loosely woven. Eseri was said to "weave Banyaruanda style," not only because she liked to decorate her mats, but because she liked them smooth and neat. When designs are made, the most usual material is the outer black bark of the plantain, or the common wild plant similar to it. This is stripped from its spongy backing and inserted on top of the bundle. It is fastened by the rope top and bottom, and cut off immediately beyond, so that it is really just loosely attached. More formal decoration, so rarely done that its preparation is known to few, uses a grass dyed black.

Baskets that contain private belongings, such as ornaments, butter, calabashes, and so forth, are usually stored in a sort of sling, which hangs from a peg set into the upper notch. This is made by the women, too, of the same rope that is used for making mats. It is made of two strands of bark, twisted and turned together. Strictly speaking, the process is to *ogoca,* which is also used for braiding, but one is commonly said to *ruka* or weave a sling. The twists are much tighter in this than in mat-weaving, and the intertwining is very close. The sling is all in one piece. There is a triangle at the bottom. The rope at each corner is then divided into two for the sides. When these are rejoined again to form the triangle for the top, they are rejoined in different order.

Woodwork

All woodcarving and woodworking is men's work. They set up such bedsteads and shelves as there may be in the house, make handles for metal tools, and carve stools, bowls, ladles, paddles, canoes, and troughs. Everyone can wield an axe, but its use is a rarity. There are scarcely any around. Only trees for canoes and center house posts demand the axe. Most cutting down of wood is done with the large curved knife. All men can handle both large and small knives efficiently. But the finer carving of utensils is done only by those who are especially skilled, and have the finer tools of the carpenter's craft, in the form of a series of adzes. All of these are used at arm's length, held by the end of the handle.

In all fine carving, the rough form of the object is blocked out of the wood, the straight adze or large knife being used to shape it, and the looped adze to finish the surface. This is as true of a canoe as of a bowl or paddle. Most products are quite simple. There is rarely any decorative carving, and polish comes through time and use rather than careful finishing.

The canoes are just plain dugouts, with no thwarts or seats. They vary in size from tiny ones hardly large enough to bear the paddler, to large ones which several people paddle, and which can carry passengers as well. For the lake people the boats are important, for many of them have fields on the islands, or on other shores.

In boat building, a rough dugout is shaped where the tree is cut down, and this is then paddled back to the village for the finer adzing. When it draws within sight of the village, its arrival is signalled by a bugle call. This is replied to by cheers and triumphal yodelling by the women.

Boat building is surrounded by all sorts of ritual precautions. When a tree is felled, if it does not fall correctly it must not be used or the boat will drown people. When the men have gone to fetch the tree for the boat, the wife of the boat owner must not sit down, or it will be a heavy job and they will not be able to bring it in. While the rough boat ia being dragged to the water, if anyone should take the wife's arm, she must not snatch it away, or the pulling rope would break. When the boat is being pulled to the lake, a little twig is set in the prow, to which the pulling ropes must be fastened. This will "lead the boat well"; otherwise they will not be able to bring it down to the water. When they reach the lake, this twig is taken out and thrown away. Whoever finds it acquires a potent instrument for black magic. If the wife of the builder has intercourse while they are at work, he will cut himself. If ants run over the log, this is a very bad omen, and the work must be abandoned and started over again on another tree, otherwise the finished boat will prove dangerous to use.

Iron Work

The work of the Chiga blacksmith includes smelting the ore, making the charcoal, the bellows, and his own tools, as well as making the implements that he forges for others.

The smithy is very crude. It may be a rough shelter of four posts with a leaf roof, or a beehive-shaped structure, much smaller and lower than a house, roughly covered over with large leaves or plantain fronds instead of grass thatching. The sparks from the forge frequently ignite the roof, so that it is useless to have it elaborate or costly.

I have never witnessed the smelting, although my nearest neighbor was a blacksmith. The ores were obtained at the far end of the lake, and these worked into crude metal. The process, as described to me, was not unlike that common to East Africa, the metal being melted in a tall mound, with openings for bellows at various points to keep the charcoal and grass fire burning high. But most of the work that Bugwahabi did was just making over tools or making them out of scraps of old metal. I never even saw him use any new metal. The only time he did so during the year was in the course of work for the government's road building.

Charcoal is prepared by burning special kinds of wood in a fire made very hot with the same grass that is used for baking pots. It is then stored in a pit ready for use. Sometimes the person who comes to the blacksmith to have a job done will bring his own charcoal. The charcoal is burned in a little pit within the forge. The fire is kept hot by blowing with bellows of clay and skins. These were worked for Bugwahabi by his son, or by whoever had come for the job, or by one of the host of onlookers who surrounded his forge on the days when he was working.

The metal is set into the fire to soften, and is then hammered with an iron hammer upon a stone anvil. It is frequently sprinkled with water from a little brush. In handling the metal, iron tongs are used. It frequently needs to be thrust back into the fire for further heating. Great care about the heating and cooling has to be exercised in working iron, and Bachiga tools are often too hastily made, or too carelessly, so that the edges often turn when they are used.

The blacksmith makes knives, razors, adzes, axes, and so forth. He also makes spears and hoes. Nowadays hoes are commonly bought from the Indian traders, who have some that are quite similar to the native in shape. They are, however, declared to be not nearly so durable. There are occasional odd pieces of metal work to be done, too. Spears and walking sticks are commonly pointed at the end with a long sheath of metal. There are also heavy bracelets and anklets, little neck ornaments worn by men who have killed many otters, leopards, or people, and the various metal clips and bangles that the women wear. Blacksmiths also make the anklets that married women wear by the hundred. These are made of wire wrapped around goats' hair. Nowadays the wire is bought from the Indians, but some of the smiths used to know how to make the wire by drawing it through a strip of metal with holes.

Pottery

Both men and women make pots, the latter making most of the small pots for household use, the men making the very large ones such as those used to make beer.

The women at Bufuka have to fetch their clay from a considerable distance, about three hours away. The clay, in small lumps, is left in the courtyard to dry in the sun. When it is to be used, it must be soaked overnight in water. Meanwhile old potsherds are pounded into a powder on the wrong side of the grindstone with a round roughing stone. The powdered sherds are poured into a trough, the clay put on top, and the whole mixed by being trodden upon. Water is sprinkled on as needed, the mass of stuff being folded over onto itself from time to time. When this mass is of the right consistency, it is folded and patted into large balls, about ten inches in diameter.

The pots are begun in the hand. First a tiny cup is made, and then the rest is added in coils. After the first coil or two have been added, the beginning of the pot is set down into the inverted broken-off neck of a large pot which has been filled with ashes and two or three large leaves.

The coils are formed by breaking a small bit of clay, kneading it in the hands and twisting it into a fat sausage, which is lengthened into the proper size for coiling—about an inch in diameter—by rolling between the palms. As the coil is added, the right hand supports it and the left pinches it into place, the thumb being toward the worker. At first the coil is bent downwards and then pinched flat, but as the work progresses it is set on the edge and merely flattened, so that each coil adds over an inch to the height of the pot. While the pot is still small the work may proceed on the near side, but as it gets larger the work is done on the far side. It always proceeds to the right, so that at first it is clockwise, and later counterclockwise.

When four or five coils have been added, the pot is smoothed into shape. The thumb is used to mould it from the outside, the other hand supporting the pot from within. Then the outside of the pot is scraped with a bit of broken calabash, which is continually dipped into water during the process. The patting and the scraping stretch and shape the pot, more than does the coiling. The base may be turned so that the working surface is toward the worker, but he also frequently gets up to get at the other sides, instead of remaining constantly on the stool from which he works. When the pot is quite large it may be transferred to a small potsherd.

The top may be finished by breaking off little bits in a sort of pinking effect, and then patting the top all around with a bit of gourd. Or it may be decorated. Either serrated grass or a bit of braiding especially woven for the purpose from papyrus is used as a stamp. This is dipped in water and rolled over the surface to be decorated, which is either the top rim or the neck.

The bottom is usually the last part finished. Work upon it must wait until the top has dried enough so that the pot can be inverted and the bottom scraped smooth. The pots must remain in the sun for several days before they are baked.

When baking the pots, a pit about a foot and a half deep is dug. It is lined up to the ground level with bits of calabash. On these, pots—of which there are usually a dozen or so—are set carefully, and then covered with a special light grass which burns quickly and very hotly. This is fired in several places. It must be carefully watched. It is important that the day and place be windless so that the grass will not burn too quickly. Later the pots are partly uncovered, and when the grass is pretty well burnt down, they are pulled out. If they are not well fired, the process may be repeated, until the pots are uniformly red. They are left to cool for a time and then taken home.

There is always a great mortality when new pots are first used. To help this somewhat, the potter hits the ground about the pit in which they are baking in several places very hard with a walking stick. Whether this really makes them or the fire settle, or is a misguided notion, I do not know. When the pots are to be used, they must first be "cooked." They are put onto the hearth lying on their sides, till they are blackened with soot. When first set up to cook food, they are tapped on the side, and a magic spell is recited over them to keep them from breaking quickly.

11

PHYSICAL SKILLS AND MOTOR HABITS

HANDEDNESS. Left-handedness is considered an amusing rather than a serious affliction. There is an idiom "to *buzobulyo*," which means "to inquire left-handedly"; it is used for the vain wasting of speech. The left-handed person is allowed to use his left hand rather than his right whenever he can conveniently manage to—except in eating. Scooping up food with the left hand, or with the wrong fingers of the right hand, is very bad manners indeed. In the use of tools and implements, the left-handed person is at occasional disadvantage, as they are made after one pattern only, but for the most part tools are symmetrical and can be used either way, requiring only that the left-handed reverse the usual direction.

Carrying. Weights are carried balanced upon the head. When carrying heavy loads, the load is balanced in or on a carrying pack of twisted papyrus pulp which is set upon the head. Walking sticks are considered an important aid to balance, particularly when carrying a heavy load. They are carried in the right hand, leaving the left free to adjust the load from time to time. Many people carry sticks habitually, tucked under the arm when not in use. Sticks have replaced the spears, which used to be made with a pointed iron-shod tip to the haft, for use as walking sticks; to what extent the practice of carrying the sticks is a mere habit surviving from the days when spears were genuinely needed, and to what extent they are a real aid in walking over difficult places, I could not determine.

In picking up and setting down heavy loads, assistance from another person is desirable. If there is no one around able to lift the weight, the carrier manages by himself, using both hands, and lifting the load first well above his head, whether he is about to lower it into position on his head, or to set it upon the ground. When the load has been set into place, the carrier holds it with his left hand, while he stoops to retrieve his stick from the ground, adjusts his cloak, and so forth.

Tumplines are never used, but women sometimes carry loads on their backs. Firewood, for example, may be slung across the shoulders when another load is being carried on the head. And babies are regularly carried fastened upon the back, leaving the mother's head and arms free.

Babies are carried in a wide leather sling, which passes around the child, set securely upon its mother's back, and is then fastened in front on the mother's chest. The two upper ends are passed under her armpits and knotted above her breasts. This holds the baby just below or at the neck, with its head dangling loose and unsupported above. The bottom edge of the sling is tucked securely under the baby's buttocks, and the two lower ends then pass about the mother's waist and tie in front, holding the bottom of the sling in place and supporting the baby in position.

In setting the baby in position on her back, the mother clutches the baby in front of her at her side, then hoists it around to the right as she bends forward, so that her back is parallel to the ground. She sets the baby prone upon her back, with its legs astraddle, and then fastens the upper ends. Then she straightens up, tucks the bottom under, and ties the lower ends. For short carries, and just standing around, the baby is often set upon the left hip, legs astraddle, and held in place by an arm.

Tiny children learn to balance on their heads. Beginning with small cups of water, they progress at their own pace to larger and heavier loads.

Bending. The flat forward-stretching back that women use when hoisting the baby into position for carrying is a general bending posture for women. The most convenient bending position appears to be this one, in which the legs, usually held somewhat apart, are straight, and the bend comes from the hips, with the back stretching forward, and both hands hang free for use. In this position women can be seen turning over grain set out on mats to dry, weeding, and so forth. From this position they can readily place the whole flat of the palm on the ground. The long forward stretch of the back is convenient also when using a short-handed hoe on a sloping field.

Kneeling. It is customary to kneel when grinding flour, chipping potsherds on a stone, and performing similar tasks. Mat making is done on the ground, bending over from a kneeling position. But for many tasks incessant stooping is preferred. My houseboy would always bend rather than kneel when washing clothes in a tub set on the ground. Eseri explained that this was entirely reasonable. She too has "no strength" when kneeling, though she can when necessary maintain a kneeling position for hours on end. I have seen people kneel rather than squat or sit when resting or engaged in some task of the hands, but this was not most usual.

In kneeling, toes may be tucked under or out; and, depending on the work being done, one may sit up from the knees, or rest back on the heels. Tiwandje, when mending a hoe in my presence, for example, used the latter form. When a girl is kneeling, she must be careful to get up modestly, first sitting down, and drawing her feet to one side, never getting into a transition posture of squatting, for this is always immodest. When getting into a kneeling position, some catch themselves with their hands, but many can sit down and then kneel without the help of their hands in balance.

Sitting. Certain formalities must be observed with regard to sitting. Some postures are considered unsuitable before one's elders or superiors. The customary polite sitting postures for girls are limited to sitting on the ground, with both legs stretched straight out in front, and skirts neatly tucked under, or sitting with one or both legs bent to one side, weight on one hip, and knees slightly forward, on the ground. The feet are held to one side and not sat upon. The former position is reported to be tiring, and cannot be kept up for hours on end. The latter is more comfortable. Shifting from one to the other, or from one side to the other, is possible and not unseemly, but must be done carefully with due regard for modesty.

Girls are chided if they slump at all, and especially for one-sided slumping. This they are told will "make the embryo grow crookedly." They can sit erect for a long time, but will lean against a post or other support if this is available. In both sitting and standing, women are noticeably more erect than men. Many men have a pronounced slump or slouch.

Men seldom sit on the ground with their legs stretched before them. Many more comfortable positions are permissible for them. For example, they may sit with their legs bent in front of them, the foot of one resting on the knee of the other. Or they may sit cross-legged. I have seen them whittling and doing other handwork in such positions (in Kasagara's case, always with his tongue out). They also sit or squat with their buttocks just off the ground, with their knees up, wide apart for better balance, and sometimes hands clasped about them. This is usual for merely sitting about, but is also a working position for whittling, tying framework, building fires, and so forth. It is not polite for men to sit in such manner in the presence of superiors.

There are some stools, but no chairs with backs. The stools, like the bedsteads, are entirely for relaxing. I rarely saw a man working with his hands while sitting on a stool; once I saw a carpenter whittling thus, but that was most unusual. Women may sit on stools before the fire when cooking, but they would not sit on stools out in the courtyard.

Women must never sit with their knees up or apart. In great privacy, before a fire in her own home, a woman may do so, but even then she will tuck her skirts up carefully from underneath to assure covering.

Swimming. Most of the Chiga, even those who live at the shore of the lake, do not know how to swim. Fatalities from drowning were by no means a rare occurrence. Most of these were due to drunkenness; boats returning form wedding parties were likely to capsize, and there have been instances of men so drunk that they drowned in the shallow water near the shore when they lost their footing. If the person is hauled out in time, attempts are made at resuscitation by violent massaging, using the technique of treading with the feet. I was told that among the *Abakongwe* there were good swimmers; there were none at all at Bufuka.

Climbing. The Chiga treat the steep slopes of their hills as though they were ordinary paths. They climb up them in perfectly upright positions, carrying burdens on their heads, and at the most supporting themselves lightly with their staffs. Downhill they prefer to run. They never look for a roundabout alternative to a steep up- and downgrade, even though the latter may be a little shorter. There is little occasion for other sorts of climbing, as the country is bare rather than wooded, and roof repairs and building are done virtually from the ground, since the top and sides of the house are in one piece.

Lying Down. Normally, people sleep and rest only on their sides. It is considered a clear mark of illness to lie on one's back, or to lie prone.

Use of the Feet. Treading with the feet is an important procedure in two distinct processes—softening hides and threshing grain, particularly small millet. Both of these are worked by an identical trick of rubbing between the feet. The operator stands on the skin, or the pile of grain, supporting himself with a stick, or sometimes two sticks, or leaning against some fixed support such as the roof or a storage bin. The feet are rolled inward alternately, each pushing a mass of the material under and toward the other, crushing it against the other foot. Each foot must actually step upon the other at the end of its roll. I also saw clay being kneaded by foot; the clay and water were in a trough. In this case, the technique was varied; the clay was stamped with the heel of one foot.

Use of the Teeth. On many occasions, the teeth serve as auxiliary tools. They are used for holding and pulling, especially in preparing basketry materials. They are also used in hairdressing, for biting open the knotted ends of curls when they are to be unwound. In eating meat, the whole piece is grasped in the teeth and then torn or cut off.

Eating. The outer edge of the palm is the most usual spoon. It is used not only for shaking dry food into the mouth, such as handfuls of beans or corn, but also for such purposes as pouring thin gruel into the mouth of an infant in beginning supplementary feeding. Adults drink such foods from a calabash cup or by means of a straw; the dregs are then scooped out with the first two fingers and thus spooned into the mouth. Thicker porridge is broken off in pieces, which are then kneaded between the fingers and used to dip up any available gravy or relish.

Rolling. Rolling between the palms of both hands is used in making the clay coils for pottery, and in twirling the fire sticks. Both of these are techniques used only rarely, and not by everyone. I do not know with what degree of skill those who do not do these particular things could manipulate them if they tried—that is, whether this is a familiar pattern of working with the hands.

Shelling Vegetables. To shell peas, the top of the pod is grasped in two fingers of the left hand. The pod is broken along the back with a twist of the right hand, which scoops out any peas that do not fall out by themselves. Husks are kept in the left hand, peas int he right, till a number have accumulated, when they are cast into different heaps. This is usually done sitting on the ground.

There are equally precise habits for husking corn and removing the kernels. The latter is done by rubbing two ears together and then scooping out the kernels with the fingers.

Hoeing, Flailing, etc. Millet is threshed by beating with a long stick. Heaps of dried peas are flailed in the same way. The worker may be standing or kneeling. In either case, the stick is wielded over the right shoulder and brought down diagonally forward, without much bending of the body. Grass for mats can be softened in this way, or by kneading with the feet. A special stick with a flattened knob is sometimes used for beating grass, though always from a standing position.

The hoe is wielded in exactly the same way. Usually it is held with the left hand above the right, and the left foot forward; it is swung diagonally across the body from over the right shoulder. (Lefthanded people swing it from the left shoulder, reversing foot positions.) Sometimes in the course of wielding the hoe, it is swung very vigorously around in a whole circle at the right side of the body, so that it comes up from in back instead of merely being raised to the shoulder. Sometimes in swinging it up only one hand is on the handle, though both are always used for the forceful down swing. The stroke is often accompanied by a kind of flinging forward of the hoe, so a long stretch of the handle slips through the hand.

The hoe is heavy, and I had some difficulty in learning to swing it smoothly and effectively. Bikomko, aged four, could already go through the motions of swinging it properly, despite its weight.

Winnowing. Winnowing is done on a flat round tray. There are two different techniques. In one, the front end of the tray is repeatedly tipped up so that the grain flies upward, the chaff being blown away by the wind, or by the winnower. Another way is to work the grain round and round on the tray, which is manipulated more or less in one plane in a sort of series of figure eights. The heavier grain is coaxed to the back this way.

The same kind of motion is used to separate dried peas from the pebbles that are always among them, though this is never altogether successful, so that they are usually sorted by hand before cooking. It is also used in playing a kind of musical instrumental rattle made of two rows of reeds bound together into a flat square about a foot long. Between the two layers are a quantity of peas or other round seeds or small pebbles, which make a curious swishing rattle when the instrument is shaken in a circular motion combined with an up and down tilt.

Grinding Flour. When grinding flour, the worker kneels at the grindstone. A small stone is used, pushed forward slowly as straight arm pressure is exerted by the palms of both hands. The flour collects at the front of the grindstone and is allowed to drop off into a tray. The curved side of one hand is used to push the grain into position for grinding.

The grindstone is also used for breaking up potsherds to mix with the clay in pottery making. A little round stone is used, and in much the same fashion, for denting the surface of the millstone to keep it in condition for grinding. This technique involves holding the little stone in the right hand, with the thumb to the left, and the first two fingers grasping it to the right. The stone is pounded up and down by a motion of the hand from the wrist, and with a slight twist of the wrist to the right on the stroke. To separate the chaff, grain is pounded in a deep mortar before grinding. One stands up for this task, working a heavy stick with both hands.

Handling Fire. Glowing coals are handled with the naked hand, by rapid shifting of position. Piles are most commonly lit, not from a flame, but by stuffing a large chunk of glowing wood or charcoal into the bowl, tamping it down with a potsherd, or even with the thumb.

Cutting. There are several different kinds of cutting, and different cutting tools. The most basic are the small straight knife, and the omuhoro, which has a curved blade and is over a foot long. These two tools are in constant everyday use. The small knife is used for cutting meat, skinning animals, cutting buro, and so forth; the larger curved one for cutting down bushes, reaping, and so forth. Either may be used in whittling.

When the large knife is used for such tasks as shaving down a handle, the stick to be trimmed is held upright with the left hand, and the knife slashed downward on the outer side. Usually the straight edge of the knife is used first, and the surface planed more closely with the curve. When the curve is used, the knife moves toward the operator on the upper surface of the wood, which is held horizontally. These are different techniques with distinct names. The first is to *beija,* meaning to carve or do carpentry; the other is to *haragata,* which means to scrape or smooth, and may also be applied to quite different forms of such operations, such as scraping the outside of a clay pot with a bit of gourd. When used to cut grass or bush, the knife is held in one hand by the handle, and swung, almost flung, with short strokes. The one side is used for chopping, the other side for grass cutting.

The short knife is held with the thumb against the blade, and the other fingers over it, the handle being disregarded. The same person may whittle sometimes towards and sometimes away from himself.

A knife, usually one especially reserved for the purpose, is used for shaving the head. The razor is always sunned for hours before use. The person doing the shaving scrapes at the other one's head, drawing the blade of the knife toward himself, and holding the skin back with the other hand to keep it from being pulled. It also helps to wet the hair from time to time.

All the men know how to carve and whittle a little. They all make tool handles, roughly shape a stick to a point, and perform other basic woodwork. But bowls, stools, and so forth are made only by experts.

Adzing. Adzing as done by the carpenter is the same sort of process as ordinary carving, but with more specialized tools. There are three sorts of adzes, one with a plain straight edge, one curved, and the third a loop. The plain and curved straight adzes are used like the large knife, the only difference being in the plane of the cutting surface. The stroke is aimed from a distance, the tool being held in one hand by the longish handle, a foot or more from the object upon which the work is being done.

The small looped adze is held differently. It is grasped by both hands and scooped towards the carpenter at work. When I watched Bandiho making a bowl, he started by chopping it out roughly with the large knife, and then worked with the regular curved adze,holding the bowl in his left hand, resting on the ground. At all times, the concave edge of the tool was toward him, even when he was working on the near outside edge of the bowl, which was being shaped to just the opposite sort of curve. But when he had the bowl in shape, he smoothed it with the little looped adze. When he began to work with this tool, he held the bowl between his feet, Though he sat with his knees up, this was still a distance away.

Chopping. When an axe has to be used, it is handled with a long swing, more or less like a hoe. It is kept in the horizontal plane, the end of the handle being grasped with both hands. There were few axes around; only those very much interested in woodworking actually owned them. I saw one in use only once, as there were no trees in the neighborhood of the village which could possibly need their use. After house posts were cut down in the forest, they were trimmed for use with more customary tools.

The lanceolate blade at the end of the awl is used particularly for the fine cutting and shredding in basketry. It is held by the blade, just as the small knife is, and usually worked away from the operator. When it is necessary to work it in the other direction, the whole hand is turned, without any change in the way in which the blade is grasped. It is held by just two fingers, the thumb above and the first finger below. It is always held flat, and never used perpendicularly to the material to be cut. It is used particularly for splitting grass for basketry, and for shredding the papyrus that forms the core of the basketry coil. The blade, held flat in the right hand, is inserted near the bottom of the long strand of grass or reed, and pushed upwards towards the tip. When necessary, to help control the split, one of the loosened strips will be held in the mouth.

Wood is split by inserting a flat blade, such as the flat part of the curved knife, as far as it will go. The other end of the wood is then banged on the ground, so as to drive the knife in deeper and increase the split, and the knife is also twisted back and forth in the crack to widen it. These processes are alternated until the split is effected.

Blades of knives and hoes have long points at the base end for insertion into the wooden handle. This pointed metal end is heated and set as far into the handle as it will go. Then the other end of the handle is pounded to work it in further. The blade is removed and heated again, and the whole process repeated. The curved knife is held by the curved part during this process, with the cutting edge covered with papyrus heart or leaves to protect the hand.

Throwing. All the throwing I ever saw was overhand—whether it was the throwing of a stick or spear, or of a bundle of grass onto a roof when thatching. This is true even of seed, which is flung over hand.

The otter spear is held in the right hand at the forward end of the long handle. The fingers go over the staff, the thumb back. The hunter out in a boat may be alone, and have to handle the paddle as well as the spear. In such a case, he will keep hold of the spear so as to have it in readiness. When thrown, the otter spear remains upright because the handle is of light bamboo.

Paddling. In large boats, the paddlers sit on the edge of the boat, using a head pad as a cushion. In a small boat, there is usually only one person, who paddles himself. He sits in the bottom, or on a tiny block of wood. Now and then one sees someone paddling standing up. If a person is alone in a boat, he always stays at the back.

One may paddle a boat from either side. When paddling on the right side, the left arm is higher, and vice versa. The lower hand encircles the paddle, with the fingers to the back. The upper may encircle it, or the shaft may slip through between any two fingers. Usually the thumb is down. There is generally about a foot between the two hands, the upper being a variable distance from the top of the paddle. When the water is very rough, the position of the arms may be reversed, and the top arm slipped down the handle at each stroke.

The usual stroke is a deep one. There are several special strokes: in one, the paddle is brought sharply down into the water, instead of reaching forward; this makes a jerking sort of movement for the boat. In another, the paddle is brought out at the back so as to make a rushing noise. This is said to be the most forceful stroke. Sometimes a double stroke is used, with one deep and the other just a sort of recovery stroke, practically useless as far as propulsion is concerned.

When several men paddle together, the synchronization is always excellent. Sometimes the sing, but not always. They all take part in steering, paddling all on one side, withholding the paddles on one side, and so forth, when necessary.

The wooden ladle used for stirring porridge is handled in somewhat the same way as a paddle.

Sewing. In all sewing, whether of hides or basketry, a hole is pierced with an awl. The thread is pushed through and pulled tight as it emerges on the side away from the worker. Then the thread is brought forward again over the edge, and reinserted for the next stitch. This makes a raised seam, not unlike our overcasting, when hides are sewn. When a patch is being attached, a rent sewn up, or a crack mended in a calabash or gourd, the thread is brought forward again through another hole. For such sewing, the holes are arranged in pairs on opposite sides of the seam.

Use of the Awl. The pointed end of the awl is used for piercing holes for sewing. The tool is clenched in the right hand, with the thumb farthest from the point. It is always thrust away from the operator, with pressure either downward or forward. There is some individual variation in ways of holding the awl for making holes. Safety pins are beginning to come into favor as a substitute or supplement for the awl, especially in making holes for mending.

Twining or Spinning. Sinews and the bark of various trees and bushes, shredded, are the favorite materials for fine cord. A regular two-ply thread is made of these.

Spinning is sometimes done against the thigh, but more often just in the hand, held free, with the right thumb moving. First, each of the two elements is twisted independently, the upper one first and then the lower. They are twisted toward the operator. They are rolled together, first slowly, a little distance apart, then sharply, in the same direction. The thumb and forefinger of the left hand holds the material, the right hand doing the spinning. As each piece of an inch or so is twisted together, the left hand completes the task by a sharp roll of the thumb.

Heavier rope is also made with a single twist. This is the heavy bark rope used in mat making, and the papyrus twists used in house building and for most bulky tying. The rope is twisted by an overhand twist to the right, using the whole of the lower right arm. The left hand holds the finished part. The twist is clockwise, away from the worker.

For the papyrus twists, fairly fresh papyrus is used. The wide strips removed from each side of the reed are used, the corner strips being discarded. The inside pulp is sometimes saved to make carrying pads. As the rope is finished, it is made into loops or skeins about a foot across. The left arm or thumb supports the skein as it grows, and as the rope is twisted it is thrown counterclockwise around the arm, resting ont he loops already formed. Usually the lower end of the loop rests on the arm, and the hand holds the upper edge, the thumb coming through to the inside. But I have seen Kabaka hold the loop with his thumb on the outside, and Ruhande holding it with his arm over the loops.

Fresh strips are added by twisting along with the old for eight inches or so. As each bundle gets unwieldy, the loose end is fastened, and a new one started. They are then laid aside to dry.

Tying. Careful tying of small knots, as in netting or fastening small strings, is done mostly with the thumb and first two fingers of the right hand. In netting, the left hand hooks around each loop as it is formed, in order to hold it open while the knot is made. A great deal of the fastening work is done simply by binding, wrapping the twine or bark round and round, and possibly tucking the end in, but not making a definite knot.

Braiding. Not only three-strand, but six-strand braiding is familiar to the Chiga. It is used in making little grass bracelets for children. These are made of a single pulpy strand, the outer surface being carefully split into six sections, left fastened together at the base. These are then braided together into a long cylinder, and the end fastened to the base to complete a circlet. Braided belts are also much favored by the women. These are preferably made of very heavy twine purchased from the pygmies. The belt is braided with a long tassel worked on to it.

Beading. Headdresses are woven of purchased beads in the style familiar to us as Indian beading. I do not know how long this has been in use here.

Decorticating. Various techniques are employed in obtaining the bark of trees and the outer skin of reeds, which are used for the various purposes.

Asa means to remove the outside of reeds from the pulpy core. This is done by splitting off the end with a knife, and then pulling off the strip thus begun by a sharp whipping motion. Ordinarily the left hand holds the base of the core, where the split is begun, and the right the severed portion of the skin which is to be split off down its full length. In preparing papyrus for making rope, the corners are sliced off down the full length first, and then the sides removed whole by the technique just described. When the papyrus is intended for the foundation coil in basketry, narrower bits are stripped off in this fashion. When bark is prepared for rope, as for mat making, initial loosening of the bark may be done by tearing at it with the teeth or beating at it with a stick, instead of cutting at it with a knife. If there are thorns, these are scraped off first with a knife. The bark is then whipped off in one piece, the left hand holding the branch or vine, the right the husk which is to be removed. It is turned inside out in the process.

On the other hand, the grass that is used as an alternative to papyrus for many purposes, and which is also three-cornered, is not stripped in this fashion by being pulled off, but is skinned off with a knife. It is used young for basketry, and possibly its greenness is what necessitates the more delicate technique. When preparing this grass, it is dried for a day by being left in the sun. Then the sprouting ends are chopped off about a foot from the tip, and

the corner removed. The sides are then removed whole by inserting a knife at about the middle of the length. The back of the knife
is pushed upward to remove the upper half of the strip, then reinserted and the blade used for the lower half. The strips, which are
3/8 to 1/2 inch wide, are then hung away, rolled up in tiny loops.

When the basketry materials are to be prepared for use, they
have to be split into narrower strips. For this purpose, tearing is
again used, only instead of a whipping motion, the teeth are employed, When the strips are to be used, they are first soaked in
water. Then the remnants of the pulpy core must be stripped off
the inside of the skin, and the irregular sides trimmed down. The
knife part of the awl is used to start the trip. After slicing it up a
little way, the good part is held at either end by the two hands, and
the loosened bit which is to be discarded is pulled off by the mouth.
This is true both for removing the pulp and the irregular side bits.
After that, the blade is used to cut the remaining strip into three
narrow strips for use, the blade as usual in such work being pushed
up and away from the worker. When bark is to be stripped off
posts to be used for building, the bark is loosened by beating and
then pulled off. Only when a very smooth finished surface is required, as for knife and hoe handles, is the surface adzed.

12

AFRICAN TRIBALISM:
SOME REFLECTIONS ON UGANDA

GWENDOLYN CARTER once commented that "there is a sense for Africa as a whole which is more real to the educated Africans of the continent than is the notion of Europe to educated Europeans, or of one America to the inhabitants of North and South America."[1] Pan-Africanism, the various All-African Conferences, common interest in the movements for freedom of all the African peoples, the African voting bloc in the United Nations, the Organization of African Unity—these are all expressions of a sense of African identity based on a common experience under colonialism and a common goal of freedom and dignity in the modern world. Among African intellectuals there is a search for common African values and worldviews, an attempt to discover, or to forge, a bond of common culture, exemplified in the concepts of Negritude, and expressed in a growing body of sophisticated contemporary literature. Yet Africa today, even just Africa "south of the Sahara," is far from a single unified cultural and ethnic whole. There are hundreds of languages; differences, both old and new, in ways of getting a living; and matrilineal, patrilineal, and even dual forms of family organization. Despite the attempt to find a common philosophical base for "African religion," there are vast differences in traditional religions in both practice and belief. There are friendly and unfriendly ancestors, great pantheons and areas with little interest in the gods, and varying incidence of witchcraft beliefs, possession cults, and initiation rites. There is the further divisive effect of intrusive religions: Islam, Protestant or Catholic churches, and blends of the new and the old. There are differences, too, in the old forms of tribal organization. Indigenous African political units ranged from small-scale chieftainships, rooted in kin and clan, to great states, often established by conquest and ruled by the superposition of alien lineages. There were also "tribes, without rulers," areas of fragmented, subdividing lineages, with no central authority or common allegiance at all, even within the boundaries of shared language and culture.

There are those who wonder to what extent national or pan-African ideas and ideals, realistic or romantic common causes can transcend the enormous diversities of cultural and "tribal" or ethnic affiliations. The boundaries of the several emerging nations were drawn not according to African political, cultural, and linguistic affinities, but by the accidents of European history. It is asked whether "tribal" loyalties—the ties that bind the individual to his rural home, that spell themselves out as obligations to his kinsmen, that impel him to have respect for traditional authority figures, or that structure developing lines of authority in patterns set by older forms of social organization—are likely to be more active factors in the current social situation than the new nationalisms. Will older antagonisms to other peoples make it difficult to forge new bonds of common allegiance along national lines? To what degree are the boundaries of the moral community—the group within which common moral fellowship is acknowledged[2]—changing, becoming wider and more inclusive? Certainly there are many cleavages, points of considerable tension on the modern scene, which seem to fall along old lines of tribal divisions. To what extent are these a tribal legacy deeply rooted in the divergent loyalties and institutions of the past, and destined to be a genuine source of long-range difficulty in Africa?

The general point of this paper is that however much tribal affiliation and identification may enter, the issues and conflicts of today are rooted in problems and social interactions of today, and are not just atavisms rooted in some preexistent past and continuing on a momentum of traditionalism. This is not to say that history does not count; it is a requisite key to understanding any transformations in the present, which can only be transformations of the past. But the manifold ways in which varying kinds of tribal identifications will be extended or deepened, the extent to which old cultures and old loyalties will remain stumbling blocks to change, or be transformed, widened, and reinterpreted, seem to me to be functions not of the past as such, but of the genuine issues and problems of the present, to which new answers must be found. At least as a heuristic principle, it seems to be fruitful to keep a careful research orientation on these issues and problems of the present, and on the direction of their development, if we are to understand the role that the past continues to play.

Both Gluckman and Epstein, who have worked in this kind of theoretical framework, have made this point. Speaking of the role of "tribal" organizations and affiliations in the urban area of the Copperbelt, in Northern Rhodesia, Epstein writes, "Intertribal relations on the Copperbelt...and the cleavages within political organizations along tribal lines, cannot be explained simply as vestiges from a tribal past which have survived into the present. On the contrary, they reflect processes at work within the urban social system."[3] He points out that while "tribalism refers to a significant category of interaction in everyday social relationships among Africans," the lines of tribal alignment tend to be transformed by the historical accidents of the present. For example, he tells us that peoples of many different tribes from Nyasaland form a community of common interest in the mining area and are regarded as though they were a tribal unit. Similarly Gluckman points out that even in the rural areas, where tribal identifications are still operating in their original regional and community settings, "we are still not dealing merely with survivals," but rather that "membership of a tribe involves participation in a working political system, and sharing domestic life with kinfolk; and that this continued participation is based on present economic and social needs, and not merely on conservatism."[4]

I should like to explore the situation in Uganda as one illustration of this complex process of interaction between modern interests and older loyalties. Uganda is not "typical" in any simple sense, but it is probably no less so than any other specific area of Africa. It embraces a characteristic heterogeneity of ethnic make-up. Its peoples speak various Bantu, Sudanic, and Nilotic languages. There are herdsmen in the north and west, fisherfolk on the great lakes, and farmers dependent on quite distinct food staples—millet in some areas, plantain in others. The present boundaries of Uganda include the great kingdoms of Buganda, Bunyoro, and Ankole, quite a number of smaller states, and a large number of non-centralized peoples who had no chiefs at all. These were disparate peoples, with no possible sense of common allegiance or obligation. Indeed, between many of these different peoples—tribes, if you like—there was an active condition of warfare at the time of British intervention, in the latter part of the nineteenth century.

Uganda was governed by the British as a protectorate. There were few permanent European residents, no great areas of European plantations, copper mines, or industrial centers, although there were some small-scale European and Indian-owned cotton mills, and later a growing focus of factory production around the electric-power center in Jinja. Most important, from the point of view of the difficulties in the current situation, is the fact that throughout the history of the protectorate, Buganda, a separate province about twice the size of the ancient kingdom of Uganda, enjoyed a special and privileged status. By the terms of the Uganda Agreement, signed in 1900, and supplemented by further legislation over the years, Buganda received a considerable measure of self-government. The Kabaka was recognized as hereditary monarch. Wide areas of appointment to office, administration of welfare departments, tax-collection and some disbursement, even lawmaking, were in the hands of the Lukiko or council, a body of chiefs and notables appointed by the Kabaka, or elected by a complicated system of indirect voting, culminating in electoral colleges in the various districts. Chiefs and other dignitaries were assigned large areas of agricultural land as their private estates, so that now about half—and the more valuable half—of the land in Buganda province is privately owned, in blocs which range from a few acres to many square miles. A good deal of this is planted in cotton and coffee, worked by share-cropping tenants or hired labor, and some of the holdings in and near Kampala are subdivided into relatively high-rental residential or business plots.

The rest of the protectorate was governed by quite different regulations. Its chiefs were British appointees, and in some areas, where there was no background of centralized authority on even a small scale, the chiefs were Ganda,[5] brought in to teach the "backward" areas how to govern themselves. Even where, as in Bunyoro, for example, or Ankole, hereditary kings were recognized by specific agreements, they did not have the self-governing powers assigned to the Baganda. And nowhere else were there parallel land allotments, so that there are no comparable large estates, nor access to individual wealth, for the peoples of the rest of Uganda.

The movement toward independence in Uganda involved a drama which is easily referred to the rubric of "tribalism." The issue was that of Ganda separatism. Establishing a Protectorate Legislative Council with increasing native representation and responsible participation in government was conceived by the Colonial Office as an important step toward the goal of independence and self-government. When a common election for delegates to this body was held, Buganda refused to participate in the election, although special provision was made to guarantee it substantial representation. Actually, there were several issues. One was the threat of being swamped in a protectorate-wide body; another was the disapproval of a direct-election system, which would have given the vote even to "foreigners" resident in Buganda (that is, members of other tribes of the protectorate and Ruanda, who in a few districts actually constitute a majority of the population); and a third was popular opposition to a body which was clearly being set up on a "multiracial" basis, with representation for Europeans and Indians.

The election boycott was successful. Only some thirty-five thousand out of a Buganda population of over a million registered for it. When arrangements for the election went ahead in spite of the Buganda protest and boycott, the Lukiko—the Buganda assembly—declared itself out of the protectorate. It passed a resolution rescinding its 1900 agreement with Britain and declaring its full independence. Despite Britain's refusal to recognize this new status, it proceeded, on January 11, 1961, to implement its resolution by assigning ministerial portfolios to cover the new functions the independent government would have to assume.

When the British persisted, and the candidates elected by the three percent who voted were seated in the legislature, the Ganda leaders changed tactics and founded their own political party, Kabaka Yekka ("the Kabaka only"), which captured the seats at the next election, and secured special home-rule privileges for Buganda and the election of the Kabaka as the first president of Uganda. Kabaka Yekka has been maintained as a strictly Baganda party, despite suggestions that it expand to include traditionalist and royalist elements in the other kingdoms of Uganda.[6]

Certainly, this is Ganda "tribalism" in the sense that it is Ganda separatism and a reflection of Ganda attitudes of difference and superiority over the other peoples of the protectorate. These attitudes are easy to discern. Land is seldom sold to members of other tribal groups, although they are welcomed as tenants, especially as seasonal commercial production tenants. Many "foreigners" play a considerable role as stewards and even political right-hand men to their landlords, but virtually none have yet been appointed as chiefs. The Ganda are, on the average, wealthier. They are Christian, and more of them are literate and even highly educated. They disdain to work with their hands, and whenever possible hire paid laborers, who flock in from all sides to work on Ganda-owned plantations and in construction trades, while landless Ganda aim at civil-service jobs and commute from the suburbs on bicycles.

The quality of Ganda superiority feelings is neatly epitomized in a fragment of a high-school students' debate, reported by Audrey Richards:

14-year-old girl: "If we are all equal we ought to give our porters food on plates with us, and not on banana leaves at the back door."

Answer, from another student: "But we are not equal. The Europeans and Ganda are clean and the others are dirty."[7]

It would seem to me quite obvious that the character and content of these attitudes are at least as much a product of the privileged economic and political position of the Ganda today as a heritage of previous tribal alignments. For one thing, Ganda superiority was not so firmly entrenched before the Uganda agreement with Britain. It is true that the kingdom was an expanding conquest state, exacting tribute from increasing numbers of its neighbors. It had an extremely powerful and rather efficient system of centralized control, with an elaborate appointive bureaucracy under a hereditary dynastic ruler. But it was not the only powerful state in the region. The Kingdom of Bunyoro especially was in a comparable position of successful conquest and ascendancy. One of the factors impelling the Ganda to make peace with the British and place themselves under their protection was the desire to gain British arms and support against their dangerous rival in the west. There is still a considerable area in Buganda which is *Bunyoro irridenta,* Lunyoro-speaking, but ruled by Ganda chiefs. The districts in question were ceded to Buganda not by treaty with the Nyoro, but by agreement with the British, in recognition of Ganda cooperation against the intransigent Nyoro, whose king died in exile, never reconciled to British rule. And the problem of these "lost counties" is still a live issue.[8]

To some extent these issues still rankle. But it seems that "tribal" (or perhaps in this instance we would be better advised to say "national" or "imperial") antagonisms must sometimes be set aside for larger issues, such as the safeguarding of the principle of monarchy. In any case, it is precisely with their old rivals—the great kingdoms of Bunyoro, Toro, and Ankole—that the Ganda ruling class made some common cause. The several hereditary monarchs met together a number of times, and urged that no change be made in the formal government of the protectorate before the status of Buganda, and the position of its monarch, was fully clarified and protected. The value of hereditary monarchy both as symbol and for bargaining power in the contemporary situation is so great that in Busoga the chiefs, once heads of about fifteen separate small states and now united by the British under an appointed Paramount, have asked that the latter be elevated in status and be named hereditary monarch. And when Uganda achieved its independence in 1962, the constitution provided for hereditary status for the various kings and federal status for their several districts, though with greater formal independent powers granted to Buganda than to the others.

"Tribalism" certainly seems an inadequate and misleading term for this whole situation. We must remember that the lines of separation between these various kingdoms were in a state of flux long before the British arrived on the scene. There were realignments by war and conquest, and by treaty among the rulers, which meant that subject populations were transferred to different masters. In addition, subject peoples themselves might move, or adopt a new ruler. As Audrey Richards puts it:

> Lineage groups have split off from parent stocks and have become attached by fictions of common descent to similar lineages in another tribe. In some cases they have acquired position as ruling dynasties over indigenous people. In others the migrants have been absorbed into the political systems of neighboring tribes by the mere act of recognizing the latter's chiefs and giving them tribute. They have done so either as refugees from one tyrannical chief trying to win protection from another, or as humble allies of a more powerful political group. Cases of families and individuals being incorporated into stranger tribes are also known.[9]

What is more, in Buganda the political organization was not set up along clan and kin lines, with permanent relationships to hereditary chiefs and subchiefs. Instead there was considerable vertical as well as horizontal mobility. Only the position of the Kabaka was hereditary, and even that was not clear-cut, because there was no simple designation of the specific heir. The ancient kingdom was almost an "open society." Chiefs were appointed and demoted by the Kabaka; preferment was by personal favor, not lineage. And as for the ordinary Muganda, too poor to play this game of power politics, even he was in a position to exercise some role in it. A new chief might be appointed over him at any time, to whom he would owe customary dues and assistance in war. But he was free to move on his own initiative, to find a master whom he preferred if he did not like his immediate overlord. Land-use rights came from this kind of voluntary feudal subjection, not from membership in a clan with vested rights to particular land areas, although there were indications of earlier conditions of such tenure, as in the designated non-alienable clan burial grounds.

Certainly this is a far cry from the usual model of traditional chieftainship and hereditary loyalties. The consequence of the Uganda agreement, and particularly of its land tenure provisions, was to shift the balance toward what Low, in his analysis of twentieth-century Buganda political history, has so aptly called "neo-traditionalism." There has been increasing power for the chiefs, with rather less for the Kabaka, and for the ordinary peasant. Many of the best-educated and most Westernized elite are the sons of wealthy landowning chiefs, with an inclination to enter the power-hierarchy rather than to fight it.[10]

Furthermore, and again to counter the model of homogeneity and comfortable unity under "tribal" conditions, there is reason to think that the Ganda are far from a united people today. It is true that there was strong general support for the Kabaka a few years ago, when he was exiled in a political dispute with Britain. But this was an indignity which could obviously rally the support of anti-British nationalists, such as the Uganda National Congress, as well as of the most ardent traditionalists. It is also true that the 1960 election boycott was successful, but there have been accusations that this was the effect of threats and intimidation, not unanimity of sentiment. And there were voices, in Buganda itself, which accused the Lukiko of refusing to go along with constitutional changes because its members were afraid of being voted out of office in genuinely democratic elections. These accusations may be partial and biased, but they are at least straws in the wind.

There are a few clearer indications of some popular resentment against the entrenched power of the landlords and chiefs—grumblings, for example, which Richards reports, that landlords line their pockets at the expense of Ganda peasants, by preferring to rent their lands to the Alur and other "foreign" tenants."[11] And there has been the long history of resentment over the violation of clan burial ground rights, expressed through the "Bataka Union" of lineage heads. When the chiefs' estates were assigned, many of them received, as part of their private lands, grounds which traditionally belonged to the different clans and lineages in perpetuity, as burial centers for all the scattered members of the clan. The "Bataka" lost their legal case for the return of these lands as long ago as 1926, but they have remained a pressure group, and apparently have had considerable popular support as a channel for the expression of various grievances. Some of these boiled over in riots in 1945 and 1949. In 1949, the Bataka submitted a petition to the Kabaka, calling among other things for greater democracy in government, including direct election of Lukiko representatives. I have no data on their political strength today. But it is surely important to note that while there are some fifty thousand Ganda landowners by now, this is just a tiny fraction of the entire Ganda population, and other bases of political differences are clearly present.

There is one other "new" cultural distinction which plays an important role in Uganda politics: religious affiliation, particularly as between Catholic and Protestant groups. This goes far enough back in Buganda history so that perhaps it ought to fall into the category of the "neo-traditional." There were serious religious conflicts between the adherents of different Christian missions, as well as with followers of Islam, in the early pre-pacification days. Once order was established, the issue was resolved by apportionment of different areas and political offices to Protestants and Catholics respectively, and Low's study indicates that for the whole first half of this century there was very little change in the distribution.[12] There are virtually no pagan chiefs, and very few large-scale landholders, who are not officially Christian. The only exception is in the area of Kkooki, where an entire small kingdom was incorporated into Buganda by its own voluntary submission, just in time to profit by the favorable terms of the Uganda agreement.

What of the other peoples of the protectorate, with their differing languages and cultures and varying adherence to older ways of life? What does "tribalism" mean to them, and to what degree have their horizons and loyalties been changing? Because of the differences in their older life ways, and in their reactions to modern currents of change, it would be very difficult to make any valid statements that would fit all of them. I should, as a matter of fact, even be hard pressed to find a definition for the tribe as such which would fit all the peoples of Uganda. However, for some at least we can say that the experiences of the recent past have acted as a catalyst for the emergence of new and wider ethnic identifications. For the Alur, for example, we can find the same kind of situational interpretation of identification and allegiance, and the same process of "super-tribalization," of recognition of "tribal" belongingness far beyond the limits of any earlier community. Actually, the Alur represent at least five different stocks, varying in language and culture. They were all subject to Alur chiefs, but the latter governed as individuals, not as members of an organized governing unit. Today, when any of these many people come to Buganda to work, they are all classified as Alur, both by the Ganda and themselves. They are fitted into a Ganda stereotype for the Alur, as rather violent people, with a penchant for fighting and strong drink, but excellent workers. And they tend to live apart in little enclaves, which may be made up of actual kinsmen, or simply of people from the same clan, chieftainship, or region.[13] The phenomenon of clustering together for security, which this represents, is a common one in the urbanization process. It has been described not only for Africa, but for other parts of the world as well, and characterizes the immigrant to America as well as it does the "tribal" migrant to a large city. In Uganda, welfare and social clubs have developed along such "super-tribal" lines, embracing, for example, all people from Ruanda and Urundi, or many different speakers of Luo dialects.

The Ganda keep all these people at a social distance, and deny them landownership or political preferment. This is itself a new rather than an old phenomenon, for the Ganda in the past incorporated aliens. Indeed, some of the leading Ganda families were originally of alien lineage. Today, "foreigners" are kept out of the power elite as much as possible. But as far as the immigrants themselves are concerned, more and more of them are staying longer and longer, just as is the case in other centers of cash income in Africa. And it is clear that whatever their past or present antagonisms to the Ganda may be, some at least among them are quite ready to be assimilated, if the Ganda would allow it. As the protocol of an interview with a Ruanda immigrant puts it, "Yes, I want to become a Ganda. I join in everything they do. When I have enough money I mean to be baptised like the Ganda."[14]

The model of tribalism must also be modified by the segmentary-lineage type of structure which was to be found among quite a few of the peoples of Uganda. For such people as the Chiga, whatever sense of ethnic unity they possess can only be an emergent one, a response to experiences of the recent past. For the Chiga as I knew them in the nineteen-thirties had no "tribal" unity whatsoever. They were simply those people who lived in the hill country of the southwest.[15] They spoke a dialect of Lunyankole sometimes with a considerable admixture of Lunyaruanda. There was no common Chiga jural or moral community. Different Chiga clans, and even sub-clans, were constantly fighting one another; there were cattle raids, feud killings, even open battles. And there was no way of avoiding such bloodshed by ritual or blood-money payments, except between closely related lineages. The only ties uniting people of different lineages were bonds of affinal kinship and pact-brotherhood, and these were individual bonds only, not political networks.

The only sense of common Chiga identity came from a common rejection of alien overlordship. They were the people whom the Hima and the Tutsi had not conquered, or who had escaped from their suzerainty. They recognized no chiefs, paid no tribute, and told with proud boasts of individuals who had accepted patronage gifts of cattle, only to run off with them instead of becoming vassals. But the battles they had fought with invading Ruanda or Ankole armies were fought by separate clans, not by the Chiga as a people. The different clans had no common ultimate identity, no claim to common origin; some spoke of coming from the north, others from Ruanda, and all knew of individuals and lineages who had moved away, migrated, for instance, northward to the grasslands below the escarpment, and so had ceased to be "Bachiga."

Independence and individualism have remained important parts of the Chiga worldview and value system. When resettlement projects were undertaken in recent years, to relieve serious population pressure on their densely settled lands, the Chiga resisted attempts to move them into Ankole. This was not because of traditional ties to their homeland, for such moves had often taken place in the past, but because those who were to move feared they would lose their independence and become subject to the hereditary ruler of Ankole.

The Chiga image of government as distasteful has not been lessened by their experience with British overrule. They are among those peoples of the protectorate whose introduction to the techniques of "self" government was through Ganda chiefs. Baxter tells us that one of the lessons they learned was that chiefs should be domineering and arbitrary.[16] Being a pragmatic people, the Chiga knuckled under to superior power, but they are no doubt ready to value their independence should they win it once more.

Perhaps there is a danger here for the future. On the other hand, the Chiga have been moving forward to participation in the money economy, to Christianity and education. They have been selling their goats and their labor in Buganda, and improving their agricultural methods by careful terracing and reforestation. Some of them have lately been the proud recipients of freehold titles to their agricultural plots. Perhaps their qualities of rugged individualism, uncomplicated by strong tribal bonds, will fit them well for democracy. I have no actual current data on which to predict whether individualism, nationalism, or a new tribalism will emerge in this area. It appears that in earlier district elections, the Chiga did vote in large numbers, indicating an interest in wider affairs; but they are reported to have voted solidly by religious blocs, "lining up" literally behind the Protestant and Catholic candidates respectively. Major Uganda national parties today represent a fusion of parties from the northeast and the southwest, again suggestive of wider allegiances. Many delicate problems may still be in the balance, of course. Only recently, people somewhat similar to the Chiga in their cultural and political status (the Konjo and the Amba of the northern part of the Western Province) have been demanding separate recognition. They claim to be discriminated against by the Toro, and would like to form a distinct administrative unit from them.[17] But this is all within the framework of the Uganda national state, not a proposed secession.

All this suggests that the Chiga are beginning to see themselves as part of Uganda. It does not tell us whether the Chiga have in fact developed any stronger identification of themselves as a tribal unit than they once had. Certainly their moral community has broadened in at least some senses, for the old warfare and fighting have gone, under the enforced Pax Britannica. With this change, there had begun the acceptance of other people's rights to their lives and to their cattle, as long ago as in the nineteen-thirties. I do not know how much further this has gone today.

In any case, I think we can say not only for the Chiga, but for most of Uganda, that whatever strength "tribal" allegiances and inter-tribal antagonisms may have can hardly be a heritage from the "tribal" past, since for the masses of the people neither loyalties nor differences were deeply rooted in a "tribal" tradition. Perhaps it is different in regions in which there was a more integral relation of the chief to his people, based on common hereditary territorial and ritual commitments. But I think the prevalence of the latter kind of unity has probably been somewhat exaggerated in our common image of Africa. In Uganda, as we have seen, the lines of what *is* one's tribe, of what security it provides and what obligations it implies, and the character of its relations with other tribes, have always been subject to fluctuation and reinterpretation. It seems to me that patterns of cohesion, division, and identification will continue to be responsive to the realities of legal, economic, and political experiences and pressures. The emergence of a stronger consciousness of ethnic unity in any "tribal" region does not have to be incompatible with the parallel growth of allegiance to a wider unity, providing there is some context in which each is meaningful, and that the interests involved are not sharply in conflict.[18]

A parallel lesson could be drawn from the implications of another meaning which is sometimes given to "tribalism." I have been considering tribalism in the sense of ethnic loyalty and identification. It is also sometimes taken to refer to commitment to traditional patterns of culture. There are, it is true, considerable differences in the extent to which different African peoples have chosen the path of culture change. Some, especially the pastoral peoples of East Africa—including the Karamajong and others of northern Uganda—have fought to maintain their traditional way of life. Most others have welcomed at least some change, have accepted the value of lamps and bicycles, and even of universities, hospitals, and scientific research. We all know the story of the ways in which changes in family form, land utilization, the position of women, and so on follow in succession once the die is cast. It is too late now for most of Africa to vote for "tribal" ways of life. It is true that we are witnessing today a strong rebirth of some aspects of indigenous culture. Pouring libations to the ancestors and wearing cloths instead of European clothes, as in Ghana today, are symptoms of this movement. But these are sophisticated symbols, not simple reversions to "tribalism." Nor are they marks of tribal separatism. Their essence is the defiance not of modern ways as such but of the image of the colonial power, and all of its culture, as superior. More meaningful are the new cultural forms, the family corporations, women's welfare "meetings," even such things as the new concrete sculpture, which are adaptations of the old to meet the problems and demands of today.

I do not believe that differences in culture as such are likely to be barriers to communication and unity of action, or to mutual tolerance and respect in Africa. The African has no tradition for crusading missionary zeal in imposing his own standards of morality and esthetics on other people. Hair styles, riddles and songs, even initiation rites like the filing of teeth, have passed readily from one people to another in the past, sometimes even as fads and fashions to be experimented with. If such differences ever become the rallying cries for conflict, it will surely be only because they will be symbols for existing conflict on another level. Of course, institutional differences, as in marriage and inheritance laws, may sometimes pose problems in relations between intermarrying groups; but these are no more (and no less) difficult of resolution than the comparable problems posed by the rapidly changing patterns of social organization within a given "tribe."

In short, I think that we can say, for tribal cultures as for tribal loyalties, that features of the past are likely to be dynamic factors in the present only as they are relevant to real issues in the present and reflect common or conflicting interests and values. It sometimes seems to me that the issues of "tribalism" which pose the greatest problems for Africans today are those that arise not from situations intrinsic to Africa but from the "tribal" conflicts of our own Western world.

NOTES

This paper was originally presented at the Conference on African Tribalism, sponsored jointly by the University of Pennsylvania and The American Society for African Culture, on April 24, 1961, at the University of Pennsylvania.

1. Gwendolyn Carter, *Independence for Africa* (New York, 1960), 163.
2. For a fuller explanation of this concept, see May and Abraham Edel, *Anthropology and Ethics* (Springfield, Ill., 1959), chap. 9.
3. A. L. Epstein, *Politics in an Urban African Community* (Manchester, 1958), 239.
4. Max Gluckman, "Tribalism in Modern British Central Africa," *Cahiers d'Etudes Africains* 1 (1960): 55.
5. Ganda here refers, as is customary current usage, to the people of Buganda, who speak Luganda, and call themselves Baganda.
6. See Cherry Gertzel, "How Kabaka Yekka Began," *Africa Report* (October 1964): 9-13.
7. A. I. Richards, *Economic Development and Tribal Change* (Cambridge, 1954), 161.
8. In 1964 the Baganda political party, Kabaka Yekka, withdrew from its coalition with the government when Prime Minister Obote approved the holding of a referendum on their status.
9. Richards, 8.
10. D. A. Low and R. C. Pratt, Buganda and British Overrule (Oxford, 1960), 138ff., 259.
11. Richards, 223.
12. Low and Pratt, 97.
13. Southall, "Alur Migrants," in Richards, 141-60.
14. Richards, 167.
15. May Edel, *The Chiga of Western Uganda* (Oxford, 1957).
16. P. T. W. Baxter, "The Kiga," in A. I. Richards, *East African Chiefs* (New York, 1960), 278-310.
17. There have been outbreaks of violence in February 1963 and June 1964.
18. A rather similar view is stated for the Congo in D. Biebuyck and Mary Douglas, *Congo Tribes and Parties* (London, 1961), 44ff.

Sketch map showing the distribution of homesteads and some of
the fields cultivated by families
from Bufuka and neighbouring
peninsulas. All the land lies in
rounded ridges and fields are
mostly along their slopes and
tops. Letters in circles indicate
the home sites and patchwork
indicates the outlying cultivated
fields.

A = Abahabga
K = Abakobga
H = Abahirane
Z = Abazigate
T = Abatora
J = other Abajura
Y = other Abayundu, not
        Abajura
X = not related

Diagram showing schematically how lineage membership is traced
All are of the Abajura

ABAHABGA

1, 2, 3, and 4 are Abahabga, a minor lineage of the Abatora
lineage of the Abajura.

All Abajura lineages are descended from Nkuba. Other lineages

·mong some of the living adult male population in Bufuka village.
·ineage of the Abayundu clan.

△ Kayundu

△ Tciceca   △

△ Nkuba

Bizigate △   △ △

△   △   △ △

△ Buhirane

△   △

△   △   △

△   △   △   △   △   other   other   other
5   6   7   8   9   Abazigate   Abajura   Abayundu

ABAHIRANE

5, 6, 7, 8 and 9 are Abahirane, a minor lineage of the
      Abazigate lineage of the Abajura.

·re descended from Kayundu through other sons and grandsons.

INDEX